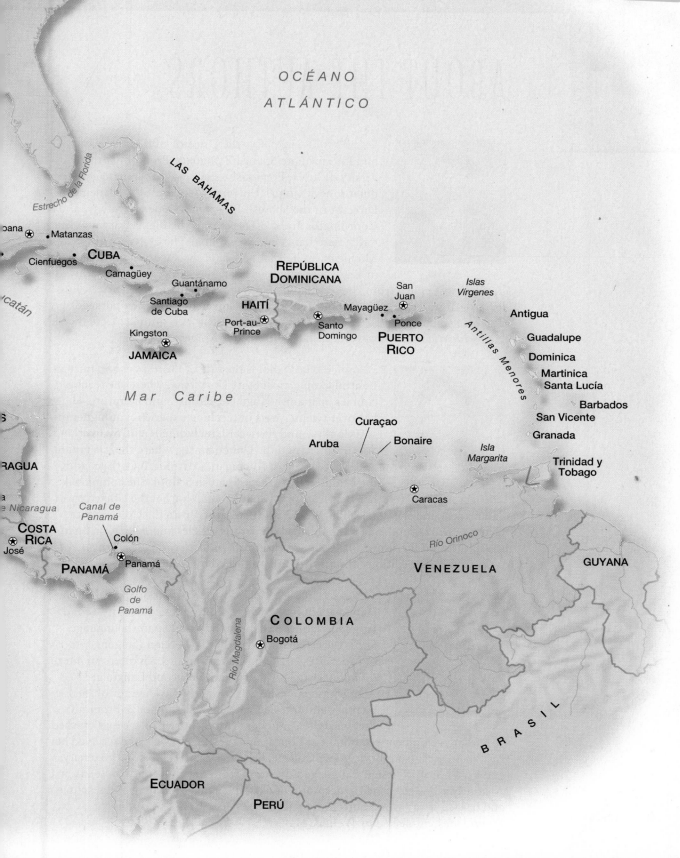

S0-AXI-748

OCÉANO

ATLÁNTICO

LAS BAHAMAS

Estrecho de la Florida

Matanzas

CUBA

Cienfuegos

Camagüey

REPÚBLICA
DOMINICANA

San
Juan

Islas
Vírgenes

Guantánamo

Santiago
de Cuba

HAITÍ

Mayagüez

Antigua

Yucatán

Port-au-
Prince

Santo
Domingo

Ponce

Guadalupe

Kingston

PUERTO
RICO

Dominica

JAMAICA

Martinica
Santa Lucía

Mar Caribe

Barbados

San Vicente

Curaçao

Granada

Aruba

Bonaire

Isla
Margarita

Trinidad y
Tobago

Caracas

Canal de
Panamá

Río Orinoco

e Nicaragua

COSTA
RICA

VENEZUELA

GUYANA

Colón

José

Panamá

PANAMÁ

Golfo
de
Panamá

COLOMBIA

Río Magdalena

Bogotá

B R A S I L

ECUADOR

PERÚ

ABOUT THE AUTHORS

Elizabeth E. Guzmán is the Director of the Elementary and Intermediate Spanish Language Program at the University of Iowa. Previously, she served as Language Coordinator at St. John's University/College of St. Benedict, Director of the Spanish Program at Yale University, and Coordinator and Co-Director of the Elementary and Intermediate Language Program at The University of Michigan. In her native Chile, she supervised instructors of English as a Foreign Language. Ms. Guzmán received her B.A. in English from Universidad de Santiago (Chile) and her M.A. in English as a Second Language from West Virginia University, and then pursued doctoral studies at the University of Pittsburgh. She is a co-author of Prentice-Hall's *Identidades* and several earlier editions of *Mosaicos*.

Paloma Lapuerta holds the title of Professor of Spanish at Central Connecticut State University, where she teaches courses in Spanish language, culture, and literature. She has over twenty years of teaching experience at higher institutions around the world, including Spain, Switzerland, South Africa, and the United States, where she has taught at the University of Michigan, Dartmouth College, and the Middlebury College Spanish School. She completed her *Licenciatura* in Spanish Philology at the University of Salamanca, and she holds a Ph.D. in Spanish literature from the University of Geneva, Switzerland. She has published numerous articles and a book on Spanish culture and literature. She is a co-author of *Identidades*, *La escritura paso a paso*, and earlier editions of *Mosaicos*, all published by Prentice Hall.

Judith E. Liskin-Gasparro is a professor of Spanish at the University of Iowa, where she teaches courses in second language acquisition, pedagogy, and Spanish language. She is the co-director of FLARE (Foreign Language Acquisition Research and Education), which offers an interdisciplinary doctoral program in Second Language Acquisition, and she was formerly the Director of the Elementary and Intermediate Spanish Language Program. Previously, she taught at Middlebury College and worked as a test development consultant at Educational Testing Service. She received her B.A. in Spanish from Bryn Mawr College, her M.A. from Princeton University, and her Ph.D. in Foreign Language Education from the University of Texas at Austin. She has published articles and books on language learning and teaching and has led many workshops for language teachers. She is a co-author of *Identidades*, published by Prentice Hall.

VOLUME 1

Fifth Edition

MOSAICOS

Spanish as a World Language

Matilde Olivella de Castells (Late)
Emerita, California State University, Los Angeles

Elizabeth E. Guzmán
University of Iowa

Paloma Lapuerta
Central Connecticut State University

Judith E. Liskin-Gasparro
University of Iowa

Prentice Hall
Upper Saddle River   London   Singapore   Toronto
Tokyo   Sydney   Hong Kong   Mexico City

Dedicamos esta edición de Mosaicos a Matilde Castells, quien puso juntas, una a una, las piezas de este libro con un talento y profesionalismo admirables.

Executive Editor: Julia Caballero
Development Editors: Elizabeth Lantz, Celia Meana
Executive Marketing Manager: Kris Ellis-Levy
Senior Marketing Manager: Denise Miller
Marketing Coordinator: William J. Bliss
Senior Managing Editor: Mary Rottino
Associate Managing Editor: Janice Stangel
Project Manager: Manuel Echevarria
Development Editor for Assessment: Melissa Marolla Brown
Media Editor: Meriel Martínez
Senior Media Editor: Samantha Alducin
Art Manager: Gail Cocker
Illustrator: Andrew Lange Illustration
Cartographer: Peter Bull Studio
Assistant Editor/EditorialCoordinator: Jennifer Murphy
Manufacturing Buyer: Cathleen Petersen

Manager, Print Production: Brian Mackey
Manager, Rights and Permissions: Zina Arabia
Manager, Visual Research: Beth Brenzel
Manager, Cover Visual Research & Permissions: Karen Sanatar
Image Permission Coordinator: Fran Toepfer
Cover Image: Ferran Traite Soler/IStockphoto.com
Photo Researcher: Diane Austin
Designer: Ximena Tamvakopoulos
Creative Design Director: Leslie Osher
Art Director, Interior: John Christiana
Editorial Assistant: Katie Spiegel
Publisher: Phil Miller
Composition/Full-Service Project Management: Macmillan Publishing Solutions
Printer/Binder: Courier Kendallville, Inc.

This book was set in 10/12.5 Sabon.

Credits and acknowledgments borrowed from other sources and reproduced, with permission, in this textbook appear on pages A54–A55.

Library of Congress Cataloging-in-Publication Data

Mosaicos : Spanish as a world language / Matilde Olivella de Castells ... [et al.]. — 5th ed.
  p. cm.
  English and Spanish.
  Includes bibliographical references and index.
  ISBN-13: 978-0-13-500153-0 (hardbound : alk. paper)
  ISBN-10: 0-13-500153-6 (hardbound : alk. paper)
  1. Spanish language—Textbooks for foreign speakers—English. I. Castells, Matilde Olivella de.

  PC4129.E5M69 2008
  468.2'421—dc22

                                                    2008046837

10 9 8 7 6 5 4

Student Edition ISBN - 10:	0-13-500153-6
Student Edition ISBN - 13:	978-0-13-500153-0
Annotated Instructor's Edition ISBN - 10:	0-205-66392-3
Annotated Instructor's Edition ISBN - 13:	978-0-205-66392-7
Volume 1 ISBN - 10:	0-205-63609-8
Volume 1 ISBN - 13:	978-0-205-63609-9
Volume 2 ISBN - 10:	0-205-63608-X
Volume 2 ISBN - 13:	978-0-205-63608-2
Volume 3 ISBN - 10:	0-205-63607-1
Volume 3 ISBN - 13:	978-0-205-63607-5

BRIEF CONTENTS

SCOPE AND SEQUENCE

Funciones y formas	Mosaicos	Enfoque cultural

Capítulo	Communicative objectives	A primera vista

Capítulo	Communicative objectives	A primera vista

Funciones y formas	Mosaicos	Enfoque cultural

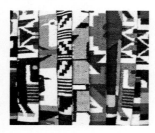  

Funciones y formas	Mosaicos	Enfoque cultural

Capítulo	Communicative objectives	A primera vista

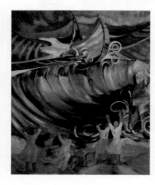

PREFACE

Welcome to the Fifth Edition of *Mosaicos*

Since the publication of its first edition more than a decade ago, *Mosaicos* has been widely acclaimed for its practical, communicative, culturally based approach to first-year Spanish. The approach has been refined over the course of several editions, and for this fifth edition we have been especially thorough in examining all aspects of the Student Text and all components of the *Mosaicos* program. The result is a fresh, twenty-first-century perspective on language teaching and learning in the context of a dynamic introduction to the Hispanic world and its people. We hope that both veteran users and those new to *Mosaicos* will discover a text that is richly contextualized, cognitively engaging, visually attractive, and readily accessible, accompanied by a wide array of resources that support student learning and make each class period valuable and enjoyable.

One of the hallmarks of the *Mosaicos* approach—and the rationale for the title—is the emphasis on the integration of the many different instructional strands that comprise a beginning Spanish course. We have made a special effort to ensure that this fifth edition effectively integrates elements that other programs often treat in isolation. We have gone farther than ever before in our effort to synthesize linguistic content with appropriate cultural contexts. We have refined and improved the open-ended *Situaciones* activities, in which students are asked to integrate their knowledge of grammatical structures and functions with thematically relevant vocabulary. Finally, we have made major revisions to the *Mosaicos* section of each chapter, in which students put linguistic and cultural knowledge together as they develop and practice their listening, speaking, reading, and writing skills.

Mosaicos reflects the wisdom and experience of the many expert language instructors who have used the program and have provided helpful suggestions over the years. But at a deeper level, it is grounded in current theories of language learning and in pedagogical principles embraced by most language instructors today. It presents vocabulary within communicative and cultural contexts. Its grammar sections move from meaning to form, providing an understanding of the language that is both functional and structural. It emphasizes the social aspects of language use by providing an abundance of carefully sequenced pair and group activities. It fosters awareness of the diversity of the Spanish-speaking world through photos, realia, maps, readings, and activities, as well as a new video program. By engaging students in the linguistic, cognitive, and social aspects of language learning, the distinctive *Mosaicos* approach draws on current knowledge about language learning to prepare first-year students to continue their study of Spanish language and culture at the intermediate level.

Highlights of the Fifth Edition

While building on the strengths of earlier editions, the fifth edition of *Mosaicos* incorporates many new and remarkable features. With its focus on learning strategies and communicative functions, it provides students and instructors with more tools than ever before to enhance and enrich the learning experience.

Vocabulary in Context

The *Mosaicos* program features a culturally and communicatively rich format for presenting and practicing new vocabulary. Through the two-page spread at the beginning of each chapter and in the *A primera vista* section that follows, students encounter new words in appropriate linguistic and cultural contexts.

The chapter-opening pages have been completely redesigned to provide a stimulating introduction both to the chapter theme and to the country or region that the chapter targets. New chapter titles highlight the text's active, functional approach to language learning, and abundant annotations on the chapter-opening pages guide instructors in introducing and recycling relevant vocabulary.

In the *A primera vista* section, new vocabulary is presented in contexts that reflect the chapter theme in various ways. Language samples, photos, line drawings, and realia are used to present new material, rather than word lists and translations. The activities that follow foster the use of new and previously learned vocabulary in natural, thematically relevant contexts. Special features include the following:

- Boldface type is used within the language samples to highlight new words and phrases that students will need to learn to use actively. (A convenient list of these words and phrases is provided at the end of each chapter.)

- Audio icons remind students that recorded versions of the language samples are available in the *Mosaicos* audio program.

- *Cultura* boxes (many new to this edition) raise awareness of the cultural contexts in which the language is used and help students learn the skills of close observation and interpretation of cultural products.

- *En otras palabras* boxes (all new to this edition) give examples of regional variations in the language.

Grammar as Function and Meaning

In the newly renamed *Funciones y formas* section of each chapter, grammar is presented as a means to effective communication. The bulleted explanations—clear, concise, and easy to understand—are designed to be studied at home, although their integration into the main body of the text enables students to use them for quick reference as they practice communication in class.

- Visuals and brief language samples are now used consistently to introduce new structures in meaningful contexts. The new structures are highlighted in boldface type.

- Short comprehension-based activities (all new to this edition) draw students' attention to the connection between meaning and linguistic form, providing a bridge from *función* to *forma*. These *Piénselo* activities are designed to help students develop their ability to think about how each structure communicates meaning by means of particular forms.

- A carefully designed sequence of communicative activities (many new or revised for this edition) follow the bulleted grammatical explanations. These activities focus attention on the communicative purpose of the linguistic structures while invoking culturally relevant contexts. All activities require students to process meaning as well as form so that they develop confidence in speaking and skill in using their linguistic knowledge to gather information, answer questions, and resolve problems.

- A large number of open-ended *Situaciones* activities (many new or revised for this edition) prompt students to integrate relevant grammatical structures with contexts drawn from the chapter theme. Two *Situaciones* role-plays are now provided for each grammar topic, and the format of these activities has been standardized so that there are always two roles (Role A and Role B). *En directo* boxes introduce colloquial expressions and encourage students to use them in the *Situaciones* and other communicative activities.

- Strategically placed *Lengua* boxes offer succinct grammatical information when it is needed to support self-expression.

- The grammatical scope and sequence has been modified in order to meet the communicative needs of beginning students more effectively. The *Algo más* boxes used in the fourth edition to present new structures have been eliminated; all essential structures are now given the full range of explanation and activities. Major topics, such as the preterit and imperfect, **ser/estar**, and object pronouns, are recycled to enhance learning, and basic topics such as regular verbs and **gustar** are presented earlier to spread essential structures more evenly over the book's fifteen chapters.

Integrated Culture

The fifth edition of *Mosaicos* builds on the successful integration of culture and language of previous editions. Each chapter focuses on a specific country or region, and numerous references to that country or region appear in the chapter's language samples, photos, maps, and realia. Related cultural content is interwoven throughout the activities and readings.

- A newly designed two-page chapter opener highlights the country or region that is the focus of the chapter. It includes a relevant work of art as well as maps and photos. A new warm-up activity (called *A vista de pájaro*) encourages students to process the visually presented information while accessing relevant prior knowledge. Numerous annotations offer instructors factual, conversational, and linguistic suggestions to pique students' interest and ease them into the chapter.

- The *Enfoque cultural* section of each chapter has new readings and accompanying activities. The first set of activities is available online as well as in the textbook. A final activity asks students to use the reading as a point of departure for expanding and sharing their knowledge. The standardized format of this section makes it possible for students to work with the readings independently so that class time may be devoted to the cultural content.

- Brief *Cultura* boxes found throughout each chapter explain cultural products, practices, and perspectives, making the cultural contexts of the vocabulary and grammatical activities meaningful and accessible to students.

Engaging New Video

A completely new video, entitled *Diarios de bicicleta*, has been scripted and filmed specifically to accompany the fifth edition of *Mosaicos*. Each episode of this engaging, often humorous video reflects the corresponding chapter's communicative objectives, recycling vocabulary and previewing functions and forms. The story line revolves around four recurring characters, but each episode is self-contained and independent of other episodes.

- The video segment for each chapter includes short excerpts that highlight the language functions introduced in the *Funciones y formas* section of the text.

- Pre-viewing, viewing, and post-viewing activities (all new to this edition) are provided in the Student Text in a special section of each chapter entitled *En acción*. Additional activities may be found in the Student Activities Manual.

A Four-Skills Synthesis

Like its predecessors, the fifth edition devotes a prominent section of each chapter to the development and practice of communication skills. These newly streamlined *Mosaicos* sections provide students with a unique opportunity to bring together the chapter's thematic content and vocabulary with its linguistic structures and cultural focus. New features, texts, and activities enhance the effectiveness of this aspect of the program.

- Specific strategies are now presented in each chapter for each of the four skills (listening, speaking, reading, and writing). The strategies build on each other within and across chapters. Activities are designed so that students systematically practice implementing the strategies presented.

- New listening activities have been created for the *A escuchar* sections. The content and genre of the listening texts, as well as the accompanying strategies, consistently support the chapter theme.

- In the *A conversar* sections, specific strategies are now provided for speaking as they are for other skill areas. The speaking activities that follow encourage structured pair interaction and help students develop interpersonal speaking skills.

- The streamlined *A leer* sections now include only one reading each. The reading selections (many new to this edition) are drawn largely from authentic texts. They reflect a variety of discourse types, ranging from expository to journalistic to literary. Activities linked to the reading strategy boost students' comprehension and reading skills.

- The process writing activities in the *A escribir* sections have been revised so that the pre- and post-writing activities now guide students through critical steps in the writing process. Where possible, these activities refer students back to the immediately preceding reading, deepening students' comprehension and awareness of text structure.

Informed by National Standards

The *Standards for Foreign Language Learning: Preparing for the 21st Century*, whose five goal areas have served as an organizing principle for language instruction for more than a decade, inform the pedagogy of the fifth edition of *Mosaicos*. Marginal notes throughout the Annotated Instructor's Edition draw attention to the way specific activities or other elements of the program help students develop proficiency in the five goal areas. A number of general strategies have been followed.

Communication.   Students are prompted to engage in meaningful conversations throughout the text, providing and obtaining information, expressing their opinions and preferences, and sharing their experiences. Readings and listening activities invite them to interpret language on a variety of topics, while *presentaciones* and writing assignments call on them to present information and ideas in both written and oral modes.

Cultures.   Many features of the text, including the maps, photos, *Cultura* boxes, and the readings in the *Mosaicos* and *Enfoque cultural* sections of each chapter, give students an understanding of the relationship between culture and language throughout the Spanish-speaking world.

Connections.   Realia, readings, the *Enfoque cultural* application activities, and conversation activities throughout the text provide opportunities to make connections with other disciplines. Students gain information and insight into the distinctive viewpoints of Spanish speakers and their cultures.

Comparisons.   *Lengua* and *En otras palabras* boxes often provide students with points of comparison between English and Spanish (and among the varieties of Spanish spoken in different parts of the world). Readings and activities frequently juxtapose U.S. and Hispanic cultural products, practices, and perspectives.

Communities.   The text encourages students to extend their learning through guided research on the Internet and/or other sources, and many of the topics explored in *Mosaicos* can stimulate exploration, personal enjoyment, and enrichment beyond the confines of formal language instruction. Instructors are reminded to encourage students to become acquainted with Spanish-speaking communities in their areas.

The Complete Program

Mosaicos is a complete teaching and learning program that includes a variety of resources for students and instructors, including an innovative offering of online resources.

For the student

Student Text
The *Mosaicos* Student Text is available in a complete, hardbound version, consisting of a preliminary chapter followed by Chapters 1 through 15. New to this edition is the option of three paperback volumes rather than the single hardcover version. Volume 1 of the paperback series contains the preliminary chapter plus Chapters 1 to 5; Volume 2, Chapters 5 to 10; and Volume 3, Chapters 10 to 15. All three volumes include the complete front and back matter.

Student Activities Manual
The Student Activities Manual (SAM), thoroughly revised for this edition, includes workbook activities together with audio- and video-based activities, all designed to provide extensive practice of the vocabulary, grammar, culture, and skills introduced in each chapter. The organization of these materials now parallels that of the student text, with an *A primera vista* section followed by *En acción* video activities, *Funciones y formas*, *Mosaicos*, and *Enfoque cultural*. A new section in each chapter (entitled *Repaso*) provides additional activities designed to help students review the material of the chapter as well as to prepare for tests.

The printed Student Activities Manual is available both in a single volume and in a series of separate volumes, paralleling the paperback volumes of the student text. The contents of the Student Activities Manual and MySpanishLab are also available online.

Answer Key to Accompany Student Activities Manual
An Answer Key to the Student Activities Manual is available separately, giving instructors the option of allowing students to check their homework. The Answer Key now includes answers to all SAM activities.

Supplementary Activities Book
Also available is a Supplementary Activities Book consisting of a range of fun, engaging activities that complement the vocabulary and grammar themes of each chapter. It offers instructors additional materials that can serve to energize and enrich their students' classroom experience.

Audio CDs to Accompany Student Text
A set of audio CDs contains recordings of the *A primera vista* language samples and the end-of-chapter vocabulary lists. It also contains audio material for listening activities included in the student text. These recordings are also available online.

Audio CDs to Accompany Student Activities Manual
A second set of audio CDs contains audio material for the listening activities in the Student Activities Manual. These recordings are also available online.

Video on DVD
Diarios de bicicleta is an original video filmed to accompany the fifth edition of *Mosaicos*. Students see the vocabulary and grammar structures of each chapter in use in realistic situations while gaining a deeper understanding of Hispanic cultures. The video also includes segments highlighting the communicative functions of each chapter. Pre-viewing, viewing, and post-viewing activities are found in the *En acción* sections of the textbook and the Student Activities Manual. The video is available for student purchase on DVD, and it is also available within MySpanishLab.

Meet the Cast

Here are the main characters of *Diarios de bicicleta*, who you will get to know when you watch the video:

Javier   Luciana   Daniel   Gaby

In addition to *Diarios de bicicleta*, two other videos are available for use in conjunction with the *Mosaicos* program. *Entrevistas* consists of interviews in which native speakers use authentic Spanish to address topics related to each chapter's theme. *Vistas culturales* contains nineteen 10–minute vignettes with footage from every Spanish-speaking country. Each of the accompanying narrations, which employ vocabulary and grammar designed for first-year language learners, was written by a native of the featured country or region. All three videos are also available online.

Online resources

MySpanishLab™

MySpanishLab is a new, nationally hosted online learning system created for students in college-level language courses. It brings together—in one convenient, easily navigable site—a wide array of language-learning tools and resources, including an interactive version of the *Mosaicos* Student Activities Manual, an electronic version of the *Mosaicos* student text, and all materials from the *Mosaicos* audio and video programs. Readiness checks, chapter tests, and tutorials personalize instruction to meet the unique needs of individual students. Instructors can use the system to make assignments, set grading parameters, listen to student-created audio recordings, and provide feedback on student work. Instructor access is provided at no charge. Students can purchase access codes online or at their local bookstore.

Companion Website

The open-access Companion Website (www.pearsonhighered.com/mosaicos) includes an array of activities and resources designed to reinforce the vocabulary, grammar, and cultural material introduced in each chapter. It also provides audio recordings for the student text and Student Activities Manual, links for Internet-based activites in the student text, and additional web exploration activities for each chapter. All contents of the Companion Website are also included in MySpanishLab.

Acknowledgments

Mosaicos is the result of a collaborative effort among the authors, our publisher, and our colleagues. We are especially indebted to many members of the Spanish teaching community for their time, candor, and insightful suggestions as they reviewed the drafts of the fifth edition of *Mosaicos*. Their critiques and recommendations helped us to sharpen our pedagogical focus and improve the overall quality of the program. We gratefully acknowledge the contributions of the following reviewers:

Rafael Arias, *Los Angeles Valley College*
Alejandra Balestra, *University of New Mexico*
Aymará Boggiano, *University of Houston*
Amanda Boomershine, *University of North Carolina-Wilmington*
Talia Bugel, *Indiana University-Purdue University Fort Wayne*
José Carrasquel, *Florida International University*
Zoila Clark, *Florida International University*
Daria Cohen, *Rider University*
Alyce Cook, *Columbus State University*
Richard Curry, *Texas A&M University*
Marta de la Caridad Pérez, *Florida International University*
Beatrice DeAngelis, *University of Pittsburgh*
Marisol del Teso Craviotto, *Miami University of Ohio*

Angela Erickson-Grussing, *St. John's University/College of St. Benedict*
Juliet Falce-Robinson, *University of California-Los Angeles*
Gayle Fiedler-Vierma, *University of Southern California*
Óscar Flores, *State University of New York-Plattsburgh*
Ausenda Folch, *Florida International University*
Myriam García, *Florida International University*
Rosa María Gómez García-Bermejo, *Florida International University*
Frozina Goussak, *Collin County Community College*
Dawn Heston, *University of Missouri-Columbia*
Casilde Isabelli, *University of Nevada-Reno*
Keith Johnson, *California State University-Fresno*
Linda Keown, *University of Missouri-Columbia*
Ruth Konopka, *Grossmont College*

Lina Llerena Callahan, *Fullerton College*
Susana Liso, *University of Virginia-Wise*
Leticia López, *San Diego Mesa College*
Libardo Mitchell, *Portland Community College-Sylvania*
Dorothy Moore, *Gettysburg College*
Michelle Orecchio, *University of Michigan*
Teresa Pérez-Gamboa, *University of Georgia*
Ana María Pinzón, *Frederick Community College*

Mónica Prieto, *Florida International University*
Nuria Sagarra, *Pennsylvania State University*
Toni Trives, *Santa Monica College*
Clara Vega, *Almance Community College*
Celinés Villalba, *University of California-Berkeley*
Lisa Volle, *Central Texas College*
Sarah Williams, *University of Pittsburgh*
Loretta Zehngut, *Pennsylvania State University*

We are also grateful for the guidance of Elizabeth Lantz, development editor, for all of her work, suggestions, attention to detail, and dedication to the text. Her support and spirit helped us to achieve the final product. Special thanks are due to Celia Meana, development editor, for helping with the art program, with the final pages, and with many other editorial details. We would also like to thank the contributors who assisted us in the preparation of the fifth edition: Daria Cohen, Marisol del Teso Craviotto, Juliet Falce-Robinson, Linda Keown, Gustavo Mejía, Teresa Pérez-Gamboa, Anne Prucha, and Lilián Uribe. Special thanks to Ninon Larché and Debbie King for their assistance in the preparation of the manuscript. We are very grateful to other colleagues and friends at Prentice Hall: Meriel Martínez, Media Editor, for helping us produce such a great video, audio programs, and Companion Website; Melissa Marolla Brown, Development Editor for Assessment, for the diligent coordination among the text, Student Activities Manual, and Testing Program; Samantha Alducin, Senior Media Editor, for managing the creation of *Mosaicos* materials for My SpanishLab™; and Jenn Murphy, Assistant Editor/Editorial Coordinator, for her work in managing the preparation of the other supplements. Thanks to Katie Spiegel, Editorial Assistant, for her hard work and efficiency in obtaining reviews and attending to many administrative details.

We are very grateful to our marketing team, Kris Ellis-Levy, Denise Miller, and Bill Bliss, for their creativity and efforts in coordinating all marketing and promotion for this edition. Thanks, too, to our production team, Mary Rottino, Janice Stangel, and Manuel Echevarria, who guided *Mosaicos* through the many stages of production; to our partners at Macmillan Publishing Solutions, especially Jill Traut, for her careful and professional editing and production services. We also thank our art team, Gail Cocker, Peter Bull, and Andrew Lange, for their amazing creativity and beautiful maps and illustrations. Special thanks to Leslie Osher, John Christina, and Ximena Tamvakopoulos for the gorgeous interior and cover designs. Finally, we would like to express our sincere thanks to Phil Miller, Publisher, and Julia Caballero, Executive Editor, for their guidance and support through every aspect of this new edition.

A Guide to *Mosaicos* Icons

	A vista de pájaro	This icon indicates a panoramic, quick overview. It accompanies the chapter opener activity and reminds students to activate background knowledge about the country or countries featured in the chapter, as well as to use the information presented in the map.
	Text Audio Program	This icon indicates that recorded material is available for students in the *Mosaicos* text audio program for students. The audio includes vocabulary and dialogues presented in *A primera vista*, as well as the listening activities presented in the text.
	Pair Activity	This icon indicates that the activity is designed to be done by students working in pairs.
	Group Activity	This icon indicates that the activity is designed to be done by students working in small groups.
	Web Activity	This icon indicates that the activity involves use of the World Wide Web. Helpful links and activities can be found on the *Mosaicos* Companion Website.

Bienvenidos

El mundo hispano les da la bienvenida.

In this chapter you will learn how to:

- introduce yourself, greet others, and say good-bye
- use expressions of courtesy
- spell in Spanish
- identify people and classroom objects
- locate people and things

- use numbers from 0–99
- express dates
- tell time
- use classroom expressions
- comment on the weather

Personas que hablan español (en millones)

Estados Unidos 35
Cuba 11,4
México 108,7
República Dominicana 9,4
Puerto Rico 3,9
Guatemala 12,7
El Salvador 6,9
Honduras 7,5
Nicaragua 5,7
Venezuela 26
Costa Rica 4,1
Colombia 44,4
Panamá 3,2
Ecuador 13,8
Perú 28,7
Bolivia 9,1
Paraguay 6,7
Chile 16,3
Uruguay 3,4
Argentina 40,3
España 40,4
Guinea Ecuatorial 0,7
Filipinas 2,9

 A vista de pájaro. Relying on your knowledge of the world, look at the map and determine whether each statement is true (**Cierto**) or false (**Falso**).

1. _____ Más de (*More than*) 350 millones de personas hablan español en el mundo.
2. _____ En Filipinas no se habla español.
3. _____ En Estados Unidos hablan español más personas que (*more ... than*) en Chile.
4. _____ En Guinea Ecuatorial se habla español.
5. _____ En Brasil se habla portugués.
6. _____ El español se habla en 23 países.

Las presentaciones

CD 1
Track 1

ANTONIO: **Me llamo** Antonio Mendoza.
Y tú, ¿cómo te llamas?

BENITO: Me llamo Benito Sánchez.

ANTONIO: **Mucho gusto.**

BENITO: **Igualmente.**

PROFESOR: **¿Cómo se llama usted?**

ISABEL: Me llamo Isabel Contreras.

PROFESOR: Mucho gusto.

LAURA: María, **mi amigo** José.

MARÍA: Mucho gusto.

JOSÉ: **Encantado.**

- Spanish has more than one word meaning *you*. Use **tú** when talking to someone on a first-name basis (a child, close friend, or relative).

  Use **usted** when talking to someone you address in a respectful or formal manner; for example, **doctor/doctora; profesor/profesora; señor/señora.** Also use **usted** to address individuals you do not know well.

- Young people normally use **tú** when speaking to each other.

- **Mucho gusto** is used by both men and women when they are meeting someone for the first time. A man may also say **encantado**, and a woman, **encantada**.

- You may respond to **mucho gusto** with either **encantado/a** or **igualmente**.

P-1 Presentaciones. **PRIMERA FASE.** Complete the following conversation with the appropriate expressions from the box on the right.

ALICIA: Me llamo Alicia. Y tú, ¿cómo te llamas?

ISABEL: Isabel Pérez. _____.

ALICIA: _____.

ALICIA: Isabel, _____.

ISABEL: Mucho gusto.

PEDRO: _____.

> Igualmente
> Mucho gusto
> Encantado
> mi amigo Pedro

SEGUNDA FASE. Move around the classroom, introducing yourself to several classmates and introducing classmates to each other.

Los saludos y las despedidas

Los saludos

CD 1
Track 2

SEÑOR: **Buenos días, señorita** Rivas.

SEÑORITA: Buenos días. **¿Cómo está usted, señor** Gómez?

SEÑOR: **Bien, gracias.** ¿Y usted?

SEÑORITA: **Muy** bien, gracias.

MARTA: **¡Hola,** Inés! **¿Qué tal? ¿Cómo estás?**

INÉS: **Regular,** ¿y tú?

MARTA: **Bastante** bien, gracias.

SEÑORA: **Buenas tardes,** Felipe. ¿Cómo estás?

FELIPE: Bien, gracias. Y usted, ¿cómo está, **señora?**

SEÑORA: **Mal,** Felipe, mal.

FELIPE: **Lo siento.**

- Use **buenos días** until lunchtime.

- Use **buenas tardes** from noon until nightfall. After nightfall, use **buenas noches** (*good evening, good night*).

- **¿Qué tal?** is a more informal greeting. It is normally used with **tú,** but it may also be used with **usted.**

- Use **está** with **usted** and **estás** with **tú.**

P-2 Saludos. You work as a receptionist in a hotel. Which greeting (**buenos días, buenas tardes, buenas noches**) is appropriate at the following times?

1. 9:00 a.m.
2. 11:00 p.m.
3. 4:00 p.m.
4. 8:00 a.m.
5. 1:00 p.m.
6. 10:00 p.m.

Las despedidas

CD 1
Track 3

adiós	*good-bye*
hasta luego	*see you later*
hasta mañana	*see you tomorrow*
hasta pronto	*see you soon*
chao	*good-bye*

■ **Adiós** is generally used when you do not expect to see the other person for a while. It is also used as a greeting when people pass each other but have no time to stop and talk.

■ **Chao** (also spelled **chau**) is an informal way of saying good-bye. It is popular in South America.

P-3 Despedidas. How would you say good-bye in these situations?
1. You'll see your friend tomorrow.
2. You arrange to meet your classmate at the library in 10 minutes.
3. Your roommate is leaving for a semester abroad.
4. You run into a good friend on campus.

Expresiones de cortesía

CD 1
Track 4

por favor	*please*
gracias	*thanks, thank you*
de nada	*you're welcome*
lo siento	*I'm sorry (to hear that)*
con permiso	*pardon me, excuse me*
perdón	*pardon me, excuse me*

■ **Con permiso** and **perdón** may be used before the fact, as when asking a person to allow you to go by or when trying to get someone's attention. Only **perdón** is used after the fact, as when you have stepped on someone's foot or have interrupted a conversation.

P-4 ¿Perdón o con permiso? Would you use **perdón** or **con permiso** in these situations?

1.

2.

3.

4.

5.

P-5 Despedidas y expresiones de cortesía. Which expression(s) would you use in the following situations?

adiós	gracias	lo siento
de nada	hasta luego	por favor

1. Someone thanks you.
2. You say good-bye to a friend you will see later this evening.
3. You ask if you can borrow a classmate's notes.
4. You hear that your friend is sick.
5. You receive a present from your cousin.
6. Your friend is leaving for a vacation in Costa Rica.

P-6 Encuentros (*Encounters*). You meet the following people on the street. Greet them, ask how they are, and then say good-bye. Switch roles and role play the encounters again.

1. su (*your*) amigo Miguel
2. su profesor/a
3. su amiga Isabel
4. su doctor/a

·)) Distinguishing Registers

CD 1
Track 5

When you talk to different people, you use different registers, that is, you address them with various degrees of formality, depending on your level of intimacy and the context of the exchange. For example, when you talk to a professor, you probably use more formal language than when you talk to classmates or friends. In Spanish, one way to mark this difference is by using **tú** (informal) and **usted** (formal).

Now you will hear four brief conversations in which people greet each other. Before you listen, complete the following chart with the pronoun you think you would use in each case.

WHEN TALKING TO YOUR …	TÚ	USTED
1. brother or sister		
2. doctor		
3. coach		
4. parents		

P-7 Conversaciones. As you listen to the four conversations, mark (✓) the appropriate column to indicate whether the greetings are formal (with **usted**) or informal (with **tú**). Do not worry if you do not understand every word.

FORMAL   INFORMAL

1. _____   _____
2. _____   _____
3. _____   _____
4. _____   _____

·)) El alfabeto

CD 1
Track 6

a	a		o	o
b	be		p	pe
c	ce		q	cu
d	de		r	ere, erre
e	e		s	ese
f	efe		t	te
g	ge		u	u
h	hache		v	ve, uve
i	i		w	doble ve, doble uve
j	jota			uve doble, ve doble
k	ka		x	equis
l	ele		y	i griega, ye
m	eme		z	zeta
n	ene			
ñ	eñe			

En otras palabras

Like English speakers, Spanish speakers have different accents that reflect their region or country of origin. For example, the letter **c** before vowels **e** and **i** and the letter **z** are pronounced like **s**, except in certain regions of Spain, where they are similar to the English *th*.

■ The Spanish alphabet includes **ñ**, a letter that does not exist in English. Its sound is similar to the pronunciation of *ni* and *ny* in the English words *onion* and *canyon*.

■ The letters **k** and **w** appear mainly in words of foreign origin.

 P-8 ¿Cómo se escribe? Ask your classmate how to spell these Spanish last names.

MODELO: Zamora
   E1: *¿Cómo se escribe Zamora?*
   E2: *Con zeta.*

1. Celaya
2. Montalvo
3. Salas
4. Bolaños
5. Henares
6. Velázquez

 P-9 Los nombres. You are at the admissions office of a university in a Spanish-speaking country. Spell out your first or last name for the clerk. Take turns.

MODELO: E1: *¿Cómo se llama usted?*
   E2: *Me llamo David Robinson.*
   E1: *¿Cómo se escribe Robinson?*
   E2: *ere-o-be-i-ene-ese-o-ene.*

Identificación y descripción de personas

CD 1
Track 7

CARLOS: **¿Quién es ese chico?**
SANDRA: **Es** Julio.
CARLOS: **¿Cómo es** Julio?
SANDRA: **Es** romántico y sentimental.

LUIS: ¿Quién es **esa chica?**
QUIQUE: Es Carmen.
LUIS: ¿Cómo es Carmen?
QUIQUE: Es activa y muy seria.

■ The verb *ser* is used to identify and describe.
  Esa chica **es** Carmen. Ella **es** activa y muy seria.
  Rodolfo **es** su amigo. **Es** atractivo.

■ Here are the forms of *ser* you will be using in this chapter.

SER *(to be)*			
yo	**soy**	*I*	*am*
tú	**eres**	*you*	*are*
usted	**es**	*you*	*are*
él, ella	**es**	*he, she*	*is*

■ To make a sentence negative, place **no** before the appropriate form of **ser**. When responding negatively to a question, say **no** twice.

Ella es inteligente.　　→　　Ella **no** es inteligente.

¿Es rebelde?　　→　　**No, no** es rebelde.

Cognados

Cognados (*cognates*) are words from two languages that have the same origin and are similar in form and meaning. Since English and Spanish have many cognates, you will discover that you already recognize many Spanish words. Here are some cognates that you may use to describe people.

■ The following cognates use the same form to describe a man or a woman.

arrogante	importante	optimista	popular
eficiente	independiente	paciente	responsable
elegante	inteligente	perfeccionista	sentimental
idealista	interesante	pesimista	tradicional

■ The following cognates have two forms. The **-o** form is used to describe a male, and the **-a** form to describe a female.

activo/a	creativo/a	introvertido/a	romántico/a
ambicioso/a	dinámico/a	moderno/a	serio/a
atlético/a	extrovertido/a	nervioso/a	sincero/a
atractivo/a	generoso/a	pasivo/a	tímido/a
cómico/a	impulsivo/a	religioso/a	tranquilo/a

■ Some words appear to be cognates but do not have the same meaning in both languages. These are called false cognates. **Lectura** (*reading*) and **éxito** (*success*) are examples. You will find other examples in future chapters.

 P-10 ¿Cómo es mi compañero/a? Choose from the preceding lists of cognates to ask the person next to you about his/her personality.

MODELO:　E1:　*¿Eres pesimista?*
　　　　　　　E2:　*No, no soy pesimista. O Sí, soy (muy) pesimista.*

Then find out how your classmate describes himself/herself.

MODELO:　E1:　*¿Cómo eres (tú)?*
　　　　　　　E2:　*Soy activo, optimista y creativo.*

P-11 Descripciones. Ask each other about your classmates. Describe them by using cognates from the preceding lists.

MODELO:　E1:　*¿Cómo es... ?*
　　　　　　　E2:　*Es...*

¿Qué hay en el salón de clase?

un reloj
una pantalla
una pizarra
un profesor
un televisor
una tiza
un borrador
un DVD
una mesa
una computadora
un libro
un marcador/un rotulador
un escritorio
un cesto
una silla
un estudiante
una estudiante
un bolígrafo
una calculadora
un cuaderno
un lápiz
una mochila
un pupitre

P-12 Identificación. With a partner, identify the items on this table.

P-13 Para la clase de español. Write down a list of the things you need for this class. Compare your list with that of your partner.

¿Dónde está?

■ To ask about the location of a person or an object, use **dónde + está**.

¿Dónde está la profesora?	Está en la clase.
¿Dónde está el libro?	Está sobre el escritorio.

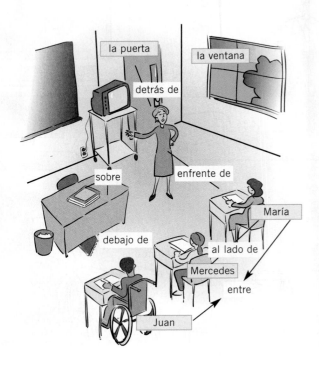

P-14 Localización. PRIMERA FASE. Indicate whether each statement is true (**Cierto**) or false (**Falso**), based on the relative position of people and objects in the drawing.

	CIERTO	FALSO
1. El televisor está detrás de la profesora.	_____	_____
2. Juan está al lado de la profesora.	_____	_____
3. El libro está sobre el escritorio.	_____	_____
4. María está entre Mercedes y Juan.	_____	_____
5. Mercedes está enfrente de la ventana.	_____	_____
6. El cesto está debajo de un pupitre.	_____	_____

 SEGUNDA FASE. Now complete the following sentences, based on the relative position of people and objects in the drawing. Compare your answers.

1. La pizarra está _____ la profesora.
2. María está _____ la profesora.
3. Mercedes está _____ Juan y María.
4. Juan está _____ Mercedes.
5. El cesto está _____ Juan.
6. El televisor está _____ la pizarra y la puerta.

·)) Listening with Visuals

CD 1
Track 8 When you are talking with someone, paying attention to the pictures or objects that the speaker points to or refers to can help you understand what is being said. These objects may be around you, or they may not, in which case you have only a mental representation of them. For example, when a friend describes his/her Spanish classroom, an image of a classroom comes to your mind based on your experience as a student.

In Spanish, make a list of the people and objects you expect to see in a classroom.

Now, as you listen to the statements about the location of people and objects, look at the drawing of the classroom on page 12 to help you understand what the speakers are saying.

Indicate (✓) whether each statement is true (**Cierto**) or false (**Falso**).

	CIERTO	FALSO
1.	_____	_____
2.	_____	_____
3.	_____	_____
4.	_____	_____
5.	_____	_____
6.	_____	_____

P-15 En la clase. Look at the seating chart below, and then follow the instructions.

María	Juan	Ester	Susana	Pedro
Carlos	Cristina	Ángeles	Alberto	Anita
Mercedes	Victoria	Roberto	Rocío	Pablo
		El profesor Gallegos		

ESTUDIANTE 1: Ask where Juan, Pedro, Cristina, Mercedes, Roberto, and Pablo are sitting.

ESTUDIANTE 2: Ask where *María, Ester, Susana, Carlos, Ángeles, Alberto, Anita, Victoria, Rocío,* and *Profesor Gallegos* are sitting.

P-16 ¿Dónde está? Take turns asking where several items in your classroom are. Answer by giving their position in relation to a person or another object.

MODELO: E1: *¿Dónde está el libro?*
E2: *Está sobre el escritorio.*

P-17 ¿Quién es? Based on what your partner says regarding the location of another student, guess who he/she is.

MODELO: E1: *Está al lado de Juan. ¿Quién es?*
E2: *Es María.*

Los números 0 a 99

CD 1
Track 9

0	cero	11	once	22	veintidós
1	uno	12	doce	23	veintitrés
2	dos	13	trece	30	treinta
3	tres	14	catorce	31	treinta y uno
4	cuatro	15	quince	40	cuarenta
5	cinco	16	dieciséis	50	cincuenta
6	seis	17	diecisiete	60	sesenta
7	siete	18	dieciocho	70	setenta
8	ocho	19	diecinueve	80	ochenta
9	nueve	20	veinte	90	noventa
10	diez	21	veintiuno		

■ Numbers from sixteen through twenty-nine are usually written as one word. Note the spelling changes and the written accent on some forms.

   18: **dieciocho**   22: **veintidós**

■ Beginning with thirty-one, numbers are written as three words.

   31: **treinta y uno**   45: **cuarenta y cinco**

■ The number *one* has three forms in Spanish: **uno, un,** and **una.** Use **uno** when counting: **uno, dos, tres...** Use **un** or **una** before nouns: **un borrador, una mochila, veintiún libros, veintiuna mochilas.**

■ Use **hay** for both *there is* and *there are.*

   Hay un libro sobre la mesa.   *There is one book on the table.*
   Hay dos libros sobre la mesa.   *There are two books on the table.*

 P-18 ¿Qué número es? Your instructor will read a number from each group. Circle the number you hear. Then compare your responses with those of your partner.

   a. 8   4   3   5
   b. 12   9   16   6
   c. 37   59   41   26
   d. 54   38   76   95
   e. 83   62   72   49
   f. 47   14   91   56

P-19 Para la oficina. You and your partner are student assistants in the Spanish department. You have to check a shipment of equipment and supplies that just arrived. Choose five items and tell your partner how many of each there are. He/She will take notes. Exchange roles.

MODELO: 4-7 mesas: *Hay cuatro mesas.*

a. 6-10 teléfonos
b. 8-12 escritorios
c. 1-2 silla(s)
d. 6-12 calculadoras
e. 10-20 cestos

f. 90-95 bolígrafos
g. 9-15 computadoras
h. 22-24 computadoras portátiles
i. 1-3 reloj(es)
j. ...

P-20 Problemas. Take turns solving the following arithmetic problems. Use **y** (+), **menos** (−), and **son** (=).

MODELO: 2 + 4 =   12 − 5 =
          Dos y cuatro son seis.   Doce menos cinco son siete.

a. 11 + 4 =
b. 8 + 2 =
c. 13 + 3 =

d. 20 − 6 =
e. 39 + 50 =
f. 80 − 1 =

g. 50 − 25 =
h. 26 + 40 =
i. 90 − 12 =

P-21 Los números de teléfono y las direcciones (*addresses*). With your partner, take turns asking each other the phone numbers and addresses of the people listed in the chart below.

Cárdenas Alfaro, Joaquín	General Páez 40	423-4837
Cárdenas Villanueva, Sara	Avenida Bolívar 7	956-1709
Castelar Torres, Adelaida	Paseo del Prado 85	218-3642
Castellanos Rey, Carlos	Colón 62	654-6416
Castelli Rivero, Victoria	Chamberí 3	615-7359
Castillo Montoya, Rafael	Santa Cruz 73	956-3382

MODELO: Castellanos Rey, Carlos
          E1: *¿Cuál es la dirección de Carlos Castellanos Rey?*
          E2: *Calle Colón, número 62.*
          E1: *¿Cuál es su teléfono?*
          E2: *(Es el) 6-54-64-16*

Cultura

In Spanish-speaking countries, the name of the street precedes the house or building number. Sometimes a comma is placed before the number.

Calle Bolívar 132
132 Bolívar Street

Avenida de Gracia, 18
18 Gracia Avenue

Telephone numbers are generally not stated as individual numbers, but in groups of two, depending on how the numbers are written or on the number of digits, which varies from country to country.

12-24-67:
doce, veinticuatro, sesenta y siete

243-89-07:
dos cuarenta y tres, ochenta y nueve, cero siete

◗)) Los meses del año y los días de la semana

CD 1
Track 10

enero	*January*	**mayo**	*May*	**septiembre**	*September*
febrero	*February*	**junio**	*June*	**octubre**	*October*
marzo	*March*	**julio**	*July*	**noviembre**	*November*
abril	*April*	**agosto**	*August*	**diciembre**	*December*

ENERO CALENDARIO

lunes	martes	miércoles	jueves	viernes	sábado	domingo
		1 AÑO NUEVO	2	3	4	5
6 LOS SANTOS REYES	7	8	9	10	11	12
13	14	15	16	17	18	19
20	21	22	23	24	25	26
27	28	29	30	31		

Days of the week and months of the year are not generally capitalized in Spanish, but sometimes they are capitalized in advertisements and invitations.

■ Monday (**lunes**) is normally considered the first day of the week.

■ To ask what day it is, use **¿Qué día es hoy?** Answer with **Hoy es…**

■ To ask about the date, use **¿Qué fecha es?** or **¿Cuál es la fecha?** Respond with **Es el (14) de (octubre).**

■ Express *on + a day of the week* as follows:

el lunes	*on Monday*
los lunes	*on Mondays*
el domingo	*on Sunday*
los domingos	*on Sundays*

■ Cardinal numbers are used with dates (e.g., **el dos**, **el tres**), except for the first day of the month, which is **el primero**. In Spain the first day is also referred to as **el uno**.

Lengua

When dates are written using only numerals, the day normally precedes the month: *11/8* = **el 11 de agosto**.

P-22 ¿Qué día de la semana es? Using the preceding calendar, take turns asking *¿Qué día de la semana es... ?*

1. el 2
2. el 5
3. el 22
4. el 18
5. el 10
6. el 13
7. el 28
8. el...

 P-23 Preguntas. Take turns asking and answering these questions.

1. ¿Qué día es hoy?
2. Hoy es... ¿Qué día es mañana?
3. Hoy es el... de... ¿Qué fecha es mañana?
4. ¿Hay clase de español los domingos? ¿Y los sábados?
5. ¿Qué días hay clase de español?

 P-24 Fechas importantes. Working with a partner, tell each other the dates on which these events take place.

MODELO: la reunión de estudiantes (10/9)
        E1: *¿Cuándo es la reunión de estudiantes?*
        E2: *(Es) el 10 de septiembre.*

1. el concierto de Marc Anthony (12/11)
2. el aniversario de Carlos y María (14/4)
3. el banquete (1/3)
4. la graduación (22/5)
5. la fiesta de bienvenida (24/8)

 P-25 El cumpleaños (*birthday*). Find out when your classmates' birthdays are. Write their names and birthdays in the appropriate space in the chart.

MODELO: E1: *¿Cuándo es tu cumpleaños?*
        E2: *(Es) el 3 de mayo.*

CUMPLEAÑOS			
enero	febrero	marzo	abril
mayo	junio	julio	agosto
septiembre	octubre	noviembre	diciembre

Lengua

You may have noticed that the word **tú** (meaning *you*) has a written accent mark, and that the word **tu** (meaning *your*) does not. In *Mosaicos*, boxes similar to this one will help you focus on when to use accent marks. You will find a complete set of the rules for accentuation in the appendix.

La hora

■ Use **¿Qué hora es?** to inquire about the time. To tell time, use **Es la...** from one o'clock to one thirty and **Son las...** with the other hours.

Es la una.	*It is one o'clock.*
Son las tres.	*It is three o'clock.*

■ To express the quarter hour, use **y cuarto** or **y quince**. To express the half hour, use **y media** or **y treinta**.

Es la una **y media.**
Es la una **y treinta.**   *It is one thirty.*

Son las dos **y cuarto.**
Son las dos **y quince.**   *It is two fifteen.*

■ To express time after the half hour, subtract minutes from the next hour, using **menos**.

Son las cuatro **menos** diez.	*It is ten to four.*

■ Add **en punto** for the exact time and **más o menos** for approximate time.

Es la una **en punto.**	*It is one o'clock on the dot/sharp.*
Son las cinco menos cuarto, **más o menos.**	*It is about a quarter to five.*

■ For *a.m.* and *p.m.*, use the following:

de la mañana	(from midnight to noon)
de la tarde	(from noon to nightfall)
de la noche	(from nightfall to midnight)

 P-26 ¿Qué hora es en... ? What time is it in the following cities?

México, p.m.   San Juan, p.m.   Buenos Aires, p.m.   Madrid, p.m.

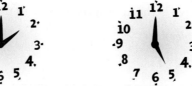 **P-27 El horario de María.** Take turns asking and answering questions about María's schedule below. Then write down your own Monday schedule, omitting the time each class meets. Exchange schedules with your partner, and find out what time each of his/her classes starts.

MODELO: E1: *¿A qué hora es la clase de español?*
                      E2: *Es a las nueve.*

LUNES			
9:00	la clase de español	12:30	el almuerzo
10:00	la clase de matemáticas	1:00	la clase de física
11:00	la clase de psicología	5:00	la clase de tenis
12:00	el laboratorio		

El tiempo

Hoy hace sol. Hace buen tiempo.

Hoy llueve. Hace mal tiempo.

■ Use **¿Qué tiempo hace?** to inquire about the weather. To answer, you may use the following expressions that start with **hace**:

Hace buen tiempo.   *The weather is good.*
Hace mal tiempo.   *The weather is bad.*

■ To express that it is sunny or that it is raining use the following:

Hace sol.   *It is sunny.*
Llueve./Está lloviendo.   *It is raining.*

P-28 ¿Qué tiempo hace hoy? Take turns with your partner asking about the weather in these cities.

MODELO: Miami: 🌑
    E1: *¿Qué tiempo hace en Miami?*
    E2: *En Miami hace buen tiempo. Hace sol.*

1. Madrid: 🌑
2. Quito: ☁
3. Lima: ☁
4. Ciudad de México: 🌑
5. Bogotá: ☁
6. Nueva York: 🌑

·)) Expresiones útiles en la clase

CD 1
Track 11

La tarea, por favor.

Vaya a la pizarra.

Conteste.

Repita.

Levante la mano.

Escriba.

Lea.

■ When asking two or more people to do something, the verb form ends in **-n**:
vaya → **vayan**, conteste → **contesten**, repita → **repitan**.

■ Although you may not have to use all these expressions, it is useful to be
able to recognize them and to respond accordingly. Other expressions that
you may hear or say in the classroom include the following:

¿Comprende(n)?	*Do you understand?*
No comprendo.	*I do not understand.*
No sé.	*I do not know.*
Más despacio, por favor.	*More slowly, please.*
Más alto, por favor.	*Louder, please.*
Otra vez.	*Again.*
¿Tienen alguna pregunta?	*Do you have any questions?*
Tengo una pregunta…	*I have a question.*
¿En qué página?	*On what page?*
¿Cómo se dice… en español?	*How do you say … in Spanish?*
¿Cómo se escribe…?	*How do you spell … ?*
Vaya(n) a la pizarra.	*Go to the board.*
Conteste(n), por favor.	*Please answer.*
Presente.	*Here (present).*

VOCABULARIO

CD 1
Tracks 12-18

Las presentaciones — Introductions

¿Cómo se llama usted?	*What's your name? (formal)*
¿Cómo te llamas?	*What's your name? (familiar)*
encantado/a	*pleased/nice to meet you*
igualmente	*likewise*
me llamo…	*my name is …*
mucho gusto	*pleased/nice to meet you*

Los saludos — Greetings

bastante	*rather*
bien	*well*
buenas tardes/buenas noches	*good afternoon/good evening, good night*
buenos días	*good morning*
¿Cómo está?	*How are you (formal)?*
¿Cómo estás?	*How are you (informal)?*
hola	*hi, hello*
mal	*bad*
muy	*very*
regular	*fair*
¿Qué tal?	*What's up? What's new? (informal)*

En el salón de clase — In the classroom

el bolígrafo	*ballpoint pen*
el borrador	*eraser*
la calculadora	*calculator*
el cesto	*wastebasket*
la computadora	*computer*
la computadora portátil	*laptop*
el cuaderno	*notebook*
el DVD	*DVD; DVD player*
el escritorio	*desk*
el lápiz	*pencil*
el libro	*book*
el mapa	*map*
el marcador/el rotulador	*marker*
la mesa	*table*
la mochila	*backpack*
la pantalla	*screen*
la pizarra	*chalkboard*
la puerta	*door*
el pupitre	*student desk*
el reloj	*clock*
la silla	*chair*
el televisor	*television set*
la tiza	*chalk*
la ventana	*window*

Las personas — People

el amigo/la amiga	*friend*
el/chico/la chica	*boy/girl*
él	*he*
ella	*she*
el/la estudiante	*student*
el profesor/la profesora	*professor, teacher*
el señor (Sr.)	*Mr.*
la señora (Sra.)	*Ms., Mrs.*
la señorita (Srta.)	*Ms, Miss*
tú	*you (familiar)*
usted	*you (formal)*
yo	*I*

La posición — Position

al lado (de)	*next to*
debajo (de)	*under*
detrás (de)	*behind*
enfrente (de)	*in front of*
entre	*between, among*
sobre	*on, above*

Verbos — Verbs

eres	*you are (familiar)*
es	*you are (formal), he/she is*
está	*he/she is, you are (formal)*
estás	*you are (familiar)*
hay	*there is, there are*
soy	*I am*

Palabras y expresiones útiles — Useful words and expressions

a	*at, to*
el año	*year*
¿Cómo es?	*What is he/she/it like?*
el día	*day*
¿Dónde está… ?	*Where is … ?*
en	*in*
ese/a	*that (adjective)*
hoy	*today*
mañana	*tomorrow*
la mañana	*morning*
más o menos	*more or less*
el mes	*month*
mi(s)	*my*
¿Quién es… ?	*Who is … ?*
la semana	*week*
sí	*yes*
su(s)	*his/her/their*
tu(s)	*your (familiar)*
un/una	*a, an*
y	*and*

See page 5 for expressions for leave-taking.
See page 6 for expressions of courtesy.
See page 10 for cognates.
See pages 14 and 16 for numbers, days of the week, and months.
See page 18 for telling time.
See page 19 for weather expressions.
See page 20 for classroom expressions.

En la universidad

Un fresco del siglo XVI en la Universidad de Salamanca

In this chapter you will learn how to:

- exchange information about classes
- identify locations at the university
- talk about academic life and daily occurrences
- ask and answer questions

Cultural focus: España

Museo Guggenheim

FRANCIA

Bilbao

Santiago de Compostela

OCÉANO ATLÁNTICO

PORTUGAL

Universidad de Salamanca

E S P A Ñ A

Barcelona

Salamanca

Segovia

Paella valenciana

Madrid ✪

Valencia

Plaza de toros

Córdoba

Sevilla

Granada

Mar Mediterráneo

La Alhambra

 A vista de pájaro. Look at the map and complete the following sentences based on what you know.

1. ___ España está en...   a. América.   b. Europa.   c. Asia.
2. ___ La capital de España es...   a. Barcelona.   b. Madrid.   c. Sevilla.
3. ___ La paella es típica de...   a. Valencia.   b. Salamanca.   c. Madrid.
4. ___ En la universidad hay...   a. estudiantes.   b. catedrales.   c. toros.
5. ___ En la plaza de toros hay espectáculos (*shows*)...   a. religiosos.   b. cómicos.   c. populares.

23

A PRIMERA VISTA

Los estudiantes y los cursos

CD 1 Track 19 Me llamo Rosa Pereda. **Estudio sociología** en la **Facultad de Humanidades** de la **Universidad** de Salamanca. Mis clases son muy temprano. **Llego** a la universidad a las ocho y media. Este semestre mis cursos son **economía, ciencias políticas, psicología, antropología** y **estadística**. La clase de economía es mi **favorita**. La clase de antropología es **difícil**, pero el profesor es muy **bueno**. La clase de psicología es **fácil** y muy **interesante**. Por las tardes **trabajo** en una **oficina**.

CD 1 Track 20 Este chico es mi amigo. Se llama David Thomas. Es **norteamericano** y estudia español en mi universidad. También estudia **literatura, historia** y **geografía**. David es un chico muy responsable y **estudioso**. Generalmente llega a la universidad a las diez. **Habla** español y **practica todos los días** con sus **compañeros** de clase, sus profesores y sus amigos de la universidad. Por la tarde, **escribe** sus **tareas** en la computadora, estudia en el **laboratorio** con uno de sus **compañeros** y **escucha** música o **mira** programas en español en la televisión.

Cultura

Some of Spain's public universities, such as the Universidad de Salamanca, the Universidad de Santiago, and the Universidad Complutense de Madrid, are among the oldest in Europe, dating back hundreds of years. Most private universities in Spain, which are much newer, have higher tuition. To be accepted to a university students take a competitive comprehensive exam, known as **Selectividad**. Many universities offer Spanish language and culture courses for foreign students.

1-1 ¿Qué sabe usted de Rosa? Refer to the information about Rosa to match the information in the right column with the information on the left.

1. ___ nombre completo	a. antropología
2. ___ universidad	b. psicología
3. ___ clase favorita	c. Salamanca
4. ___ clase difícil	d. economía
5. ___ clase fácil	e. Rosa Pereda

1-2 ¿Y David? Indicate whether each statement about David is true (**Cierto**) or false (**Falso**).

1. _____ Es norteamericano.
2. _____ Habla español.
3. _____ Estudia literatura, historia y geografía.
4. _____ Llega a la universidad a las nueve.
5. _____ Practica español con sus amigos.
6. _____ Escucha música por la mañana.

24

La Universidad de San Marcos, en Lima, Perú, se fundó en 1551.

David y Carmen hablan de sus clases

CD 1
Track 21

DAVID: Hola, Carmen. ¿Cómo estás?

CARMEN: Hola, David. **¿Cómo te va?**

DAVID: Bueno…bastante bien, pero mi clase de historia es muy difícil.

CARMEN: ¿Quién es tu profesor?

DAVID: Se llama Pedro Hernández. Es inteligente y dedicado, pero la clase es **aburrida** y **saco malas notas.**

CARMEN: ¡Vaya! Lo siento. ¿Estudias lo suficiente?

DAVID: Estudio mucho.

CARMEN: **¡Qué lástima!** Mis cinco clases son excelentes. Y tú, **¿cuántas clases tienes?**

DAVID: **Tengo sólo** cuatro.

CARMEN: ¡Uy! Son las once. Tengo un **examen** de economía **ahora**. Hasta luego.

DAVID: Hasta pronto. **¡Buena suerte!**

1-3 ¿En qué clase…? Match the words on the left with the appropriate class on the right.

1. ___ *Don Quijote* de Cervantes   a. geografía
2. ___ números   b. biología
3. ___ mapa digital   c. literatura
4. ___ animales   d. historia
5. ___ Freud   e. matemáticas
6. ___ Napoleón   f. psicología

1-4 Mis clases. PRIMERA FASE. Make a list of your classes. Indicate the days and time each class meets and whether it is easy or difficult, interesting or boring. You will find some subjects in the list below.

economía	comunicaciones	negocios
bioquímica	sociología	historia del arte
física	cálculo	informática
artes plásticas	estadística	seminario de…
contabilidad	astronomía	filosofía

CLASE	DÍAS	HORA	¿CÓMO ES?

 SEGUNDA FASE. Tell your partner about your classes. Take turns completing the following ideas.

1. Llego a la universidad a la(s)…
2. Mi clase favorita es…
3. El profesor/La profesora se llama…
4. La clase es muy…
5. Practico español en…
6. En mi clase de español hay…

 1-5 Las clases de mis compañeros/as. PRIMERA FASE. Use the following questions to interview your partner. Take notes. Then switch roles.

1. ¿Qué estudias este semestre?
2. ¿Cuántas clases tienes?
3. ¿Cuál es tu clase favorita?
4. ¿Qué día y a qué hora es tu clase favorita?
5. Tu clase de español, ¿cómo es? ¿Es fácil o difícil? ¿Es interesante o aburrida?
6. ¿Trabajas con computadoras? ¿Dónde?
7. ¿Sacas buenas notas?
8. ¿Tienes muchos exámenes?

 SEGUNDA FASE. Introduce your partner to another classmate and state one piece of interesting information about him/her. Your classmate will ask your partner about his/her classes.

MODELO: USTED: *Él es Pedro. Estudia ciencias políticas y tiene cuatro clases este semestre.*

SU COMPAÑERO/A: *Mucho gusto. ¿_____?*

CD 1
Track 22

La universidad

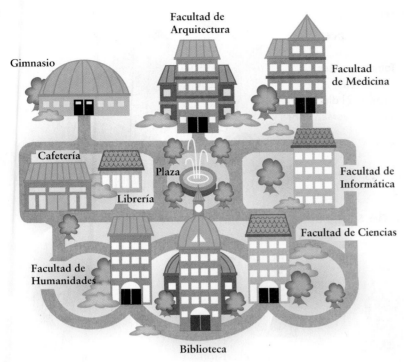

Facultad de
Arquitectura

Gimnasio

Facultad
de Medicina

Cafetería

Plaza

Librería

Facultad de
Informática

Facultad de Ciencias

Facultad de
Humanidades

Biblioteca

Carmen

Lorena

Álvaro

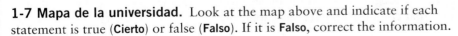
Juan

1-6 ¿En qué facultad estudian? PRIMERA FASE. Match the names of the university students pictured at the right with the school where they study.

1. ___ Juan
2. ___ Carmen
3. ___ Lorena
4. ___ Álvaro

a. Facultad de Medicina
b. Facultad de Arquitectura
c. Facultad de Humanidades
d. Facultad de Ciencias

SEGUNDA FASE. Exchange the information with a classmate and indicate two classes that each student is probably taking.

MODELO: E1: *¿Dónde estudia Carmen?*
E2: *Carmen estudia en la Facultad de... Probablemente tiene clase de... y de...*

1-7 Mapa de la universidad. Look at the map above and indicate if each statement is true (**Cierto**) or false (**Falso**). If it is **Falso,** correct the information.

1. _____ La plaza está en el centro del campus.
2. _____ La Facultad de Humanidades está junto a (*next to*) la biblioteca.
3. _____ La cafetería está detrás del gimnasio.
4. _____ La Facultad de Ciencias está delante de (*in front of*) la Facultad de Informática.
5. _____ La librería está al lado de la cafetería.
6. _____ La Facultad de Medicina está al lado del gimnasio.

Las actividades de los estudiantes

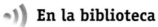 ## En la biblioteca

CD 1
Track 23

Unos **alumnos** estudian en la biblioteca. **Toman apuntes** y trabajan en sus tareas. A veces **buscan** palabras en el **diccionario**. Frecuentemente **conversan** sobre sus clases.

 ## Los fines de semana

CD 1
Track 24

Los estudiantes **toman algo** en un **café**.

Miran televisión en **casa**.

Bailan en una **discoteca** con amigos.

Caminan en la **playa**.

Montan en bicicleta.

1-8 Para escoger. Look at the illustrations above. Then choose the word or phrase that completes the sentence logically.

1. Los estudiantes ___ en la biblioteca.
   a. toman café   b. estudian   c. hablan
2. Buscan palabras en ___ .
   a. el reloj   b. el diccionario   c. el laboratorio
3. Miran televisión en ___ .
   a. la biblioteca   b. la playa   c. casa
4. Montan en bicicleta ___ .
   a. los fines de semana   b. en el café   c. en una discoteca

En la librería

CD 1
Track 25

ESTUDIANTE: **Necesito comprar** un diccionario para mi clase de literatura española.

DEPENDIENTE: ¿**Grande** o **pequeño**?

ESTUDIANTE: Grande, y todo en español.

DEPENDIENTE: **Este** diccionario es muy bueno.

ESTUDIANTE: ¿**Cuánto cuesta**?

DEPENDIENTE: Cuarenta y ocho **euros**.

1-9 ¿Qué necesita? Complete the following statements, based on the previous conversation.

1. El estudiante necesita...
2. Es un diccionario...
3. Es para su clase de...
4. El diccionario cuesta...

1-10 ¿Cuánto cuesta? During your semester abroad, you go to the university bookstore. Ask the salesclerk how much the following items cost.

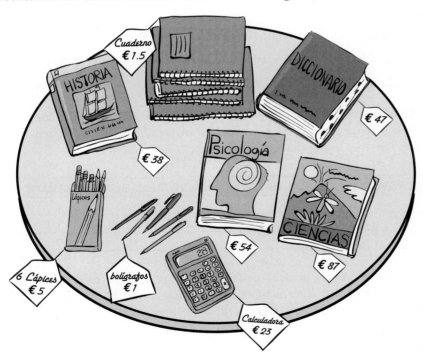

Cultura

Since 2002, the euro has been the official monetary unit of the so-called Eurozone, which includes (as of January 2008) Austria, Belgium, Cyprus, Finland, France, Germany, Greece, Ireland, Italy, Luxembourg, Malta, the Netherlands, Portugal, Slovenia, and Spain. In some other European countries and the United Kingdom, the euro, although not official, is accepted in stores. The euro currency sign is € and the banking code is EUR.

MODELO:

ESTUDIANTE: *¿Cuánto cuesta el mapa?*

DEPENDIENTE/A: *Cuesta cincuenta euros.*

1-11 Entrevista (*Interview*). Ask where and when your classmate does each of the following activities.

MODELO: practicar baloncesto (*basketball*)
E1: *¿Dónde practicas baloncesto? ¿Y cuándo?*
E2: *Practico baloncesto en la plaza por las tardes.*

ACTIVIDAD	DÓNDE	CUÁNDO
1. estudiar para un examen difícil		
2. mirar televisión		
3. tomar café/chocolate		
4. bailar salsa		
5. escuchar música		
6. comprar un diccionario/CDs/materiales para tus clases		

 1-12 Las actividades de sus compañeros. PRIMERA FASE. Go around the classroom and interview three people. Ask two different questions of each of them. Take notes to report later. Answer the questions of classmates who interview you.

1. ¿Qué haces (*do you do*) los fines de semana?
2. ¿Dónde miras televisión?
3. ¿Qué compras en la librería?
4. ¿Dónde estudias normalmente?
5. ¿Trabajas los fines de semana? ¿Dónde trabajas?

SEGUNDA FASE. Now share your classmates' answers with the rest of the class.

MODELO: *María estudia normalmente en casa. No trabaja los fines de semana.*

1-13 ¿Qué hacen? (*What do they do?*) You will hear three people talking about their activities during the week and on weekends. Before you listen, list your own activities in the chart.

CD 1
Track 26

MIS ACTIVIDADES DE TODOS LOS DÍAS	MIS ACTIVIDADES DEL FIN DE SEMANA

Now pay attention to the general idea of what is said in the recording. As you listen, decide which activities each person is talking about. Then write the number of the speaker (1, 2, 3) next to the appropriate topic.

____ los estudios
____ el tiempo libre (*free time*)
____ el trabajo

EN ACCIÓN

Diarios de bicicleta: La chivita

Antes de ver

1-14 In this video segment, you will be introduced to four college students, some of whom do not know each other. Write down four expressions you think they may use to greet and introduce each other.

Mientras ve

1-15 As you watch, indicate whether the following statements refer to Javier (**J**), Daniel (**D**), Luciana (**L**), or Gabi (**G**).

1. ___ Son sus diarios de bicicleta.
2. ___ Es compañera de Gaby.
3. ___ Viaja en bicicleta.
4. ___ Es puntual, simpático y cómico.
5. ___ Olvida (*forgets*) su teléfono en la cafetería.

Después de ver

1-16 Check off the expressions you prepared in *Antes de ver* that were used in this segment.

FUNCIONES Y FORMAS

1. Talking about academic life and daily occurrences: Present tense of regular -ar verbs

Sara   Marta

REPORTERO:	Perdón. Soy Pablo Brito del canal 11 de televisión. ¿Su nombre, por favor?
SARA:	Yo soy Sara y ella es Marta.
REPORTERO:	¿Tienen ustedes una vida muy activa?
MARTA:	Sí, nosotras somos (*are*) atletas. **Practicamos** muchos deportes. Sara **participa** en maratones y **practica** el tenis. Yo **practico** el fútbol y el baloncesto.
SARA:	Y los fines de semana **montamos** en bicicleta.
REPORTERO:	¡Qué interesante! Gracias, señoritas.

Piénselo. Check (✔) all the statements that are true, based on the reporter's interview with Sara and Marta.

1. ____ Pablo es un reportero de radio.
2. ____ Marta y Sara **practican** muchos deportes (*sports*).
3. ____ Marta **participa** en maratones.
4. ____ Marta **practica** el fútbol.
5. ____ Sara **practica** el baloncesto.
6. ____ Sara y Marta **montan** en bicicleta.

▪ To talk about actions, feelings, and states of being, you need to use verbs. In both English and Spanish, the infinitive is the base form of the verb that appears in vocabulary lists and dictionaries. In English, infinitives are preceded by *to*: *to speak*. Infinitives in Spanish belong to one of three groups, depending on whether they end in **-ar**, **-er**, or **-ir**. Verbs ending in **-ar** are presented here, and verbs ending in **-er** and **-ir** are presented in the next section.

HABLAR (*to speak*)			
yo	habl**o**	nosotros/as	habl**amos**
tú	habl**as**	vosotros/as	habl**áis**
él, ella, Ud.	habl**a**	ellos, ellas, Uds.	habl**an**

▪ Use the present tense to express what you and others generally or habitually do or do not do. You may also use the present tense to express an ongoing action. Context will tell you which meaning is intended.

Ana **trabaja** en la oficina.   { *Ana works in the office.*
{ *Ana is working in the office.*

Luis **practica** el piano todos los días.   *Luis practices the piano every day.*

▪ Here are some expressions you may find useful when talking about the frequency of actions.

siempre	*always*	**muchas veces**	*often*
todos los días/meses	*every day/month*	**a veces**	*sometimes*
todas las semanas	*every week*	**nunca**	*never*

▪ Some common **-ar** verbs are **bailar, buscar, caminar, comprar, conversar, escuchar, estudiar, llegar, mirar, montar, necesitar, participar, practicar, sacar, tomar**, and **trabajar**.

1-17 Preferencias. PRIMERA FASE. Rank these activities from 1 to 9, according to your preferences (1 = most interesting, 9 = least interesting).

_____ bailar en una discoteca
_____ mirar televisión en casa
_____ estudiar otras culturas
_____ comprar DVDs y CDs
_____ caminar en la playa

_____ montar en bicicleta cuando hace sol
_____ escuchar música rock
_____ conversar con los amigos con mensajes de texto
_____ bajar (*download*) música de Internet

SEGUNDA FASE. Now compare your answers with those of a classmate. Follow the model.

MODELO: E1: *Para mí, bailar en una discoteca es número 1. ¿Y para ti?*
E2: *Para mí, caminar en la playa es número 1.*

1-18 Mi rutina. PRIMERA FASE. Indicate (✓) the activities that are part of your routine at school.

1. _____ Llego a la universidad a las nueve de la mañana.
2. _____ Converso con mis amigos por teléfono.
3. _____ Tomo notas en todas las clases.
4. _____ Hablo con mis compañeros en la cafetería.
5. _____ Estudio en la biblioteca por las mañanas.
6. _____ Trabajo en mis tareas todas las noches.
7. _____ Miro programas cómicos en la televisión.
8. _____ A veces practico un deporte con mis amigos/as.

SEGUNDA FASE. Now compare your answers with those of a classmate. The expressions in *En directo* will help you react as your classmate tells you about himself/herself. Report your findings to the class.

MODELO: *Daniel y yo somos (muy) similares. Él y yo miramos programas cómicos en la televisión./Daniel y yo somos (muy) diferentes. Yo estudio por las mañanas; él estudia por las tardes.*

1-19 A preguntar. PRIMERA FASE. Find four different classmates, each of whom does one of the following activities. Write each name on the appropriate line. The expressions in *En directo* will help you carry on the conversation.

MODELO: mirar televisión por la noche
   E1: *¡Oye! ¿Miras televisión por la tarde?*
   E2: *Sí, miro televisión por la tarde. O*
      No, no miro televisión por la tarde.

PERSONA	ACTIVIDAD
_____	estudiar español todos los días
_____	llegar a la universidad a las 9:30 a.m.
_____	escuchar música clásica en casa por la noche
_____	trabajar en una oficina por la tarde

SEGUNDA FASE. Now report to the class your findings about your classmates' activities.

1-20 Mis actividades. PRIMERA FASE. Mark (✓) the space that indicates how often you do the following activities:

ACTIVIDADES	A VECES	MUCHAS VECES	SIEMPRE	NUNCA
estudiar con amigos				
sacar buenas notas				
montar en bicicleta los fines de semana				
mirar televisión por la tarde				
bailar los sábados				
tomar café				

SEGUNDA FASE. Now tell each other how often you do these activities, and then ask where your partner does them.

MODELO: E1: *Yo estudio con amigos a veces, ¿y tú?*
E2: *Yo siempre estudio con amigos.*
E1: *¿Dónde estudian ustedes?*
E2: *Estudiamos en la biblioteca.*

1-21 Un día típico en la vida de Luisa. PRIMERA FASE. Describe what Luisa does on a typical day.

MODELO: *Luisa llega a la oficina a las nueve menos diez.*

1.

2.

3.

4.

SEGUNDA FASE. Now, based on a typical day in her life, describe Luisa's personality. Then explain what you normally do on a regular day.

Este bar de Madrid tiene una selección de tapas deliciosas.

SITUACIONES

1. **Role A.** Your friend works in the afternoon. Ask a) where he/she works; b) the days of the week and the hours that he/she works; and c) if the job (**trabajo**) is interesting/boring/difficult/easy. Then answer your friend's questions about your job.

   Role B. Tell your friend that you work in the afternoon. Answer your friend's questions about your job. Then ask three questions about his/her job (**trabajo**).

2. **Role A.** You need to read *Don Quijote de la Mancha* by Miguel de Cervantes for your World Literature class, so you go to the university library. Tell the librarian that you need a book, and answer the librarian's questions about title (**título**) and author (**autor**).

   Role B. You are a librarian at the university library. A student tells you that he/she needs a book. Ask the title of the book (**¿cuál es el título?**) and the author (**autor**). Comment on the book.

2. Talking about academic life and daily occurrences: Present tense of regular *-er* and *-ir* verbs

REPORTERO: Y ustedes, ¿qué hacen durante el día?

PEDRO: Antonio estudia ciencias en la universidad. **Asiste** a sus clases y luego **corre** al laboratorio, donde trabaja todos los días. Habla con el profesor y **aprende** mucho. Los estudiantes de ciencias **leen** mucho, **escriben** trabajos de investigación y sacan buenas notas. Yo soy un estudiante de arquitectura, y mis compañeros y yo **leemos** y **escribimos** mucho también. Yo casi (*almost*) **vivo** en la biblioteca cuando estudio para los exámenes.

Piénselo. Check (✓) all the statements that are true, based on the reporter's interview with Pedro.

1. _____ Antonio estudia arquitectura.
2. _____ Antonio trabaja en el laboratorio y **aprende** (*learns*) mucho.
3. _____ Los estudiantes **leen** y **escriben** mucho.
4. _____ Antonio no **asiste** (*attends*) a sus clases.
5. _____ Los estudiantes de ciencias sacan buenas notas.
6. _____ Pedro estudia arquitectura.
7. _____ Pedro **vive** (*lives*) en el laboratorio.

■ You have learned in this chapter that the present tense is used to express activities and ongoing actions. You have also learned the present tense forms for verbs whose infinitives end in **-ar**. Now you will learn those forms for verbs whose infinitives end in **-er** and **-ir**.

■ Note that **-er** and **-ir** verbs have the same endings, except for the **nosotros/as** and **vosotros/as** forms.

APRENDER (*to learn*)			
yo	aprend**o**	nosotros/as	aprend**emos**
tú	aprend**es**	vosotros/as	aprend**éis**
él, ella, Ud.	aprend**e**	ellos, ellas, Uds.	aprend**en**

VIVIR (*to live*)			
yo	viv**o**	nosotros/as	viv**imos**
tú	viv**es**	vosotros/as	viv**ís**
él, ella, Ud.	viv**e**	ellos, ellas, Uds.	viv**en**

■ Other common **-er** and **-ir** verbs are **comer** (*to eat*), **comprender, correr, leer, responder** (*to respond*), **asistir,** and **escribir.**

■ The verb **ver** (*to see*) has an irregular **yo** form: **veo, ves, ve, vemos, veis, ven.**

Veo películas los fines de semana.   *I see movies on weekends.*

■ Use **deber** + *infinitive* to express that you should/must/ought to do something.

Los atletas **deben beber** mucha agua.   *Athletes should drink lots of water.*

1-22 Mi profesor/a modelo. PRIMERA FASE. Indicate which of the activities are part of the routine of an ideal instructor inside and outside the classroom.

	SÍ	NO
1. Lee el periódico (*newspaper*) en clase.	_____	_____
2. Escucha los problemas de los estudiantes.	_____	_____
3. Bebe café y come en la clase.	_____	_____
4. Escribe buenos ejemplos en la pizarra.	_____	_____
5. Nunca prepara sus clases.	_____	_____
6. Siempre asiste a clase.	_____	_____
7. Responde a las preguntas de los estudiantes.	_____	_____
8. Habla con los estudiantes en su oficina.	_____	_____

SEGUNDA FASE. Compare your answers with those of a classmate. Together write two more activities typical of an ideal instructor and ask your instructor if they are part of his/her academic routine.

1-23 Para pasarlo bien (*To have a good time*). PRIMERA FASE. Indicate which of the following activities your classmates do to have a good time.

1. _____ Leen libros en español todas las semanas.
2. _____ Escriben mensajes de texto.
3. _____ Practican deportes con los amigos.
4. _____ Asisten a clase a las ocho de la mañana.
5. _____ Corren en el gimnasio y en el parque.
6. _____ Ven películas y programas de televisión en casa.
7. _____ Comen en restaurantes elegantes.
8. _____ Beben sólo Coca-Cola en las fiestas.

SEGUNDA FASE. Compare your answers with those of a classmate. Then exchange information with another pair (**pareja**) about the activities you all do to have a good time. Use the expressions in *En directo* to help you react naturally to your classmates' responses.

MODELO: PAREJA 1: *Nosotros bailamos en discotecas para pasarlo bien.*
                      ¿Y ustedes?
          PAREJA 2: *Bebemos café y conversamos con los amigos.*

En directo

To react to what someone has said:

¡Qué interesante!

¡Qué divertido!
How funny!

¡Qué aburrido!
How boring!

1-24 Lugares y actividades. Ask what your classmate does in the following places. He/She will respond with one of the activities listed. Then ask what your classmate does not do in those places.

MODELO: en la clase
E1:   *¿Qué haces en la clase?*
E2:   *Veo películas en español.*
E1:   *¿Qué no haces en la clase?*
E2:   *No leo el periódico.*

LUGARES	ACTIVIDADES
en la playa	beber cerveza
en un café	tomar el sol
en una discoteca	bailar salsa
en una fiesta	mirar televisión
en el cine	leer el periódico
en la casa	ver películas de horror
en un restaurante	escuchar música clásica
en la biblioteca	comer un sándwich y tomar un café

1-25 A preguntar. **PRIMERA FASE.** Find four different classmates, each of whom does one of the following activities. Write each name in the chart below.

MODELO: ver películas en casa
E1:   *¿Ves películas en casa?*
E2:   *Sí, veo películas en casa./ No, no veo películas en casa.*

PERSONA	ACTIVIDAD
_____	asistir a conciertos de música rock
_____	beber café todos los días
_____	vivir en casa con la familia
_____	escribir mensajes de texto por la noche

SEGUNDA FASE. Now report to the class your findings about your class-mates' activities.

1-26 ¿Qué deben hacer? Read the situations in the column on the left and select the best advice from the column on the right.

1. ___ Maricela desea sacar buenas notas.
2. ___ Carlos corre en el parque.
3. ___ Luisa y Jorge están (*are*) muy nerviosos.
4. ___ Los estudiantes desean comer tapas.
5. ___ Óscar desea aprender a bailar.
6. ___ Carolina desea preparar tacos, burritos y enchiladas.

a. Debe trabajar en un restaurante mexicano.
b. Deben visitar España.
c. Debe estudiar todos los días.
d. Debe tomar clases de baile.
e. No deben beber café con cafeína.
f. Debe beber mucha agua.

SITUACIONES

1. **Role A.** You see a classmate at a coffee shop with laptop and books spread out on the table. Ask if he/she a) drinks coffee every day; b) often studies in the coffee shop; c) reads the newspaper there; and d) writes on the computer in the coffee shop.

   Role B. You are sitting at a table with your laptop and books at your favorite coffee shop. A classmate comes in and walks over. Answer your classmate's questions about what you usually do there.

2. **Role A.** On the way to Spanish class you run into a classmate and ask how he/she is. Your classmate confides that he/she isn't getting good grades in Spanish. Suggest that he/she a) should always attend class; b) must read the chapter every week; c) should study in the library; and d) ought to look for a good dictionary.

   Role B. In the hallway you run into the person who sits next to you in Spanish class. When he/she asks how you are, say you're so-so. Explain that you are not getting good grades in Spanish and that you are not learning the vocabulary. Listen to your classmate's advice and thank him/her.

3. Specifying gender and number: Articles and nouns

MANUEL: Hola, Rocío. Tengo **un** plan. ¿Estudiamos español en **la** universidad esta tarde? Necesito **un** diccionario para **la** tarea.

ROCÍO: ¡Buena idea! ¿En **la** biblioteca? **El** profesor de español es bueno, pero es **una** clase difícil. ¿Invitamos a mi amigo Marcos?

MANUEL: Fenomenal. Usamos **la** pizarra y **el** escritorio **del** salón 12 de **la** biblioteca.

Piénselo. Match the words on the right with those on the left. Use the dialogue and the endings of the nouns as clues.

1. ___ clase
2. ___ diccionario de español
3. ___ pizarra
4. ___ escritorio
5. ___ universidad

a. el
b. la
c. un
d. una

Gender

▪ Nouns are words that name a person, place, or thing. In English all nouns use the same definite article, *the*, and all singular nouns use the indefinite articles *a* and *an*. Spanish nouns, whether they refer to people or to things, have either masculine or feminine gender. Masculine singular nouns use **el** or **un** and feminine singular nouns use **la** or **una**.

The terms *masculine* and *feminine* are used in a grammatical sense and have nothing to do with biological gender.

	MASCULINE	FEMININE	
SINGULAR DEFINITE ARTICLES	el	la	*the*
SINGULAR INDEFINITE ARTICLES	un	una	*a/an*

■ Generally, nouns that end in **-o** are masculine and require **el** or **un**, and those that end in **-a** are feminine and require **la** or **una**.

el/un libr**o**	**el/un** cuadern**o**	**el/un** diccionari**o**
la/una mes**a**	**la/una** sill**a**	**la/una** ventan**a**

■ Nouns that end in **-dad**, **-ción**, **-sión** are feminine and require **la** or **una**.

la/una universi**dad**	**la/una** lec**ción**	**la/una** televi**sión**

■ Nouns that end in **-ma** are generally masculine.

el/un progra**ma**	**el/un** proble**ma**
el/un dra**ma**	**el/un** poe**ma**

■ In general, nouns that refer to males are masculine, and nouns that refer to females are feminine. Masculine nouns ending in **-o** change the **-o** to **-a** for the feminine; those ending in a consonant add **-a** for the feminine.

el/un amig**o**	**la/una** amig**a**
el/un profesor	**la/una** profesor**a**

■ Nouns ending in **-ante** and **-ente** may be feminine or masculine. Gender is signaled by the article (**el/la estudiante**).

■ Use definite articles with titles when you are talking about someone. Do not use definite articles when addressing someone directly.

La señorita Andrade es **la** secretaria en el Departamento de Lenguas Europeas. **El** profesor Campos es **el** director del departamento.

Ms. Andrade is the secretary in the Department of European Languages. Professor Campos is the chair of the department.

Todos los días, el profesor Campos dice "Buenos días, señorita Andrade". Ella contesta, "Buenos días, profesor Campos".

Every day, Professor Campos says "Good morning, Ms. Andrade." She responds, "Good morning, Professor Campos."

Number

	MASCULINE	FEMININE	
PLURAL DEFINITE ARTICLES	**los**	**las**	*the*
PLURAL INDEFINITE ARTICLES	**unos**	**unas**	*some*

■ Add **-s** to form the plural of nouns that end in a vowel. Add **-es** to nouns ending in a consonant.

la silla	→ las silla**s**	el cuaderno	→ los cuaderno**s**
la actividad	→ las actividad**es**	el señor	→ los señor**es**

■ Nouns that end in **-z** change the **z** to **c** before **-es**.

el lápi**z**   →   los lápi**ces**

■ To refer to a mixed group, use masculine plural forms.

los chic**os**   *the boys and girls*

1-27 Conversaciones incompletas. Complete the dialogues.

1. Supply the definite articles (**el, la, los, las**).
   E1: ¿Dónde está María?
   E2: Está en __ clase de __ profesora Sánchez.
   E1: ¡Qué lástima! Necesito hablar con ella. Es urgente.
   E2: Bueno, ella está en __ salón de clase hasta __ una, y por
       __ tarde trabaja en __ laboratorio.
   E1: ¿Y a qué hora llega?
   E2: Llega a __ dos, más o menos.

2. Supply the indefinite articles (**un, una, unos, unas**).
   E1: Necesito comprar ___ calculadora y ___ lápices.
   E2: Y yo necesito ___ bolígrafo y ___ diccionario, pero ¿qué diccionario compro?
   E1: Para el curso de español, ___ profesores usan ___ diccionario pequeño y otros usan
       ___ diccionario grande. ¿Por qué (*Why*) no hablas con tu profesor?

3. Supply the definite or indefinite articles.
   E1: Tengo ___ examen de matemáticas mañana y necesito sacar ___ buena nota en esa clase.
   E2: ¿Quién es ___ profesor?
   E1: Es ___ doctora Solís.
   E2: ¡Ah! Es ___ profesora excelente.
   E1: Sí, pero ___ clase es muy difícil. Estudio y escribo ___ tareas todos
       ___ días, pero no saco buenas notas.
   E2: ¡Vaya! Lo siento mucho.

1-28 ¿Qué necesitan? Take turns saying what these classmates need.

MODELO: Alicia tiene que buscar unas palabras. *Necesita un diccionario.*

1. Mónica tiene que tomar apuntes en la clase de historia.
2. Carlos y Ana deben hacer la tarea de matemáticas.
3. Alfredo tiene que estudiar para el examen de geografía.
4. Isabel tiene que escribir una composición para su clase de inglés.
5. Blanca y Lucía tienen que encontrar (*find*) dónde está Salamanca.
6. David tiene que escuchar una canción (*song*) para su clase de música.

SITUACIONES

1. **Role A.** You have missed the first day of class. Ask a classmate a) at what time the class meets; b) who the professor is; and c) what you need for the class.

   Role B. Tell your classmate a) that the class is at 8:00 in the morning; b) the name of the professor and what he/she is like; and c) at least three items that your classmate needs for the class.

2. **Role A.** You work for the student newspaper at your college and have been asked to interview two students to find out how they typically spend their weekends. After introducing yourself, find out a) if they work, and where; b) what they study; and c) what they do (**hacen**) on Saturdays and Sundays.

   Roles B, C. Tell the interviewer a) if you work and, if so, where; b) the classes you take; and c) what you do on weekends, where, and with whom.

4. Expressing location and states of being: Present tense of *estar*

Elisa   Humberto

ELISA: ¿Humberto? Te habla Elisa.

HUMBERTO: ¡Elisa! ¡Qué sorpresa! ¿Dónde **estás**?

ELISA: **Estoy** en el aeropuerto de Barajas, en Madrid. ¿Y tú?

HUMBERTO: Mi padre y yo **estamos** de vacaciones en Nueva York. En este momento, mi padre **está** en la tienda *Best Buy*. ¿Y cómo **están** todos en tu familia?

ELISA: Todos **estamos** muy bien. ¡Qué bueno escucharte! Lo siento, Humberto, pero el vuelo (*flight*) sale (*leaves*) pronto. Hablamos más mañana. Adiós.

Piénselo. Indicate whether each statement is true (**Cierto**) or false (**Falso**), based on the conversation. If it is **Falso**, correct the information.

1. _____ Humberto **está** en el aeropuerto.
2. _____ Elisa **está** de vacaciones en Nueva York.
3. _____ Humberto **está** en una ciudad grande con una persona de su familia.
4. _____ La tienda *Best Buy* de esta conversación **está** en Madrid.
5. _____ Elisa y Humberto **están** contentos de hablar por teléfono.

■ You have already been using some forms of **estar**. Here are all the present tense forms of this verb.

ESTAR (*to be*)			
yo	**estoy**	nosotros/as	**estamos**
tú	**estás**	vosotros/as	**estáis**
Ud., él, ella	**está**	Uds., ellos, ellas	**están**

■ Use **estar** to express the location of persons or objects.

¿Dónde **está** Humberto? *Where is Humberto?*

Está en Nueva York. *He is in New York*

■ Use **estar** to talk about states of health or being.

¿Cómo **está** la familia de Elisa? *How is Elisa's family?*

Está muy bien. *They are very well.*

1-29 En la cafetería. In the cafeteria, you run across a former classmate. Complete the conversation, using the correct forms of **estar**. Then indicate in the parentheses if **estar** signals location (**L**) or a state of being (**S**).

ROBERTO: Hola, Carlos. ¿Qué tal? ¿Cómo _____?

CARLOS: _____ muy bien. ¿Y tú?

ROBERTO: Muy bien, muy bien. ¿Y cómo _____ tu hermana *(sister)* Ana?

CARLOS: Bien, gracias. Ella y mamá _____ en España ahora.

ROBERTO: ¡Qué suerte! Y nosotros _____ en la universidad, ¡y en la semana de exámenes!

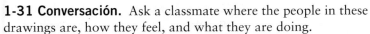

1-30 Horas y lugares favoritos. PRIMERA FASE. Ask your classmate his/her favorite time of day or day of the week. Then ask where he/she usually is at that time or on that day.

MODELO: E1: *¿Cuál es tu hora favorita del día?*
E2: *Las 10:00 de la mañana.*
E1: *Generalmente, ¿dónde estás a las 10:00 de la mañana?*
E2: *Estoy en... . ¿Y cuál es tu hora favorita?*
E1: *... .*
E2: *¿Y dónde estás?*
E1: *Estoy en... .*

SEGUNDA FASE. Compare your responses with those of your partner. Identify any similarities and/or differences in your preferences.

1-31 Conversación. Ask a classmate where the people in these drawings are, how they feel, and what they are doing.

MODELO: E1: *¿Dónde está María Luisa?*
E2: *Está en la biblioteca.*
E1: *¿Cómo está?*
E2: *Está regular.*
E1: *¿Qué hace?*
E2: *Estudia.*

María Luisa

1. Berta   Lorena

2. Carlos   el Dr. Núñez

3. Marcelo   Eduardo

5. Asking and answering questions: Interrogative words

Andrea Pérez conversa con su consejera (*advisor*) en la universidad. La consejera necesita rellenar (*fill out*) algunos formularios con información sobre Andrea. Aquí están algunas de las preguntas de la consejera y en la columna de la derecha, las respuestas de Andrea.

CONSEJERA	ANDREA
¿Cómo se llama la residencia estudiantil donde vives?	Se llama Casa Cervantes.
¿Dónde está?	Está en la Avenida España.
¿Cuándo son tus clases?	Por la mañana y por la tarde.
¿Cuánto cuesta tu transporte por mes?	Aproximadamente 35 euros.
¿Quién es tu compañera de cuarto?	Cristina Zapatero.
¿Por qué deseas (*want to*) estudiar psicología?	Para ayudar (*help*) a otras personas.

Piénselo. Match Andrea's responses in the left column with the questions her advisor asked her in the right column. **OJO:** You will be able to answer some of the advisor's questions with the information from the conversation above.

1. ___ Es el profesor Agustín Reyes-Torres.
2. ___ Se llama Cristina Zapatero.
3. ___ En la Casa Cervantes.
4. ___ 400 euros al mes.
5. ___ Por la tarde.

a. **¿Dónde** vives?
b. **¿Cuándo** es tu clase de psicología?
c. **¿Quién** es tu profesor favorito?
d. **¿Cómo** se llama tu compañera de cuarto?
e. **¿Cuánto** cuesta vivir en la residencia?

■ Interrogative words are used to ask questions or to obtain specific information. You have already been using many of these words.

¿cómo?	*how/what?*	**¿cuál(es)?**	*which?*
¿dónde?	*where?*	**¿quién(es)?**	*who?*
¿qué?	*what?*	**¿cuánto/a?**	*how much?*
¿cuándo?	*when?*	**¿cuántos/as?**	*how many?*
¿por qué?	*why?*	**¿para qué?**	*why?/what for?*

■ If a subject is used in a question, it normally follows the verb.

¿Dónde trabaja Elsa?   *Where does Elsa work?*

■ Use **por qué** to ask *why* and **porque** to answer *because.*

¿Por qué está Pepe en la biblioteca?   *Why is Pepe at the library?*

Porque necesita estudiar.   *Because he needs to study.*

■ Use **qué + ser** when you want to ask for a definition or an explanation.

¿Qué es la sardana?   *What is the sardana?*

Es un baile típico de Cataluña.   *It is a typical dance of Catalonia.*

■ Use **cuál(es) + ser** when you want to ask which one(s).

¿Cuál es tu mochila?	*Which (one) is your backpack?*
¿Cuáles son tus papeles?	*Which (ones) are your papers?*

■ Questions that may be answered with **sí** or **no** do not use a question word.

¿Trabajan ustedes los sábados?	*Do you work on Saturdays?*
No, no trabajamos.	*No, we do not.*

■ Another way to ask a question is to place an interrogative tag after a declarative statement.

Tú hablas inglés, **¿verdad?**	*You speak English, don't you?*
David es norteamericano, **¿no?**	*David is an American, isn't he?*

> ### Lengua
>
> To request repetition or clarification of a statement, use **¿Cómo?** or **¿Perdón?** The use of **¿Qué?**, the equivalent of English *What?*, is generally considered rude by native speakers.

1-32 Preguntas. First look at the cues in the right column and then complete the questions with **quién, cuándo, cuántos/as, cuál,** or **por qué,** as logical. Use your questions to interview two people as you walk around the room.

1. ¿ _____ clases tomas?	Tomo…
2. ¿ _____ son tus clases?	Por la…
3. ¿ _____ es tu clase favorita?	La clase de…
4. ¿ _____ es tu profesor/a favorito/a?	El profesor/La profesora…
5. ¿ _____ estudias español?	Porque…
6. ¿ _____ estudiantes hay en tu clase de español?	Hay…

1-33 Entrevista. Ask your classmate questions to find out the following information. Use the appropriate expressions to show disbelief, coincidence, how interesting the answers are, and so on.

1. número de clases que toma este semestre
2. su clase favorita y razón (y por qué)
3. número de alumnos en la clase favorita
4. nombre del profesor favorito/de la profesora favorita
5. lugar donde estudia generalmente y cuántas horas estudia por (*per*) día
6. lugar donde trabaja

SITUACIONES

1. **Role A.** You have just run across a friend you have not seen all year. Inquire about your friend's life in college including a) the location and size of his/her college/university; b) courses this semester; and c) his/her activities.

   Role B. You are talking with a friend you have not seen in a long time. Answer your friend's questions about your life in college. Then ask your friend some questions to get the same information.

2. **Role A.** It is the beginning of the term, and you need to add a psychology class. One of your friends is in a class that looks promising. Ask a) who the professor is; b) if there is a lot of homework; c) when the class meets; and d) if there is an exam soon. Then ask if you should know (**saber**) anything else (**algo más**) about the class.

   Role B. Your friend wants some information about your psychology class. Reply as specifically as possible to all of his/her questions. Then offer some additional information about the class.

MOSAICOS

A escuchar

ESTRATEGIA	**Listen for the gist**
	When you are having a conversation or are listening to other people talking in your native language, you may get the gist of what is said without understanding every word or paying attention to every detail. You do this by relying on what you do understand, your knowledge of the topic, and your subconscious expectations of what happens in a conversational exchange. You will find these techniques helpful when listening to Spanish.

Antes de escuchar

1-34 Preparación. You will hear two students talking about their classes. Before listening to the recording, think about the topics they may talk about and make a list of the things you may expect to hear, based on your experience as a student.

Escuchar

1-35 ¿Comprende usted? First read the following statements. Then listen to the conversation between Ana and Mario and indicate whether each statement is true (**Cierto**) or false (**Falso**).

CD 1
Track 27

1. _____ Mario y Ana estudian en la misma (*same*) universidad este semestre.
2. _____ Mario toma clases de ciencias y de humanidades.
3. _____ Ana lee en la biblioteca para sus clases.
4. _____ Ana toma clases por la tarde.
5. _____ Mario realmente visita otros países en una de sus clases.

Después de escuchar

1-36 Ahora usted. Tell your classmate what you usually do on the following days and times. Your classmate will take notes. Then switch roles. Finally, verify with each other that the notes you took are correct.

LUNES	MARTES	MIÉRCOLES	JUEVES	VIERNES
8:00 a.m.	3:00 p.m.	5:00 p.m.	9:00 p.m.	1:00 p.m.

A conversar

Antes de conversar

1-37 Preparación. Write the questions answered by the clerk at your campus bookstore.

1. _____ La dirección de la librería es Calle Mayor, número 50.
2. _____ Sí, tengo libros de historia de España en español.
3. _____ Sí, tengo diccionarios en español.
4. _____ El diccionario bilingüe cuesta 40 euros.

Conversar

1-38 Entre nosotros. You are a Spaniard studying in Malaga. Your American friend would like to purchase some gifts to take home: a fancy pen, a book on the history of Spain, a Spanish dictionary, and a map of Spain. Read the following ad and call the bookstore to find out if it has what your friend needs. Your classmate will play the role of the bookstore clerk. Remember to follow the formalities of phone conversations with someone you do not know.

En directo

To answer the phone in Spain:

¿Diga?

To greet someone formally:

Buenos días./Buenas tardes.

To ask if they have what you need:

Necesito/Busco un/una...

LIBRERÍA CERVANTES

Papelería • Impresos • Artículos para escritorio

Libros de texto • Revistas

Casa especializada en estilógrafos y bolígrafos

Plaza Constitución, 3
29005   Málaga
Teléfono 221 19 99

Después de conversar

1-39 Un poco más. Call your American friend to explain whether the bookstore has each item he/she needs and the price.

A leer

Antes de leer

1-40 Preparación. Indicate which courses from the list students in the following majors (**carreras**) should take.

anatomía
conflictos sociales
depresión
diseño gráfico

drogas tóxicas
estructura del español
fisiología
historia de la lengua

medicinas alternativas
muralistas mexicanos

MEDICINA	BELLAS ARTES	FARMACIA	PSICOLOGÍA	FILOLOGÍA

Leer

1-41 Primera mirada. Circle the letter that completes each statement, based on the information in this web page.

1. Esta es una...   **a.** página de un libro.   **b.** página web.
2. El logo indica que esta institución es...   **a.** muy nueva.   **b.** muy antigua.
3. Esta página web presenta una lista de...   **a.** carreras.   **b.** clases.
4. La información de esta página web es...   **a.** muy específica.   **b.** muy general.
5. Esta institución tiene...   **a.** un campus.   **b.** más de un campus.

1-42 Segunda mirada. Answer the following questions, according to the information in the text.

1. Al final (*the bottom*) de esta página web hay varias teclas (*keys*). ¿Qué tecla usan los estudiantes para conversar con personas que trabajan en la Universidad de Salamanca?
2. Imagínese que usted necesita información sobre su carrera en la Universidad de Salamanca. ¿Qué facultad tiene la información que usted necesita?

Después de leer

1-43 Ampliación. Explore the **Servicio Central de Idiomas** page on the Universidad de Salamanca website by following the link on the *Mosaicos* web page and answer the questions that accompany the link. Be prepared to share your answers with the rest of the class.

A escribir

Antes de escribir

1-44 Preparación. As part of the course work in your Spanish class, you have been asked to correspond by e-mail with a university student in Spain. Think about and write down the information you would like to include in your first e-mail. Brainstorm...

1. some basic questions that this Spanish student may have about your college life.
2. some words and ideas that will help you answer those questions.
3. the order in which you will organize these ideas.

Escribir

1-45 Manos a la obra. Now write the Spanish student an e-mail about life at your college or university. Use the information you gathered in *Preparación*. Consider including the following points, if you have not already listed them.

1. introducing yourself
2. telling how things are going for you
3. describing your school and your classes: class number and names, when you are taking them, how interesting (or not) your classes and professors are
4. describing your daily routine at school, what you do after classes and on weekends, where and with whom you do these activities, and so on

Después de escribir

1-46 Revisión. After writing your e-mail, you may discuss it with a classmate. Then go over it carefully.

1. Make sure you have provided all the information your Spanish friend may need or any other you deem necessary. Pay attention to the content of your message and to the order in which you presented the information.
2. Revise any errors in language use, spelling, punctuation, accentuation, and so on.
3. Finally, make any changes that will help make your email clear and comprehensible to your e-mail pen pal.

ENFOQUE CULTURAL

Escuelas y universidades en España

El sistema escolar español es diferente del sistema de Estados Unidos y está dividido en cuatro partes: Educación Infantil, Educación Primaria, Educación Superior Obligatoria y, finalmente, el Bachillerato. En España, los niños y niñas hacen la Educación Infantil (que no es obligatoria sino voluntaria) hasta los seis años. Después empiezan la Educación Primaria, que es obligatoria y dura seis cursos, de los seis a los doce años de edad.

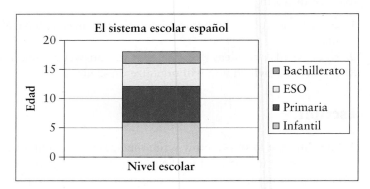

Entre los doce y los dieciséis años, los niños y niñas españoles cursan la Escuela Superior Obligatoria (ESO). La ESO completa la escolaridad obligatoria, pero muchos españoles continúan estudiando dos años más para terminar el Bachillerato, que los prepara para continuar con los estudios universitarios.

Rectorado de la Universidad Complutense

En España hay muchas universidades. La Universidad de Salamanca es una de las más antiguas del mundo y una de las más importantes de Europa. Esta universidad tiene un excelente programa de español para extranjeros y sus cursos de verano (durante junio, julio y agosto) tienen mucho prestigio.

De otra parte, la Universidad Complutense de Madrid es la más grande de España y también es muy antigua. Tiene un campus muy grande que se llama Ciudad Universitaria. Este nombre es muy apropiado, porque tiene más de 100.000 estudiantes.

El fútbol es un deporte muy popular en España.

En general, en las universidades españolas los estudiantes practican muchos deportes, pero la competencia entre universidades no es tan intensa como en Estados Unidos. Los deportes más populares entre los estudiantes universitarios españoles son el fútbol, el baloncesto y el atletismo, pero muchos estudiantes practican otros deportes también.

Los estudiantes universitarios españoles, como los de Estados Unidos, se divierten bailando en discotecas y clubes. Pero la música que escuchan no es necesariamente igual. A los jóvenes españoles les gusta escuchar música de rock en español. Hay muchos grupos de rock españoles. "El canto del loco" y "Fito y Fitipaldi" son dos grupos de rock español muy populares. A muchos jóvenes también les gusta bailar el flamenco, la música tradicional de Andalucía. En Sevilla, por ejemplo, hay clubes donde sólo tocan sevillanas, una música típica de esta ciudad. Finalmente, en su tiempo libre, muchos estudiantes españoles van de tapas y, por ejemplo, la Ciudad Universitaria está cerca de muchos bares de tapas.

1-47 Comprensión. PRIMERA FASE. **Reconocimiento de palabras clave.** Find in the text the Spanish word or phrase that best expresses the meaning of the following concepts:

preschool _____

middle school _____

high school _____

summer school _____

soccer _____

track _____

dance _____

SEGUNDA FASE. **Oraciones importantes.** Underline the statements that contain ideas found in the text. Then indicate where in the text those ideas appear.

1. Some Spanish students finish school at sixteen, while others continue with their education until they are eighteen.
2. Kindergarten is compulsory in Spain at the age of six.
3. Spanish universities are mostly private institutions.
4. The University of Salamanca has a long history.
5. The University of Madrid is so big that it is like a small city in itself.
6. Spanish universities offer their students the opportunity to practice sports.
7. Fito and Fitipaldi are two famous Spanish Formula drivers.
8. Many Spanish students enjoy dancing to traditional Spanish music.

TERCERA FASE. **Ideas principales.** Write a brief paragraph in English summarizing the main ideas expressed in the text.

1-48 Use la información. Prepare a poster to present to the class comparing what you have learned about the educational system of Spain to that of your own country. Use visuals to illustrate the different stages of the educational system, a few of the oldest and most important universities, and some of the activities that are popular with students in their free time.

VOCABULARIO

Las materias o asignaturas	Subjects
la antropología	anthropology
las ciencias políticas	political science
la economía	economics
el español	Spanish
la estadística	statistics
la geografía	geography
la historia	history
la informática/	computer
la computación	science
la literatura	literature
la psicología	psychology
la sociología	sociology

Los lugares	Places
la biblioteca	library
el café	cafe, coffee shop
la cafetería	cafeteria
la casa	house, home
la discoteca	dance club
el gimnasio	gymnasium
el laboratorio	laboratory
la librería	bookstore
la oficina	office
la playa	beach
la plaza	plaza, square
la universidad	university

Las Facultades	Schools, departments
de Arquitectura	of Architecture
de Ciencias	of Sciences
de Humanidades	of Humanities
de Informática	of Computer Science
de Medicina	of Medicine

Las personas	People
el alumno/la alumna	student
el compañero/	partner,
la compañera	classmate
el dependiente/	
la dependienta	salesperson
ellos/ellas	they
nosotros/nosotras	we
ustedes	you (plural)

Las descripciones	Descriptions
aburrido/a	boring
antiguo/a	old
bueno/a	good
difícil	difficult
estudioso/a	studious
excelente	excellent
fácil	easy
favorito/a	favorite
grande	big
interesante	interesting
malo/a	bad
norteamericano/a	North American
pequeño/a	small

Verbos	Verbs
aprender	to learn
asistir	to attend
bailar	to dance
beber	to drink
buscar	to look for
caminar	to walk
comer	to eat
comprar	to buy
comprender	to understand
conversar	to talk, to converse
correr	to run
deber	should
escribir	to write
escuchar	to listen (to)
estar	to be
estudiar	to study
hablar	to speak
leer	to read
llegar	to arrive
mirar	to look (at)
montar (en bicicleta)	to ride (a bicycle)
necesitar	to need
participar	to participate
practicar	to practice
sacar buenas/malas notas	to get good/bad grades
tomar	to take; to drink
tomar apuntes/notas	to take notes
trabajar	to work
ver	to see
vivir	to live

Palabras y expresiones útiles	Useful words and expressions
ahora	now
algo	something
¡Buena suerte!	Good luck!
¿Cómo te va?	How is it going?
con	with
¿Cuánto cuesta?	How much is it?
el diccionario	dictionary
este/a	this
el examen	test
el fin de semana	weekend
para	for, to
pero	but
¡Qué lástima!	What a pity!
sólo	only (adv.)
también	also
la tarea	homework
tengo/tienes	I have/you have
¿verdad?	right?

See page 33 for expressions of frequency.
See page 44 for question words.

Mis amigos y yo

Yo soy/Myself, por Cristina Cárdenas, una pintora norteamericana de origen mexicano

In this chapter you will learn how to:

- describe people, places, and things
- state where and when events take place
- express origin and possession
- express likes and dislikes

Cultural focus: **Estados Unidos**

CANADÁ

OCÉANO PACÍFICO

Un rapero latino,
Daddy Yankee

Los actores hispanos
Antonio Banderas y Salma Hayek

San Francisco

E S T A D O S
U N I D O S

Chicago

New York
Philadelphia

OCÉANO ATLÁNTICO

Los Angeles
Phoenix
Tucson

Santa Fe

Una margarita
con guacamole y chips

Houston

San Antonio

MÉXICO

Golfo de
México

Miami

Calle Ocho, Miami

El Álamo, San Antonio, Texas

 A vista de pájaro. Using the map and photos, as well as what you may already know, provide the following facts about Hispanics.

1. Tres hispanos famosos
2. El grupo hispano más numeroso en Estados Unidos
3. La ciudad (*city*) en Estados Unidos con más puertorriqueños
4. El estado con más mexicanos
5. Un producto hispano
6. Un tipo de música latina

A PRIMERA VISTA

Mis amigos y yo

¿Quiénes somos?

CD 1
Track 35

Me llamo Mario Quintana. Soy de
Puerto Rico y **tengo** veintidós **años. Me
gusta** escuchar música y mirar televisión.
Estudio en una universidad de Nueva
York y **deseo** ser profesor de historia.
Los chicos en estas fotografías son mis
amigos. Ellos también son **hispanos** y
estudian en la universidad. **Todos** somos
bilingües.

Esta chica es Amanda Martone.
Es **alta, delgada** y **morena.** Tiene
los **ojos** de color café y el **pelo
negro** y muy **largo.** Amanda es
una chica muy **agradable.** Estudia
mucho y desea ser economista.
Su familia es dominicana, pero
vive en Estados Unidos.

Cultura

Puerto Rico was a Spanish
colony for almost four centuries until it was ceded to
the United States following
the Spanish-American War
in 1898. Puerto Rico is a
freely associated common-
wealth (*estado libre
asociado*) of the United
States, and its people have
been U.S. citizens since
1917. Most Puerto Ricans
on the mainland live in
New York; New Jersey,
Pennsylvania, and Illinois
also have large Puerto
Rican communities.
However, Puerto Rico
remains geographically and
culturally part of Latin
America and almost all of its
residents speak Spanish as
their primary language. English is also widely spoken.
Being bilingual opens doors
to better economic opportunities in Puerto Rico and on
the mainland.

Esta chica se llama Ana Villegas.
No es alta ni baja. Es de **estatura
mediana** y usa **lentes de contacto.** Es
pelirroja y tiene los ojos **oscuros.**
Ana es **callada, trabajadora** y muy
inteligente. Sus padres son
cubanos.

Este chico se llama Ernesto Fernández.
Ernesto es moreno y tiene los ojos
castaños y el pelo **corto.** Es **bajo, fuerte,**
muy **conversador** y **simpático. Le gusta
usar** la computadora para conversar
con sus amigos de aquí y de México.

Esta chica es Marta Chávez Conde. Es española y tiene veintiún años. Es **rubia**, tiene los ojos **azules** y es muy **divertida**. Este año está en Estados Unidos con su familia.

2-1 Asociaciones. To whom do the descriptions on the left refer?

1. _____ Tiene el pelo largo.
2. _____ Tiene veintidós años.
3. _____ Es de España.
4. _____ Es bajo y fuerte.
5. _____ Usa lentes de contacto.
6. _____ Habla mucho.
7. _____ Tiene los ojos de color café.
8. _____ Tiene el pelo negro y es muy agradable.
9. _____ Tiene los ojos azules y el pelo rubio, es muy divertida.
10. _____ Desea ser profesor de historia.

a. Mario Quintana
b. Amanda Martone
c. Ernesto Fernández
d. Ana Villegas
e. Marta Chávez Conde

2-2 ¿Quién es? PRIMERA FASE. Read the texts on pages 56–57 again and write a list of at least eight expressions that you may use to describe people, including physical appearance (*apariencia*) and personality traits (*personalidad*).

SEGUNDA FASE. Now, without mentioning his/her name, describe a classmate in at least three sentences, using the vocabulary from the *Primera fase*, or any other that you may need. The rest of the group will try to guess who this person is. The group can ask questions if more information is needed to guess the student's identity.

MODELO: E1: *Es de estatura mediana y delgado. Tiene el pelo negro. Es fuerte y callado.*
E2: *¿Es… ?*

2-3 ¿Qué me gusta? Tell your classmate if you like each of the following activities. Then compare your responses.

comer en restaurantes italianos   estudiar español   practicar tenis/fútbol/béisbol
escribir correos electrónicos   trabajar los fines de semana   tener animales en casa
bailar los sábados por la noche   tomar café por la noche

MODELO: estar en casa por las noches
E1: *¿Te gusta estar en casa por las noches?*
E2: *Sí, me gusta. /No, no me gusta.*

Las descripciones

¿Cómo son estas personas?

fuerte   débil

joven   vieja/mayor

lista

tonto

trabajador   perezoso

simpático

antipático

triste   alegre

pobre   rica

casado

soltero

¿Cómo son estos animales?

CD 1
Track 37 Este perro es **feo** y **gordo**.

Esta gata es **bonita** y **delgada**.

> **Lengua**
>
> The word **la pierna** (*leg*) is used with both humans and animals. *Foot* is **el pie** (humans) and **la pata** (animals).

2-4 Opuestos. Complete the following statements about these famous people.

MODELO: *Shakira no es mayor, es joven.*

1. ____ Penélope Cruz no es gorda, es...
2. ____ El presidente de la compañía no es perezoso, es...
3. ____ Jennifer López no es antipática, es...
4. ____ Madonna no es tonta, es...
5. ____ Bill Gates no es pobre, es...
6. ____ Enrique Iglesias no es feo, es...

a. trabajador
b. lista
c. delgada
d. rico
e. guapo
f. simpática

> **En otras palabras**
>
> Depending on the region, Spanish speakers may use **bonita**, **linda**, or **guapa** to refer to a female. **Bien parecido**, **buen mozo**, **guapo** are usually used to refer to a male.

¿De qué color son estas cosas?

CD 1
Track 38

Este auto es **rojo** y es muy bueno.

Esta flor es **amarilla** y **blanca**. Es muy bonita.

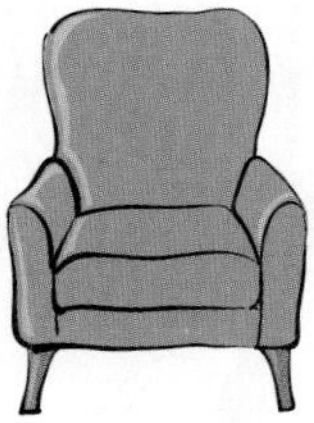

La silla **azul** es alta.

La silla **verde** es baja.

Otros colores

CD 1
Track 39

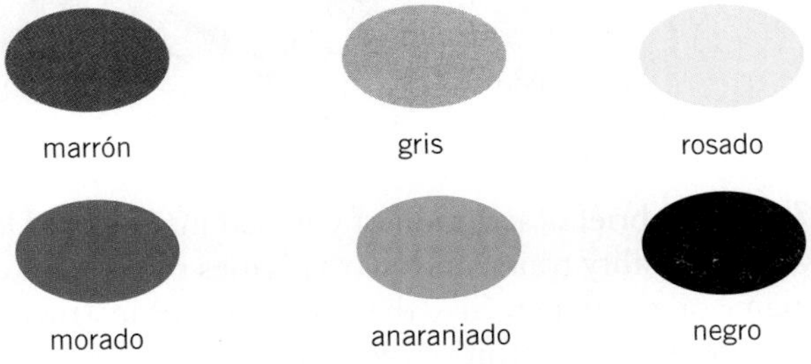

> **En otras palabras**
>
> Depending on the country and what is described, Spanish has various words to express the color brown: **café**, **marrón**, **carmelita**, **castaño/a**, and **pardo/a**. The words **naranja** and **rosa** are also used instead of **anaranjado/a** and **rosado/a**.

2-5 ¿De qué color son estas banderas (*flags*)? PRIMERA FASE. Read each description and then write the name of the country under its flag.

1. La bandera de Bolivia es roja, amarilla y verde.
2. La bandera de Estados Unidos es roja, blanca y azul.
3. La bandera de España es roja y amarilla.
4. La bandera de México es verde, blanca y roja.
5. La bandera de Colombia es amarilla, azul y roja.

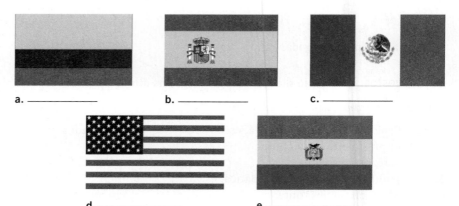

a. _____   b. _____   c. _____

d. _____   e. _____

SEGUNDA FASE. Take turns choosing a color and stating how many objects of that color are in the classroom. Your classmate will guess the color.

MODELO: E1:   *Hay dos mochilas y ocho pantalones vaqueros (jeans).*
          E2:   *Es el azul.*

2-6 Vamos a describir. Describe the people in these photos.

Eva

Alicia y Raquel

Alejandro

José Luis

2-7 ¿Quién soy? Write a brief description of yourself including at least three physical traits, two personality traits, and two activities that you like to do. Do not include your name on the paper. Give the paper to your instructor. He/She will ask each student to pick a description, read it, and try to guess who wrote it.

El origen

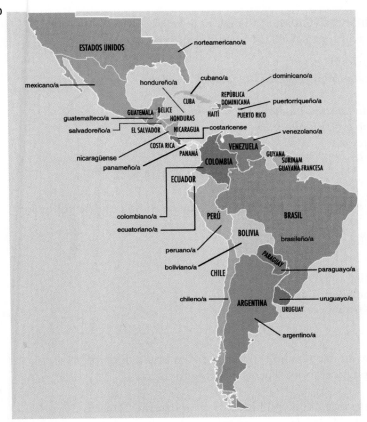

)) ¿De dónde son... ?

CD 1
Track 40

Cultura

Hispanics in the United States come from countries all over the world. Some are recent immigrants, but others have roots here that go back centuries. For example, Mexicans were living in what is now Texas, New Mexico, Arizona, Colorado, Nevada, and California, among other places, long before those territories became part of the United States after the Mexican War (1846–1848). Puerto Ricans have been U.S. citizens since 1917.

Lengua

These are other examples of nationalities:

alemán/alemana (*German*), **canadiense, francés/francesa, japonés/japonesa, marroquí, nigeriano/a, polaco/a, portugués/ portuguesa.**

2-8 Nacionalidades. PRIMERA FASE. Indicate the nationalities of the following people.

MODELO: *Carolina Herrera es una diseñadora famosa de Venezuela.*
        Es <u>*venezolana*</u>.

1. Albert Pujols es un jugador de béisbol de República Dominicana.
   Es _____ .
2. Salma Hayek es una actriz de México, protagonista de *Frida*. Es _____.
3. Rigoberta Menchú es una activista de Guatemala, Premio Nobel de la Paz, 1992. Es _____.
4. Julio Bocca es un bailarín de Argentina. Es _____.
5. Isabel Allende es escritora, originaria de Chile, autora de *La casa de los espíritus*. Es _____.
6. Oprah Winfrey es una presentadora de televisión de Estados Unidos.
   Es _____.
7. Gabriel García Márquez es un escritor de Colombia, autor de *Cien años de soledad*, Premio Nobel, 1982. Es _____.
8. Ricky Martin es un cantante de Puerto Rico. Es _____.

SEGUNDA FASE. Which of the personalities in the *Primera fase* is interesting to you? Why?

MODELO: *Para mí, ...es interesante. Es un actor famoso/una actriz famosa.*

 2-9 Adivinanzas (*Guesses*). Think of a well-known person. A classmate will try to guess the identity by asking you questions.

MODELO: E1:   *¿De dónde es?*
E2:   *Es estadounidense./Es de Estados Unidos.*
E1:   *¿Cómo es?*
E2:   *Es de estatura mediana, rubio y muy rico.*
E1:   *¿Qué es?/¿En qué trabaja?*
E2:   *Es actor.*
E1:   *¿Es Brad Pitt?*
E2:   *¡Sí!*

 2-10 Entrevista. **PRIMERA FASE.** Interview a classmate to find out the following information:

1. his/her name
2. his/her age
3. what he/she is like
4. the things he/she likes to do
5. where he/she is from
6. ...

SEGUNDA FASE. Write an introduction to the interview and a description of this person, including physical traits. Then share it with the class.

2-11 ¡Hola! **PRIMERA FASE.** You will hear a student describe himself. Before you listen, mark (✓) in the *Antes de escuchar* column the information you think he may provide.

CD 1
Track 41

	ANTES DE ESCUCHAR	**DESPUÉS DE ESCUCHAR**
1. name		
2. age		
3. parents' names		
4. physical description		
5. country where he was born		
6. place where he intends to work		

SEGUNDA FASE. Now, listen and pay attention to the general idea of what is said. Then, in the *Después de escuchar* column, indicate which information the speaker provided.

EN ACCIÓN

Diarios de bicicleta: ¿Una cantante divina?

Antes de ver

2-12 PRIMERA FASE. How well do you remember? Indicate whether the following statements refer to Javier (**J**) or to Daniel (**D**).

1. ____ Es mexicano.   2. ____ Es muy puntual.   3. ____ Es colombiano.

SEGUNDA FASE. In this segment a singer is scheduled to audition for a role in an up-coming musical. Guess what she looks like by underlining one sentence in each pair.

1. Es bonita. Es fea.
2. Es joven. Es vieja.
3. Tiene el pelo corto. Tiene el pelo largo.
4. Tiene los ojos verdes. Tiene los ojos negros.

Mientras ve

2-13 Indicate whether each statement is **cierto** (**C**) or **falso** (**F**) according to the video segment. Correct the statements that are false.

1. ____ Los amigos están en la cafetería.
2. ____ Luciana y Gabi necesitan escuchar audiciones para un nuevo musical.
3. ____ Beatriz Condes canta una canción tradicional mexicana.
4. ____ Beatriz Condes canta mal.

Después de ver

2-14 At the end of the video segment, a new character appears. Write five sentences in Spanish describing her.

FUNCIONES Y FORMAS

1. Describing people, places, and things: Adjectives

Eduardo es alt**o** y atlétic**o**.

Adriana es baj**a** y es muy elegant**e**.

Ana, Patricia y Teresa estudian mucho. Son inteligent**es** y trabajador**as**.

Carlos, Luis y Carmen son sociable**s** y activ**os**. Conversan y bailan mucho en los clubes.

Piénselo. Complete the descriptions of the people in the drawings by supplying their names.

1. _____ es joven y delgad**a**.
2. _____ , _____ y _____ son interesant**es** y estudios**as**.
3. _____ es moren**o** y guap**o**.
4. _____ , _____ y _____ son popular**es** y activ**os**.
5. _____ es colombian**o**.
6. _____ , _____ y _____ son español**as**.

- Adjectives are words that describe people, places, and things. Like articles (**el, la, los, las**) and nouns (**chica, chicas; libro, libros**), they generally have more than one form. In Spanish an adjective must agree in gender (masculine or feminine) and number (singular or plural) with the noun or pronoun it describes. Adjectives that describe characteristics usually follow the noun.
- Most masculine adjectives end in **-o**, and most feminine adjectives end in **-a**. To form the plural, these adjectives add **-s**.

	MASCULINE	FEMININE
SINGULAR	el chic**o** alt**o**	la chic**a** alt**a**
PLURAL	los chic**os** alt**os**	las chic**as** alt**as**

■ Adjectives that end in **-e** and some adjectives that end in a consonant have the same form for both masculine and feminine. To form the plural, adjectives that end in **-e** add **-s**; those that end in a consonant add **-es**.

	MASCULINE	FEMININE
SINGULAR	un libro interesante	una revista (*magazine*) interesante
	un cuaderno azul	una mochila azul
PLURAL	unos libros interesantes	unas revistas interesantes
	unos cuadernos azules	unas mochilas azules

■ Other adjectives that end in a consonant add **-a** to form the feminine and **-es** or **-as** to form the plurals.

	MASCULINE	FEMININE
SINGULAR	el alumno español	la alumna española
	el alumno hablador	la alumna habladora
PLURAL	los alumnos españoles	las alumnas españolas
	los alumnos habladores	las alumnas habladoras

■ Adjectives that end in **-ista** are both masculine and feminine. To form the plurals, add **-s**.

Pedro es muy optim**ista**,	*Pedro is very optimistic,*
pero Alicia es pesim**ista**.	*but Alicia is pessimistic.*
Ellos no son materia**listas**.	*They are not materialistic.*

2-15 ¿Cómo son estas personas? Choose the correct completion to describe the following people. More than one answer may be possible.

1. Muchos alumnos de mi universidad son…
   a. latinoamericano.   b. hispanos.   c. norteamericanas.   d. mexicanos.
2. Mi profesora favorita es muy…
   a. joven.   b. activo.   c. inteligente.   d. delgado.
3. Mi amigo Nicolás es muy…
   a. tonta.   b. fuerte.   c. callado.   d. antipática.
4. Las dos chicas más inteligentes de la clase son…
   a. activos y sociables.   b. trabajadoras y estudiosas.   c. altos y morenos.   d. interesante y optimista.

2-16 Cualidades necesarias. Your school is hiring recent graduates to help recruit students interested in studying other languages and cultures. Mark (✔) the qualities you think these new employees should have and then describe them to a partner, making sure that adjectives agree with nouns. Your partner will mention additional qualities.

MODELO: dos empleados bilingües en inglés y español
     E1: *Los empleados bilingües hablan bien inglés y español. Son activos y extrovertidos.*
     E2: *Sí. Son simpáticos, no son antipáticos. Hablan con los estudiantes y los padres de los estudiantes.*

1. dos especialistas en computadoras para el laboratorio de lenguas

   ____ activo   ____ bilingüe   ____ competente   ____ pasivo
   ____ agradable   ____ callado   ____ extrovertido   ____ trabajador

2. una recepcionista para la Oficina de Admisiones

   ____ eficiente   ____ imparcial   ____ perezoso   ____ simpático
   ____ hablador   ____ interesante   ____ perfeccionista   ____ tímido

2-17 Personas importantes. PRIMERA FASE. With your partner, take turns describing the people in the photos. Use at least three of the following descriptions: *atlético, cómico, extrovertido, guapo, inteligente, liberal, serio, simpático, tiene el pelo…, tiene los ojos…, trabajador, …*

Jimmy Smits es un actor famoso de cine (*movies*) y televisión.

Tish Hinojosa es una cantante mexicano-americana. Canta y escribe canciones también.

Julia Álvarez es una novelista y poeta dominicana. También es profesora.

Alex Rodríguez es un jugador de béisbol muy bueno.

 SEGUNDA FASE. Now, take turns describing someone important in your life. Your partner will ask questions to get more information about that person.

En directo

To address someone on the phone about an ad:

Hola, buenos días, llamo por el anuncio…

To respond:

¡Ah, sí, hola! Buenos días…

To greet someone you know on the phone:

Hola, ¿qué tal?

Soy María… /Habla María…

To respond:

Ah, ¡hola!

¿Qué tal, María?/¿Cómo estás?

SITUACIONES

1. **Role A.** You have just rented an apartment near campus and are looking for a roommate (**compañero/a de apartamento**). You receive a call from an interested student. Verify the student's name and ask a) where he/she is from; b) what his/her personality traits are; c) if he/she works and, if so, where; and d) what he/she likes to do in his/her free time (**tiempo libre**).

   Role B. Through an ad (**anuncio**) on a campus bulletin board, you see that someone is looking for a roommate (**compañero/a de apartamento**). You call that person. Answer his/her questions in detail and ask any questions you may have.

2. **Role A.** Your friend calls to tell you that he/she has been dating someone new. Ask a) where your friend's new boyfriend/girlfriend (**novio/a**) is from; b) what he/she is like; c) what he/she studies; d) if he/she has a car and, if so, what it looks like (color, size); and e) at least one other question of your own invention.

   Role B. You call your friend to talk about your new boyfriend/girlfriend. Your friend asks a lot of questions. Answer in as much detail as possible.

2. Identifying and describing; expressing origin, possession, location of events, and time: Present tense of *ser*

Marc Anthony **es** un artista neoyorquino muy talentoso y versátil. **Es** cantante y actor. Sus padres **son** de Puerto Rico. También **es** compositor. Canta y escribe canciones de salsa, de pop y de pop latino, y **es** un actor muy bueno de cine y de teatro. Sus (*His*) conciertos **son** en Estados Unidos y en muchos países latinoamericanos.

Piénselo. Read the sentences about Marc Anthony on the left. Select the meaning expressed by **es** or **son** in each sentence from the list on the right.

1. ____ Marc Anthony **es** de ascendencia puertorriqueña.
2. ____ El próximo (*next*) concierto de Marc Anthony **es** en California.
3. ____ La esposa de Marc Anthony **es** Jennifer López.
4. ____ Las películas de Marc Antony **son** muy populares.
5. ____ Este álbum de Marc Antony **es** de Daniel. Es su álbum favorito.
6. ____ Marc Anthony **es** muy famoso como artista de salsa y de pop.

a. identificación
b. descripción
c. nacionalidad/origen
d. posesión
e. eventos (localización, hora)

■ You have practiced some forms of **ser** and have used them for identification (**Esta señora es la profesora de historia**) and to tell time (**Son las cuatro**). Here are other uses of this verb.

SER (*to be*)			
yo	**soy**	nosotros/as	**somos**
tú	**eres**	vosotros/as	**sois**
Ud., él, ella	**es**	Uds., ellos/as	**son**

■ As you have seen, **ser** is used with adjectives to describe an intrinsic feature of a person, place, or thing.

¿Cómo **es** ella?   *What is she like?*

Es atlética y extrovertida.   *She is athletic and outgoing.*

¿Cómo **es** el apartamento?   *What is the apartment like?*

El apartamento **es** pequeño pero **es** muy cómodo.   *The house is small, but it is very comfortable.*

Lengua

Adjectives of nationality that end in a consonant form the feminine by adding **-a**.

español → española

Note that the feminine and plural forms do not have a written accent.

portugués → portuguesa
portugueses → **portugues**as

alemán → alemana
alemanes → **aleman**as

Adjectives of nationality are not capitalized.

Lengua

De + el contracts to **del**, but **de + la** and **de + los/las** do not contract.

El diccionario **es del** profesor, no **es de la** estudiante.
The dictionary is the professor's, not the student's.

■ **Ser** is used to express nationality; **ser + de** is used to express origin.

NATIONALITY

Gonzalo **es** chileno.	*Gonzalo is Chilean.*
Adriana **es** venezolana.	*Adriana is Venezuelan.*

ORIGIN

¿De dónde **son** Gonzalo y Adriana?	*Where are Gonzalo and Adriana from?*
Gonzalo **es** de Chile.	*Gonzalo is from Chile.*
Adriana **es** de Venezuela.	*Adriana is from Venezuela.*

■ **Ser + de** is used to express possession. The equivalent of the English word *whose?* is **¿de quién?**

¿De quién es el apartamento?	*Whose apartment is it?*
El apartamento **es de** Marta.	*The apartment is Marta's.*

■ **Ser + de** is also used to express the material of which something is made.

El reloj **es de** oro.	*The watch is (made of) gold.*
Las sillas **son de** madera.	*The chairs are made of wood/wooden.*

■ **Ser** is also used to express where an event takes place or time of an event.

El concierto **es** en el estadio.	*The concert is (takes place) in the stadium.*
La clase **es** a las nueve.	*The class is (takes place) at nine.*

2-18 ¿Cómo somos? PRIMERA FASE. Look at the following descriptions and write an X under the appropriate heading.

	SÍ	NO
1. Yo soy muy estudioso/a y trabajador/a.	_____	_____
2. A veces soy callado/a.	_____	_____
3. Soy norteamericano/a.	_____	_____
4. Mis abuelos son de otro (*another*) país.	_____	_____
5. Mi familia es muy religiosa y tradicional.	_____	_____
6. Mi mejor amigo/a es extrovertido/a y conversador/a.	_____	_____
7. Mis amigos y yo somos sociables y activos.	_____	_____
8. Mis clases este semestre son interesantes.	_____	_____

 SEGUNDA FASE. Now compare your answers with your partner's. Ask questions to get additional information.

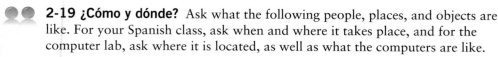

2-19 ¿Cómo y dónde? Ask what the following people, places, and objects are like. For your Spanish class, ask when and where it takes place, and for the computer lab, ask where it is located, as well as what the computers are like.

MODELO: tu profesor/a de inglés
        E1: *¿Cómo es tu profesor de inglés?*
        E2: *Es alto, moreno y muy simpático.*

1. tus amigos
2. tu cuarto (*bedroom*)
3. tu compañero/a de cuarto (*roommate*)
4. el auto de tu mejor amigo/a
5. la clase de español
6. el laboratorio de computadoras

2-20 ¿Qué es esto? Take turns to describe an object and its location in the classroom. Your partner will ask you questions and guess what it is.

MODELO: E1: *Es grande, es de plástico, está al lado de la ventana.*
        E2: *¿De qué color es?*
        E1: *Es roja.*
        E2: *¿Es la mochila de Juan?*

> ### Lengua
>
> **Madera** (*wood*), **plástico**, **tela** (*fabric*), **metal**, **oro** (*gold*), **vidrio** (*glass*) are some words used to describe what something is made of.

2-21 Eventos y lugares. You are working at the university's information booth, and a visitor (your classmate) stops by. Answer his/her questions. Then switch roles.

MODELO: la exposición del club de fotografía

VISITANTE: *Perdón/Disculpe, ¿dónde es la exposición del club de fotografía?*

EMPLEADO/A: *Es en la biblioteca.*

VISITANTE: *¿Dónde está la biblioteca?*

EMPLEADO/A: *Está en la calle Madison, enfrente del edificio (building) de biología.*

1. el concierto de música salsa
2. la conferencia (*lecture*) sobre el arte mexicano
3. el banquete para los estudiantes internacionales
4. la reunión de profesores
5. la fiesta del club de español
6. la ceremonia de graduación

SITUACIONES

1. **Role A.** You meet a student from a Spanish-speaking country in one of your classes. Introduce yourself and find out a) the student's name; b) his/her city and country of origin; c) characteristics of his/her city; and d) what his/her friends are like.

   Role B. You are an international student from a Spanish-speaking country. Answer your classmate's questions and then ask questions to get the same information he/she obtained from you.

2. **Role A.** A friend has invited you to a party at his/her house on Saturday. Ask a) where the house is located; b) what it looks like (so you can find it easily); and c) what time the party is.

   Role B. You have invited a friend to a party at your house on Saturday. Answer your friend's questions. Then explain that the house belongs to your parents (**padres**), and tell your friend why your parents are not at home that weekend.

3. Expressing inherent qualities and changeable conditions: *Ser* and *estar* with adjectives

Todos los estudiantes **están** aburridos porque la profesora **es** aburrida.

Piénselo. Read the statements below and classify them as to whether they describe either a) a personality trait/physical characteristic or b) a feeling or perception that may change.

1. ____ La profesora **es** aburrida. Sus clases no son interesantes.
2. ____ Sofía **está** delgada en ese vestido (*dress*) negro.
3. ____ Los estudiantes **están** nerviosos. Tienen un examen difícil hoy.
4. ____ Normalmente, las modelos **son** altas y muy delgadas.
5. ____ Hoy los niños **están** contentos. Van (*They are going*) al parque.
6. ____ Roberto **es** estudioso y trabajador. Estudia mucho todos los días.

■ **Ser** and **estar** are often used with the same adjectives. However, the choice of verb determines the meaning of the sentence.

■ **Ser +** *adjective* states the norm—what someone or something is like.

Jorge **es** delgado.	*Jorge is thin.* (He is a thin man.)
Sara **es** muy nerviosa.	*Sara is very nervous.* (She is a nervous person.)
El libro **es** nuevo.	*The book is new.* (It is a new book.)

■ **Estar +** *adjective* expresses a change from the norm, a condition, or how one feels about the person or object being discussed.

Jorge **está** delgado.	*Jorge is/looks thin.* (He lost weight recently, or he looks thin in a picture or because of the clothes he is wearing.)
Sara **está** muy nerviosa.	*Sara is very nervous.* (She is feeling nervous.)
El libro **está** nuevo.	*The book is/looks new.* (It is used, but it seems like a brand new book.)

■ The adjectives **contento/a, cansado/a, enojado/a** are always used with **estar.**

Ella **está contenta** ahora.	*She is happy now.*
Los niños **están cansados.**	*The children are tired.*
Carlos **está enojado.**	*Carlos is angry.*

■ Some adjectives have one meaning with **ser** and another with **estar.**

Ese señor **es** malo.	*That man is bad/evil.*
Ese señor **está** malo.	*That man is ill.*
La chica **es** lista.	*The girl is clever/smart.*
La chica **está** lista.	*The girl is ready.*
La manzana **es** verde.	*The apple is green.*
La manzana **está** verde.	*The apple is not ripe.*
La profesora **es** aburrida.	*The professor is boring.*
La profesora **está** aburrida.	*The professor is bored.*

2-22 ¿Qué pasa aquí? Look at the drawings and then complete the descriptions about each one with the appropriate form of **ser** or **estar.**

1. Esteban _____ (1) un joven listo y estudioso. Este semestre saca buenas notas, excepto en la clase de economía. _____ (2) una clase muy difícil. Esteban _____ (3) nervioso porque mañana hay un examen sobre la Comunidad Económica Europea, pero él no _____ (4) listo. Debe estudiar toda la noche.

2. ¡Pobres niños! (*Poor children!*) La fruta _es_ (5) buena y saludable (*healthful*), pero estas manzanas _están_ (6) verdes, no _están_ (7) buenas. Ahora los niños no _están_ (8) contentos. Una niña _está_ (9) mala porque le duele el estómago (*her stomach hurts*).

¡Qué asco!

¡Horrible!

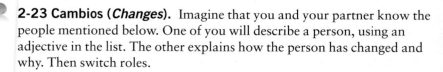

2-23 Cambios (*Changes*). Imagine that you and your partner know the people mentioned below. One of you will describe a person, using an adjective in the list. The other explains how the person has changed and why. Then switch roles.

MODELO: Arturo/fuerte
    E1: *Arturo es fuerte.*
    E2: *Pero por su enfermedad (*illness*), ahora está muy débil.*

PERSONAS	CARACTERÍSTICAS	RAZONES
1. Ramón	alegre	por sus problemas
2. Laura y Gustavo	callado/a	por la dieta
3. Cristina	conversador/a	por el ejercicio
4. Andrés	débil	por el exceso de estudio
5. Ana y Sofía	extrovertido/a	por la falta (*lack*) de motivación
6. Teresa	feliz	por su depresión
	fuerte	por sus buenas notas
	introvertido/a	
	optimista	
	perezoso/a	
	pesimista	
	trabajador/a	
	triste	

2-24 Termómetro emocional. PRIMERA FASE. Indicate (✓) how you feel in each situation. Then write two adjectives to further describe how you feel and how you think your classmate feels in these situations.

LUGARES	ABURRIDO/A	CONTENTO/A	TRANQUILO/A	NERVIOSO/A	YO	MI COMPAÑERO/A
en la cafetería con mis compañeros						
en los exámenes finales						
en la oficina de un profesor/una profesora						
en un concierto con mis amigos						
en una fiesta formal						
en mi casa por la noche						

 SEGUNDA FASE. Now compare your responses with those of your partner and write down one similarity and one difference between the two of you. Report to the class.

MODELO: en la clase de español
E1: *En la clase de español, yo estoy contento/a. Tú también estás contento/a en la clase de español, ¿verdad?*
E2: *Tienes razón. Yo estoy contento/a. O Estás equivocado/a. Yo estoy aburrido/a.*
E1: [a la clase] *Yo estoy contento/a en la clase de español, pero Amanda está aburrida.*

SITUACIONES

1. **Role A.** You have traveled to another city for a job interview. A friend of a friend who lives in that city has offered to show you around. Make arrangements over the phone to meet this person, whom you do not know. Find out what the person looks like, so you will be able to spot him/her at your meeting place.

   Role B. You have offered to get together with a friend of a friend who has a job interview in your city. You do not know this person, so when you arrange over the phone to meet, you have to find out what the person looks like and something about his/her personality, so you can decide what to show him/her.

2. **Role A.** Show your classmate a photo. Identify the people and explain what they are like. Then respond to your friend's questions and comments about them.

   Role B. After your classmate tells you about the people in the photo, ask and comment about a) how they seem to be feeling, based on their facial expressions or what they are doing and b) where they appear to be.

4. Expressing ownership: Possessive adjectives

Mis amigos y yo

Condorito—the main character of the comic strip magazine of the same name—introduces some of his closest friends. Look at the group portrait to follow what he says.

Condorito y sus amigos

Mi nombre es Condorito. Soy un cóndor simpático, listo y sincero.

Yayita y **su** pequeña Sobrina (*niece*) Yuyito son **mis** dos grandes amores (*sweethearts*). **La** sobrina **de** Yayita es muy atractiva, pero es muy dependiente de **su** tía (*aunt*)y de **su** abuelo Don Tremendón. **Nuestra** relación es especial. Nosotros pasamos mucho tiempo juntos.

Mi sobrino (*nephew*) Coné es amoroso, pero un poco llorón (*whiner*). **Su** mejor amiga es Yuyito. La actividad favorita **de ellos** es comer chocolate y jugar en el parque. Finalmente, Doña Tremebunda es la madre de **mi** novia Yayita. Honestamente no me gusta mucho hablar con ella porque es muy materialista. También es dominante y ambiciosa. Y **tu** familia y amigos, ¿cómo son?

Cultura

Condorito, a comic strip created by the Chilean cartoonist René Ríos (Pepo), is popular throughout Latin America. The main character, Condorito, is an anthropomorphic condor who uses his wit, rather than his work or talents, to solve the problems of everyday life. The multifaceted Condorito, usually in black pants and red shirt, adopts new identities to tell the latest gossip in town. With his ability to transcend social class, nationality, and ideology, he can be a peasant, a scientist, or a beggar, an Egyptian or an Argentinian. The comic strip in which he appears portrays with humor the personality and struggles of the Chilean people. For more information go to the *Mosaicos* web page.

Piénselo. Complete the following statements, using the information in Condorito's description.

1. Condorito tiene una novia. ____ nombre es _____ .
   a. Tu... Yayita   **b.** Mi... Doña Tremebunda   **c.** Su... Yayita

2. Condorito dice (*says*): *Nuestra relación es especial.* ¿A qué relación se refiere Condorito en esta afirmación?
   a. La relación de Condorito con Yayita y su familia.
   b. La relación de Yayita con la familia de ella.
   c. La relación entre Coné, Yayita, la familia de Yayita y él (Condorito).

3. Coné es ____ Condorito.
   a. la hija de   **b.** el sobrino de   **c.** el hijo (*son*) de

4. Condorito prefiere no pasar tiempo con Doña Tremebunda. ¿Por qué?
   a. por la apariencia física de ella   **b.** por la personalidad de ella
   c. por el hijo de ella

■ Possessive adjectives modify nouns to express possession. They always precede the noun they modify.

   mi amigo   **tu** familia

POSSESSIVE ADJECTIVES	
mi(s)	*my*
tu(s)	*your (familiar)*
su(s)	*your (formal), his, her, its, their*
nuestro(s), nuestra(s)	*our*
vuestro(s), vuestra(s)	*your (familiar plural)*

■ Possessive adjectives change number to agree with the thing possessed, not with the possessor.

   mi *clase*, mis *clases*

■ The **nosotros/as** and **vosotros/as** forms must agree also in gender.

   nuestro *profesor*, nuestros *amigos*; nuestra *profesora*, nuestras *amigas*

■ **Su** and **sus** have multiple meanings. To ensure clarity, you may use **de** + *the name of the possessor* or *the appropriate pronoun* instead of *su/sus*. For example, the multiple meanings of *su compañera* can be expressed as follows:

la compañera +
- **de ella** (la compañera de Elena)
- **de él** (la compañera de Jorge)
- **de usted**
- **de ustedes**
- **de ellos** (la compañera de Elena y Jorge)
- **de ellas** (la compañera de Elena y Olga)

En otras palabras

The word for *car* in Spanish varies, depending on the country or region. The most widely accepted word is **el auto**, commonly used in the southern half of South America. In Mexico, Central America, the Caribbean, and the northern countries of South America, **el carro** is frequently used. **El coche** is used in Spain.

2-25 Mi mundo (*world*). **PRIMERA FASE.** Write down two things that you own (**pertenencias**) and two people whom you value very much. You may use the words in the box or choose others.

Pertenencias:	un carro	una computadora portátil	un iPod
Personas:	un amigo/ una amiga	un profesor ideal/ una profesora ideal	un actor/ una actriz

PERTENENCIAS
1. _____
2. _____

PERSONAS
1. _____
2. _____

SEGUNDA FASE. Take turns describing your selections. Take notes so that you can share with the class the similarities and differences between you and your classmate.

Pertenencias

E1: *Yo tengo un auto. Es rápido y moderno. Y tú, tienes un auto?*
E2: *Sí.*
E1: *¿Y cómo es tu auto?*
E2: *Mi auto es rojo y muy viejo.*

Personas

E1: *Mi madre es importante en mi vida (life). Es muy alegre y activa. Y tu mamá, ¿cómo es?*
E2: *Mi madre es tranquila y muy inteligente.*

2-26 Mi familia. Which of these statements apply to your family and friends?
Mark (✓) your answers in the spaces under **Yo**. Then interview a classmate.

	YO	MI COMPAÑERO/A
1. Mi familia es grande.	_____	_____
2. Otros miembros de mi familia viven en nuestro barrio (*neighborhood*).	_____	_____
3. A veces pasamos las vacaciones con mis abuelos (*grandparents*).	_____	_____
4. Siempre conversamos sobre temas políticos.	_____	_____
5. A veces no estamos de acuerdo y discutimos.	_____	_____
6. Nuestros amigos visitan la casa frecuentemente.	_____	_____

2-27 Nuestra universidad. PRIMERA FASE. In preparation for the *Segunda fase*,
write some words that generally describe the following aspects of your
university.

1. los profesores: _____

2. las clases: _____

3. los estudiantes: _____

4. los equipos (*teams*) de fútbol, baloncesto, béisbol, etc.: _____

5. el campus: _____

SEGUNDA FASE. Now write 1 or 2 sentences about each topic in the *Primera fase*.
Be prepared to present your sentences to the class. The class will decide which
sentences a) describe the school most accurately and b) present an appealing
view of the school for prospective students.

SITUACIONES

1. **Role A.** You are a Spanish professor. You inform a student about a lecture by
   another professor. Explain that a) the professor is visiting the university;
   b) there is a lecture by the professor (**una conferencia del profesor**) on
   Thursday; c) it will take place in the library.

   Role B. Your professor invites you to a lecture. Find out a) the time of the
   lecture; b) the speaker's name; and c) the topic (**tema**).

2. **Role A.** You are a student from Peru studying in the United States. You phone
   your parents and ask how they are. Tell about your host parents (**madre
   americana/padre americano**), brother (**hermano**), and sister (**hermana**). Describe
   their ages, appearance, personalities, and occupations.

   Role B. You live in Peru, and your child is studying in the United States. When
   he/she calls, ask about a) the host family schedule (**horario**) and b) activities of
   the host family.

En directo

To initiate the conversation:

Oye (*Hey*), **mi hermano
americano es...**

¿Sabes? (*You know?*) **Mi
hermano americano es...**

To acknowledge information
by showing surprise:

Ah, ¿sí?

¡No me digas!
Oh, really?, No way!, Wow!

5. Expressing likes and dislikes: *Gustar*

The following is a transcript of a chat over the Internet between Marisa, a Mexican student living in Mexico City, and Carla, a Mexican American living in El Paso, Texas.

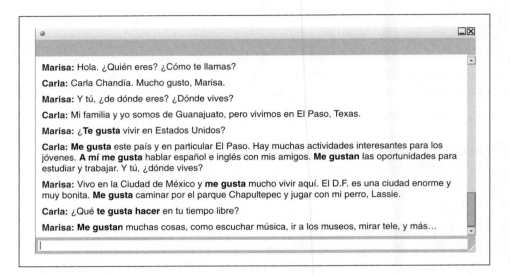

Marisa: Hola. ¿Quién eres? ¿Cómo te llamas?

Carla: Carla Chandía. Mucho gusto, Marisa.

Marisa: Y tú, ¿de dónde eres? ¿Dónde vives?

Carla: Mi familia y yo somos de Guanajuato, pero vivimos en El Paso, Texas.

Marisa: ¿**Te gusta** vivir en Estados Unidos?

Carla: **Me gusta** este país y en particular El Paso. Hay muchas actividades interesantes para los jóvenes. **A mí me gusta** hablar español e inglés con mis amigos. **Me gustan** las oportunidades para estudiar y trabajar. Y tú, ¿dónde vives?

Marisa: Vivo en la Ciudad de México y **me gusta** mucho vivir aquí. El D.F. es una ciudad enorme y muy bonita. **Me gusta** caminar por el parque Chapultepec y jugar con mi perro, Lassie.

Carla: ¿Qué **te gusta hacer** en tu tiempo libre?

Marisa: **Me gustan** muchas cosas, como escuchar música, ir a los museos, mirar tele, y más…

Piénselo. Indicate whether each paraphrase best refers to Marisa (**M**) or Carla (**C**).

1. ____ **Me gustan** las posibilidades académicas que ofrece Estados Unidos.
2. ____ **Me gusta** vivir en la capital de México.
3. ____ **Me gusta** ser bilingüe.
4. ____ **Me gustan** las actividades al aire libre (*open air*).
5. ____ **Me gusta** el arte.

■ To express what you like to do, use **me gusta** + *infinitive*. To express what you don't like to do, use **no me gusta** + *infinitive*.

Me gusta hablar español.	*I like to speak Spanish.*
No me gusta mirar televisión.	*I don't like to watch television.*
Me gusta practicar deportes y salir con mis amigos.	*I like to play sports and go out with my friends.*

■ To express that you like something or someone, use **me gusta** + *singular noun* or **me gustan** + *plural noun*.

Me gusta la música clásica.	*I like classical music.*
Me gustan las personas alegres.	*I like happy people.*

■ To ask a classmate what he/she likes, use **¿Te gusta(n)… ?** To ask your instructor, use **¿Le gusta(n)… ?**

¿Te gusta/Le gusta tomar café?	*Do you like to drink coffee?*
¿Te gustan/Le gustan los chocolates?	*Do you like chocolates?*

■ To state what another person likes, use **a** + *name of person* + **le gusta(n)…** When you are talking about the preferences of more than one person, use **a** + *name of person* + **les gusta(n)…**

A Diego le gustan las fiestas.   *Diego likes parties.*

A Carlos le gusta el fútbol.   *Carlos likes soccer.*

A Diego y a Carlos les gusta ir de vacaciones con sus padres.   *Diego and Carlos like to go on vacation with their parents.*

2-28 Mis preferencias. PRIMERA FASE. Mark (✓) your preferences in the following chart.

ACTIVIDAD	ME GUSTA MUCHO	ME GUSTA UN POCO	NO ME GUSTA
escribir correos electrónicos en español			
comer en restaurantes de comida mexicana			
bailar salsa			
escuchar música rock en español			
aprender sobre la cultura de otros países			
visitar lugares históricos			

SEGUNDA FASE. Now, compare your answers with those of a classmate. Share with the class one similarity and one difference between you and your partner in terms of your preferences.

2-29 ¿Te gusta… ? PRIMERA FASE. Ask if a classmate likes the following. Be sure to ask follow-up questions as appropriate.

1. el gimnasio de la universidad
2. los teléfonos celulares con conexión a Internet
3. la informática
4. los autos de este año
5. los animales
6. los conciertos de música clásica

SEGUNDA FASE. Write a brief note to another classmate in which you share two pieces of information about yourself and two pieces of information you discovered about your partner.

2-30 ¿Qué te gusta hacer? PRIMERA FASE. Write down some questions that you would ask a classmate to find out the following:

1. what he/she likes to do in his/her free time
2. in what restaurant he/she likes to eat with his/her family

SEGUNDA FASE. Interview two classmates and ask each of them the questions you prepared in the *Primera fase. Com*pare their responses and be prepared to share with others your conclusions regarding how your classmates spend their time.

SITUACIONES

1. **Role A:** You are at a park where you hear someone giving Spanish commands to a dog. Break the ice and introduce yourself. Ask a) the person's name; b) the dog's name and age; and c) if the dog is friendly (**manso**). Compliment the dog (smart, strong, very pretty, etc.). Tell the person that you like dogs very much and that you also like cats. Answer the questions this person asks.

   Role B: You are in the park training your dog and someone approaches. Answer this person's questions and ask if he/she has a dog, and if so, what it looks like. Say that you don't like cats because they are not active or fun. Finally, ask where this person is from and where he/she is studying Spanish.

2. **Role A:** You are at Panchero's, a Mexican restaurant. While you are waiting to be seated, you hear someone speaking Spanish to a child. Introduce yourself and ask the child's name and age. Compliment the parent on his/her beautiful child. Also ask the parent if he/she likes Panchero's and likes to eat at American restaurants like McDonald's.

   Role B: You and your two-year-old daughter are waiting to be seated at Panchero's, a Mexican restaurant. Someone asks you about your child. React to the person's comments and answer his/her questions.

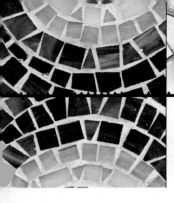

MOSAICOS

A escuchar

Listen for specific information

When you ask a person specific questions, he/she may provide not only the answers you need, but also additional information. To listen efficiently, focus on the answers you requested. This will help you obtain the information you need.

Antes de escuchar

2-31 Preparación. You will listen to a student telling her mother about how different her roommates are. Before listening to their conversation, write the name(s) of your own roommate(s) and a sentence that describes each of them.

Escuchar

CD 1
Track 42

2-32 ¿Comprende usted? Listen to the conversation between a student and her mother. Mark (✓) the appropriate column(s) to indicate whether the following statements describe Rita, Marcela, or both.

	RITA	MARCELA
1. Estudia economía.		
2. Le gusta bailar.		
3. Es alta, morena y tiene los ojos negros.		
4. Es muy seria, baja y delgada.		
5. Estudia arte moderno.		

Después de escuchar

2-33 Ahora usted. Complete the following sentences to say how you feel about your roommate(s).

1. Me gusta(n) mi(s) compañero/a(s) de cuarto porque...
2. A veces no me gusta(n) mi(s) compañero/a(s) de cuarto porque...
3. Mi(s) compañero/a(s) de cuarto y yo somos semejantes/diferentes porque...

A conversar

Describe a person

Descriptions are most effective when they are well organized. When describing a person, you may want to include demographic information (e.g., age, nationality/origin), physical characteristics, and personality traits. A well-organized description presents information by category, beginning with an introductory phrase to prepare your listener.

Antes de conversar

 2-34 Preparación. *Mafalda*, like *Condorito*, featured earlier in this chapter, is a popular comic strip in the Spanish-speaking world. Go to the *Mosaicos* web page, choose one of the characters shown there, and read the description about him/her.

Conversar

 2-35 Entre nosotros. Describe the physical characteristics and personality traits of the *Mafalda* character you read about in **2-34**. Your partner will ask questions or comment as appropriate. Then switch roles.

Después de conversar

2-36 Un poco más. Find out about another popular comic character, like those mentioned in the *Cultura* box below, and tell the class about him/her.

Cultura

Mafalda is the name of a character in a comic strip of the same name created by the Argentinian cartoonist Quino. Extremely popular in the Spanish-speaking world, she is a six-year-old girl deeply concerned with political issues and world peace. Her naive yet sharp criticism of society has made her an icon for the defense of human rights. For more information go to the *Mosaicos* web page.

En directo

To introduce information about physical characteristics:

En cuanto a lo físico,... / Físicamente, es...

To introduce information about personality:

Es una persona... /Tiene un carácter...

Cultura

Many Hispanics who emigrate to other countries maintain connections to their culture by reading and listening to music in Spanish. In areas with large Hispanic populations, Spanish-language newspapers and magazines are available.

These carry some of the many comic strips popular in the Hispanic world, including *Mafalda* (Argentina), *Condorito* (Chile), and *Mortadelo y Filemón* (Spain). You will find information about these comic strips on the Internet.

A leer

ESTRATEGIAS

Scan a text for specific information

When you read in Spanish, your goal should be to read for ideas, not for the meaning of every word. One way to read for ideas is to search for particular pieces of information that you think will be in the text. Often the comprehension questions after the text will help you decide what information to search for as you read. This approach to reading, called *scanning*, works best if you a) focus on the information you are seeking and b) read the text through quickly at least twice, looking for specific information each time.

Antes de leer

2-37 Preparación. PRIMERA FASE. Read the title of the text and examine its format. (This is the reading strategy you learned in *Capítulo 1*.) What type of text is it?

1. a series of e-mail messages
2. personal ads
3. ads for items for sale

SEGUNDA FASE. Scan the text and use your highlighter to mark the following information in each paragraph.

1. el nombre de la persona
2. la edad (*age*) de la persona
3. la dirección electrónica de la persona

Leer

2-38 Primera mirada. Read the personal ads that follow and scan them for the information needed in the form. In some cases, it may not be possible to provide all the information requested.

	PERSONA 1	PERSONA 2	PERSONA 3	PERSONA 4
nombre				
edad				
nacionalidad				
estado civil				
personalidad (1 ó 2 adjetivos)				
le gusta...				

Amigos sin fronteras

Soltera, sin hijos y sin compromiso. Me llamo Susana y tengo 24 años. Soy guatemalteca. Busco amigos extranjeros, solteros, separados o divorciados, jóvenes o mayores. Soy amable, cariñosa y muy trabajadora. Por mi trabajo, viajo mucho, pero me gusta la compañía de otras personas. Soy bilingüe. Hablo español e inglés. Escriban a sincompromiso@comcast.net.

Soy Ricardo Brown. 21 años, sincero, dedicado. Me gustan las fiestas. Soy soltero. Deseo conocer a una chica de unos 23 años, preferiblemente venezolana como yo. Prefiero una mujer activa e independiente. Me gusta practicar deportes y explorar lugares nuevos. Escríbanme a amigosincero@msn.com.

Me llamo Pablo Sosa, tengo 31 años, y soy chileno. Soy agradable y muy trabajador. Me gusta hacer mi trabajo a la perfección, pero soy tolerante. Los autos convertibles son mi pasión. Deseo mantener correspondencia por correo electrónico con jóvenes del extranjero para intercambiar información sobre los convertibles europeos o americanos. Mi dirección electrónica es locoporlosautos@yahoo.com.

Soy Xiomara Stravinsky, decoradora y fotógrafa argentina. Me gusta el arte, especialmente el impresionismo. Tengo 27 años y soy divorciada. Soy dinámica, agradable y generosa, pero tengo pocos amigos porque tengo dos trabajos y paso muchas horas con mis clientes. Necesito un cambio en mi vida. ¿Deseas ser mi amigo/a? Por favor, escríbeme a xiomarastravinsky@hotmail.com.

Lengua

The letter **y** changes to **e** when it precedes a word beginning with **i** or **h**.

inglés y español, but **español e inglés**

inteligente y agradable, but **agradable e inteligente**

Después de leer

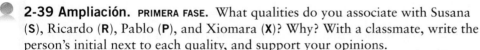

2-39 Ampliación. **PRIMERA FASE.** What qualities do you associate with Susana (**S**), Ricardo (**R**), Pablo (**P**), and Xiomara (**X**)? Why? With a classmate, write the person's initial next to each quality, and support your opinions.

a. ____ sociable
b. ____ simpático/a
c. ____ divertido/a
d. ____ perfeccionista

e. ____ mayor
f. ____ flexible
g. ____ trabajador/a
h. ____ ocupado/a

SEGUNDA FASE. Find the best match for Susana, Ricardo, Pablo and Xiomara from the following responses received.

1. Tengo 22 años y me gustan todos los deportes. Mis padres viven en Caracas pero yo vivo en Miami.
2. Enseño arte en la escuela secundaria. Tengo tiempo para mis amigos los fines de semana.
3. Soy de Nicaragua. Soy muy sociable y deseo perfeccionar mi inglés.
4. Trabajo para *Autos de hoy*, una revista de Internet.

A escribir

Consider audience and purpose

Writing is an act of communication between writer and reader. Writers usually have a purpose in mind, such as compiling information, informing the reader, describing something or someone, or expressing a point of view. Readers rely on their prior knowledge and on the quantity and quality of information presented to derive meaning from the text.

As you write, keep in mind your purpose and make the necessary adjustments to form and content to facilitate your audience's comprehension of the message.

Antes de escribir

2-40 Preparación. PRIMERA FASE. Read the following ad written by a movie fan in your local Spanish-language newspaper.

> Fanático del cine necesita amigos para discutir películas los fines de semana. Tengo 24 años y estudio cinematografía. Me fascinan las películas de acción y también las románticas. Soy fuerte, activo, atlético y aventurero. Me gusta practicar deportes, especialmente el tenis y el esquí. Siempre estoy muy ocupado, pero tengo unas horas todas las semanas para conversar sobre películas y hacer deportes. Interesados, favor de enviar correo electrónico a fanaticodelcine@yahoo.com.

SEGUNDA FASE. You decide to respond to the ad. First, think about the following questions and mark (✓) your responses accordingly.

1. What is the purpose that *fanaticodelcine* has in mind when he writes the e-mail?
   a. ＿＿ to find a girlfriend
   b. ＿＿ to find someone (male or female) to talk with about movies

2. What would your purpose be if you responded to his personal ad?
   a. ＿＿ to share your interest in movies with someone who is knowledgeable about the topic.
   b. ＿＿ to date *fanaticodelcine*

TERCERA FASE. Now jot down information that will help you meet the goal of becoming the conversation partner of *fanaticodelcine*.

1. your age
2. your place of origin
3. words (adjectives) that describe you physically
4. expressions (adjectives) that describe your personality
5. activities (verbs) that you like to do that may match the needs of the person in the ad

Escribir

2-41 Manos a la obra. Write an e-mail to *fanaticodelcine* using the information you prepared in the *Tercera fase* of **2-40**.

Para:

Asunto: Anuncio

Hola,_____

Respondo a tu anuncio del periódico.(*Provide your name.*)
_____

Primero, aquí tienes alguna información personal.(*Provide personal information.*)_____
_____
_____
_____

En segundo lugar, estas son algunas de las actividades que, al igual que tú, yo hago en mi tiempo libre.(*Provide activities that you, like fanaticodelcine, like to do in your free time.*)_____
_____
_____
_____

En tercer lugar, los fines de semana… (*Tell what you like to do.*)_____
_____
_____
_____

Finalmente, deseo ser tu amigo/a. Por favor, escríbeme un correo electrónico a mi dirección:_____
_____

Hasta pronto.
_____

Después de escribir

2-42 Revisión. After writing your e-mail, read it again and check the following:

1. Did you include all the information *fanaticodelcine* needs? Do you think your information will be interesting to him?
2. Did you use punctuation correctly? Did you verify that there are no spelling or grammatical mistakes that may hinder comunication?
3. Make any necessary changes that will make your e-mail clear and comprehensible to *fanaticodelcine*.

ENFOQUE CULTURAL

Los hispanos y la expansión de Estados Unidos

Inicialmente, Estados Unidos está formado por trece colonias de Inglaterra. Estas trece colonias ocupan principalmente el noreste y la región del Atlántico. Las trece colonias se independizan de Inglaterra en la larga y violenta Guerra de Independencia. George Washington es un líder muy importante de esta guerra. El 4 de julio de 1776, el Congreso Continental firma la Declaración de Independencia en Filadelfia y George Washington es el primer presidente de la nueva república.

La expansión de Estados Unidos

Moneda de 25 centavos en honor de Luisiana, 2002

La primera expansión de las trece colonias hacia el oeste ocurre en 1803 durante la presidencia de Thomas Jefferson. En este año, el gobierno de Estados Unidos compra a Francia el inmenso territorio de Luisiana por 23 millones de dólares. Esta región ocupa unos 2.100.000 km^2. La compra de Luisiana incorpora todo el valle del Río Misisipi al territorio de Estados Unidos.

En 1810, el presidente James Madison anexa al territorio de Estados Unidos la región de Florida Occidental. Esta región está en la costa norte del Golfo de México y hoy pertenece a los estados de Luisiana, Misisipi, Alabama y Florida. Pero anteriormente, pertenece a España, Francia y también a Inglaterra. Durante un tiempo se llama la República Independiente de Florida Occidental. España disputa esta anexión, pero en 1819 acepta ceder todo el territorio de Florida, incluyendo la península de Florida.

Bonnieblue, la bandera de la República Independiente de Florida Occidental

Dinero de República Independiente de Texas

Entre 1845 y 1853, Estados Unidos anexa extensos territorios mexicanos. La anexión de Texas en 1845 causa la guerra entre México y Estados Unidos. En 1848, México cede otra parte muy grande de su territorio, incluyendo partes de Texas, Colorado, Arizona, Nuevo México y Wyoming, además de toda la extensión de California, Nevada y Utah. En 1853 Estados Unidos compra un área adicional en la frontera de México y el presidente Franklin Pierce paga diez millones de dólares. Los habitantes mexicanos de estas regiones son los ancestros de muchos latinos de Estados Unidos.

En 1898 Puerto Rico se convierte en un protectorado de Estados Unidos a causa de la guerra de Estados Unidos contra España. Los habitantes de Puerto Rico son ciudadanos de Estados Unidos desde 1917.

El escudo de Puerto Rico tiene el símbolo de San Juan y la inscripción en latín: "Su nombre es Juan".

En otras palabras

Expresiones puertorriqueñas:

No le des **cabuya**.
Don't give him/her ammu-nition to bother you.

Yo no compro la lotería porque tengo una **macacoa** terrible.
I don't buy lottery tickets because I have terrible luck.

Dejó su cuarto hecho un **majarete**.
He/She left his/her room a complete mess.

En otras palabras

Expresiones chicanas (*Mexican-American*):

Ando brujo.
I am broke.

¡Ándale, güero!
Let's go, blondie!

2-43 Comprensión. PRIMERA FASE. **Reconocimiento de palabras clave.** Find in the text the Spanish word or phrase that best expresses the meaning of the following concepts:

1. war   _____
2. valley   _____
3. ancestors   _____
4. border   _____
5. coat of arms _____
6. citizen   _____

SEGUNDA FASE. **Oraciones importantes.** Underline the statements that contain ideas found in the text. Then indicate where in the text those words appear.

1. The colonies became independent after a long and violent war.
2. The Continental Congress signed the Declaration of Independence in Philadelphia.
3. George Washington was a good soldier, but a poor politician.
4. The purchase of the Mississippi Valley turned out to be a poor decision by President Jefferson.
5. Spain gave up its claim to Florida and West Florida without any resistance.
6. The United States and Mexico went to war over the annexation of Texas.
7. Puerto Ricans are citizens of the United States.

TERCERA FASE. **Ideas principales.** Write a brief paragraph in English summarizing the main ideas expressed in the text.

 2-44 Use la información. Prepare an oral presentation describing the current flag or a historic flag of one of the states that has a Hispanic heritage. Consult the *Mosaicos* web page where you will find a worksheet and relevant links to collect information about the flag.

VOCABULARIO

CD 1
Tracks 43-47

Las descripciones — **Descriptions**

agradable	*nice*
alegre	*happy, glad*
alto/a	*tall*
antipático/a	*unpleasant*
bajo/a	*short* (in stature)
bilingüe	*bilingual*
bonito/a	*pretty*
callado/a	*quiet*
cansado/a	*tired*
casado/a	*married*
contento/a	*happy, glad*
conversador/a	*talkative*
corto/a	*short* (in length)
débil	*weak*
delgado/a	*thin*
divertido/a	*funny, amusing*
enojado/a	*angry*
estatura mediana	*average, medium* (height)
feo/a	*ugly*
fuerte	*strong*
gordo/a	*fat*
guapo/a	*good-looking, handsome*
joven	*young*
largo/a	*long*
listo/a	*smart; ready*
mayor	*old*
moreno/a	*brunette*
nervioso/a	*nervous*
nuevo/a	*new*
oscuro/a	*dark*
pelirrojo/a	*redhead*
perezoso/a	*lazy*
pobre	*poor*
rico/a	*rich, wealthy*
rubio/a	*blond*
simpático/a	*nice, charming*
soltero/a	*single*
tonto/a	*silly, foolish*
trabajador/a	*hardworking*
triste	*sad*
viejo/a	*old*

Las nacionalidades — **Nationalities**

alemán/alemana	*German*
argentino/a	*Argentinian*
boliviano/a	*Bolivian*
canadiense	*Canadian*
chileno/a	*Chilean*
colombiano/a	*Colombian*
costarricense	*Costa Rican*
cubano/a	*Cuban*
dominicano/a	*Dominican*
ecuatoriano/a	*Ecuadorian*
español/a	*Spanish*
estadounidense	*U.S. citizen*
francés/francesa	*French*
guatemalteco/a	*Guatemalan*

hispano/a	*Hispanic*
hondureño/a	*Honduran*
japonés/japonesa	*Japanese*
marroquí	*Moroccan*
mexicano/a	*Mexican*
nicaragüense	*Nicaraguan*
nigeriano/a	*Nigerian*
panameño/a	*Panamanian*
paraguayo/a	*Paraguayan*
peruano/a	*Peruvian*
polaco/a	*Polish*
portugués/portuguesa	*Portuguese*
puertorriqueño/a	*Puerto Rican*
salvadoreño/a	*Salvadorian*
uruguayo/a	*Uruguayan*
venezolano/a	*Venezuelan*

Los colores — **Colors**

amarillo/a	*yellow*
anaranjado/a	*orange*
azul	*blue*
blanco/a	*white*
marrón	*brown*
gris	*gray*
morado/a	*purple*
negro/a	*black*
rojo/a	*red*
rosado/a, rosa	*pink*
verde	*green; not ripe*

Verbos — **Verbs**

desear	*to wish, to want*
ser	*to be*
usar	*to use*

Palabras y expresiones útiles — **Useful words and expressions**

el auto, el coche, el carro	*car*
de	*of, from*
¿de quién?	*whose?*
del	*of the* (contraction of *de* + *el*)
la flor	*flower*
le gusta(n)	*you* (formal) *like; he/she likes*
los lentes de contacto	*contact lenses*
me gusta(n)	*I like*
mucho (*adv.*)	*much, a lot*
mucho/a (*adj.*)	*many*
el ojo	*eye*
el pelo	*hair*
te gusta(n)	*you* (familiar) *like*
Tengo... años.	*I am . . . years old.*
tiene	*he/she has; you* (formal) *have*
todos/as	*everybody*

See the English-Spanish and Spanish-English glossaries for other adjectives of nationality.
See page 74 for possessive adjectives.

El tiempo libre

En este cuadro anónimo del siglo XVIII, vemos la boda de un hombre y una mujer.
Ella es la princesa inca Nusta Beatriz y él es un noble español, D. Martín de Loyola.

In this chapter you will learn how to:

- discuss daily activities and leisure
- talk about food
- express where you are going
- make plans

Cultural Focus: Perú

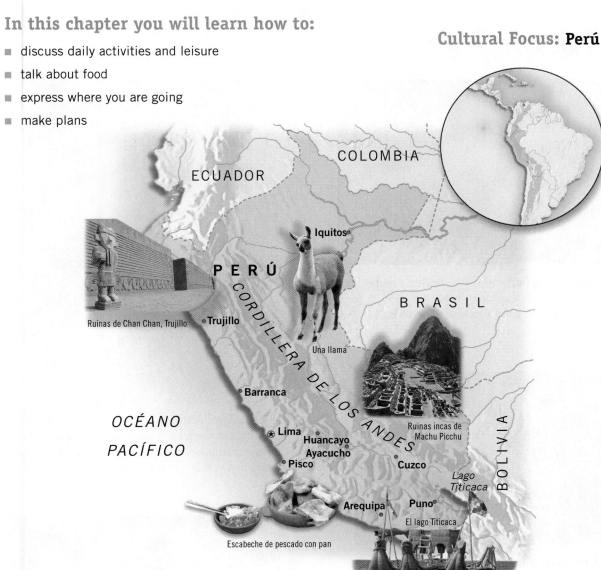

COLOMBIA

ECUADOR

Iquitos

P E R Ú

CORDILLERA DE LOS ANDES

Ruinas de Chan Chan, Trujillo

Trujillo

Una llama

B R A S I L

Barranca

OCÉANO PACÍFICO

Lima

Huancayo

Ayacucho

Pisco

Ruinas incas de Machu Picchu

Cuzco

Lago Titicaca

B O L I V I A

Arequipa

Puno

El lago Titicaca

Escabeche de pescado con pan

A vista de pájaro. Based on what you know about Peru, indicate if the statement is true (**Cierto**) or false (**Falso**).

1. _____ Perú está al sur de Colombia.
2. _____ La capital de Perú está en la costa del Atlántico.
3. _____ La comida de Perú es muy variada.
4. _____ Algunos peruanos son de origen inca y español.
5. _____ El Amazonas está entre Perú y Ecuador.
6. _____ La llama es un animal débil.

A PRIMERA VISTA

·)) Las diversiones

CD 2
Track 1

En muchos **países** hispanos hay **fiestas** y **reuniones**. Los **jóvenes** bailan, escuchan **música** o conversan. A veces **tocan la guitarra** y **cantan canciones** populares.

Estas **mujeres van** a la playa en su **tiempo libre** y también **durante** las **vacaciones**. Allí, caminan y conversan **mientras** otras personas **toman el sol**, **nadan** en **el mar**, corren o **descansan**.

Este **hombre** lee el **periódico al aire libre** en un parque de su **ciudad**. Y usted, ¿lee el periódico? ¿Qué periódicos o **revistas** lee?

Muchos jóvenes van al **cine**, especialmente los fines de semana. También es común **alquilar películas** para ver en casa.

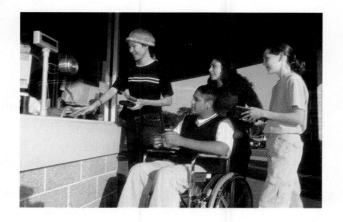

3-1 Asociaciones. Which leisure activities do you associate with the following places?

1. _____ la playa
2. _____ la fiesta
3. _____ el cine
4. _____ la biblioteca
5. _____ la casa

a. ver una película
b. leer el periódico
c. tomar el sol
d. mirar televisión
e. bailar y conversar

3-2 Nuestro tiempo libre. PRIMERA FASE. What do all of you do in the following places? Take turns asking one another, and take notes on the responses.

MODELO: las fiestas
E1: *¿Qué haces en las fiestas?*
E2: *En las fiestas bailo mucho. ¿Y tú?*
E1: *Bailo y hablo con mis amigos.*
E2: *Y tú (E3), ¿qué haces en… ?*

	COMPAÑERO/A 1	COMPAÑERO/A 2	COMPAÑERO/A 3	YO
1. en la universidad después de clase				
2. en la biblioteca pública de tu ciudad				
3. en casa el fin de semana				
4. en un parque de tu ciudad				
5. en la playa durante las vacaciones				
6. en la discoteca con tus amigos				

SEGUNDA FASE. With the other members of your group, prepare a report to share with the class about the activities most popular among group members.

MODELO: *En nuestro grupo, dos personas practican fútbol después de clases.*

3-3 ¿Qué hacen Pedro y Carmen? PRIMERA FASE. Look at the drawings and explain what Pedro and Carmen do on weekends.

SEGUNDA FASE. Write an e-mail to Rafael, your new friend in Peru, explaining what you and your friends do on weekends.

Hola Rafael,

¿Cómo estás? Nosotros estamos muy bien. Los fines de semana mis amigos y yo _____

_____

_____

_____ .

¡Hasta pronto!

_____

)) Los planes

CD 2
Track 2 **Una conversación por teléfono entre Manuel y Lola**

LOLA: ¿Aló?

MANUEL: Hola, mi amor, **¡felicidades** por tu cumpleaños!

LOLA: Ay, gracias, Manuel.

MANUEL: **¿Qué te parece** si **vamos** al cine esta tarde y **después** a un restaurante para **cenar?**

LOLA: Me parece **fabuloso.** ¿Qué película vamos a ver?

MANUEL: Hay una nueva de Alfonso Cuarón.

LOLA: Muy bien. Me gustan mucho sus películas. ¿Dónde **ponen** la película?

MANUEL: **Cerca de** El Jardín Limeño, tu restaurante peruano favorito.

LOLA: **Estupendo,** ¿entonces **luego** vamos a cenar allí?

MANUEL: **¡Claro!** ¿Nos vemos en tu casa a las cinco?

LOLA: Sí, sí, perfecto. ¡Hasta luego!

3-4 Una invitación. PRIMERA FASE. Using the preceding dialogue as a model, role-play a phone call to invite a classmate to join you in a weekend activity. He/She should accept or decline the invitation.

SEGUNDA FASE. Repeat the activity with two other classmates. Then explain to the class your weekend plans and how many people are joining you.

MODELO: *El sábado por la tarde Juan, Verónica y yo vamos al gimnasio para ver un partido de básquetbol.*

En otras palabras

Telephone greetings vary from country to country. **¿Diga?** and **¿Dígame?** are used to answer the phone in Spain; **¡Bueno!** in Mexico; **¿Aló?** in Argentina, Peru, and Chile; **¡Oigo!** and **¿Qué hay?** in Cuba. Terms of endearment such as **mi amor, corazón, mi vida, querido/a,** and **mi cielo** also reflect regional preferences.

En directo

To extend an invitation:

Te llamo para ver si quieres (*if you want*) + *infinitive...*

Tengo una idea. ¿Por qué no + *nosotros/as form...of the verb...?*

To accept an invitation:

¡Estupendo! ¿Dónde quedamos? *Where do we meet?*

Sí, gracias/¡Ah, qué bien!/ ¡Qué buena idea!

¡Qué bueno!

¡Fabuloso!

To decline an invitation:

Lo siento, pero no tengo tiempo/tengo mucho trabajo/tengo mucha tarea...

Ese día no puedo (*I can't*), **tengo un examen.**

Cultura

Traditionally, Mexico, Spain, and Argentina have had important film industries, but films are made in other Spanish-speaking countries as well. Outstanding Spanish-language film directors like Pedro Almodóvar and Icíar Bollaín in Spain, Alfonso Cuarón and Alejandro González in Mexico, Sergio Cabrera in Colombia, and Juan Carlos Tabío in Cuba, among others, are internationally known.

3-5 ¿Adónde vamos? PRIMERA FASE. You and your partner are in a study abroad program in Lima and are looking for something to do together over the weekend. Underline three activities in the cultural section of the newspaper that you find interesting. Then fill in the chart, including the day and time for each activity.

AGENDA CULTURAL
La guía de Lima

Cine

El amor en los tiempos del cólera. Dir. Mike Newell. C.C. Británico. Calle Bellavista 531. Miraflores. 7:30 pm. Libre.

Teatro

La casa de Bernarda Alba. Grupo de Teatro Lorca. C.C. Británico. Av. La Marina 2554. San Miguel. 7:30 pm. Libre.
Entre visillos. Basada en "La cantante calva", de Eugenio Ionesco. Auditorio Municipalidad de San Isidro. La República 455. El Olivar. 8 pm. Boletería.

Música

Los andinos en concierto. Huainos, yaravíes, mulizas. ICPNA. Jr. Cuzco 446. Lima. 7 pm. S/. 10.00.
Noche flamenca. Ballet La flor de Sevilla. ICPNA. Av. Angamos Oeste 120. Miraflores. 7:30 p.m. S/. 25.00.
Amalia Sánchez en concierto. A beneficio del C.C. de Rehabilitación de Ciegos. C.C. Ricardo Palma. Larco 770. Miraflores. 8 pm. S/. 10.00.

Exposición

Maestros en acción. Asociación de Docentes de la ENSABAP. Bellas Artes de La Molina. Av. Rinconada del Lago 1515. 7 pm.

Libro

Lectura de poemas de Óscar Liria. Av. La Paz 646. 7:30 pm. Libre.

Conferencia

La mujer en el arte. Con Lola Reyes. C. C. San Marcos. Parque Universitario. Lima. 6:30 pm. Libre.

Literatura

Perú en la literatura francesa. Con Pierre Brillat. Alianza Francesa. Av. Arequipa 4595. Miraflores. 8 pm. S/.15.00, S/.10.00.

Cultura

Huainos, *yaravíes*, and *mulizas* are Peruvian songs of pre-Columbian origin that are popular in the Andean region of the country. They are often performed and danced in the *peñas*, music clubs that promote traditional (Afro-Andean and Creole) music. In the *peñas* people dance all night long and enjoy excellent regional food.

¿ADÓNDE VAMOS?	¿QUÉ VAMOS A VER/HACER/ESCUCHAR?	¿CUÁNDO?

SEGUNDA FASE. Explain your plans to another pair. Decide if you can do some of the activities together.

■)) La comida

CD 2
Track 3 **En el restaurante.** Ahora Lola y Manuel están en el restaurante El Jardín Limeño para **celebrar el cumpleaños** de Lola. Hablan con el **camarero.**

CAMARERO:	Buenas noches. ¿Qué desean los señores?
MANUEL:	Lola, ¿qué vas a comer?
LOLA:	Para mí, una **ensalada** primero y después **pollo** con **verduras.**
MANUEL:	Yo, para empezar, **ceviche** de pescado. Y luego un **bistec** con **papas.**
CAMARERO:	¿Y para beber?
LOLA:	Vamos a beber **vino** blanco. Y también **agua** con gas, por favor.
CAMARERO:	¿Algo más?
MANUEL:	Nada más, gracias.

ESPECIALIDADES DE LA CASA

ENTRADAS

Ensalada de la casa	S/.10
Ceviche de pescado	S/.15
Papa a la huancaína	S/.10
Causa a la limeña	S/.12

PLATOS PRINCIPALES

Chupe de camarones	S/.22
Ají de gallina	S/.18
Lomo saltado	S/.17
Bistec con papas	S/.17
Pollo con verduras	S/.16

POSTRES

Suspiro de limeña	S/.8
Alfajor	S/.8
Mazamorra morada	S/.6

BEBIDAS

Chicha morada	S/.4
Jugo de maracuyá	S/.4
Inca Kola	S/.3

Cultura

Peruvian cooking mostly uses regional ingredients and follows preparation methods inherited from indigenous cultures. Ceviche is a typical dish of Peru and other countries in Latin America. It is generally made with seafood that is not cooked but rather marinated in lime juice and spices.

yuca frita

adobo de chancho

papas cocidas

aceitunas

frijoles

ceviche de pescado

tamales

rocotos rellenos

La comida peruana es muy variada. Sobre esta mesa hay ceviche de pescado, tamales, papas cocidas, rocotos (pimientos) rellenos, adobo de chancho (cerdo), yuca frita, frijoles y aceitunas.

En directo

Expressions to take an order:

¿Qué desean los señores?

¿Qué van a tomar/beber?

Expressions to order food:

Para mí, una ensalada, arroz con…

Me gustaría/Quisiera comer/tomar…
I would like to eat/ drink…

Yo quiero/deseo…

Cultura

The *Cultura* box above mentions one of the most typical dishes in Perú, *el ceviche*. Some other typical Peruvian dishes include *papa a la huancaína* (sliced boiled potatoes covered with a spicy creamy cheese sauce); *causa a la limeña* (seasoned mashed potato stuffed with tuna, egg, shrimp, or avocado); *chupe de camarones* (shrimp chowder); *ají de gallina* (shredded chicken casserole with walnuts, parmesan cheese, and Peruvian hot peppers); *suspiro de limeña* (a dessert made with milk and eggs); *alfajor* (two-layer cookies with *dulce de leche* between the layers; *mazamorra morada* (purple corn pudding).

Más comidas y bebidas

CD 2
Track 4

el desayuno

el cereal
la leche
el té
el café caliente
el jugo de naranja
el pan tostado/las tostadas
los huevos fritos

el almuerzo

la ensalada de lechuga y tomate
el sándwich de jamón y queso
una cerveza fría
las papas fritas
el refresco
la fruta
la hamburguesa

la comida/la cena

el pescado
el arroz
el helado
el pollo
el agua
los vegetales/ las verduras
la sopa
los espaguetis

3-6 Calorías. PRIMERA FASE. Which item in each group contains the most calories?

1. la sopa de tomate, una hamburguesa, la sopa de pollo
2. el pollo frito, el pescado, la ensalada
3. los vegetales, las frutas, las papas fritas
4. la cerveza, la leche desnatada (*skim*), el café
5. el helado de chocolate, el cereal, el arroz

SEGUNDA FASE. Mention items in the *Primera fase* that you eat or drink frequently. Do you both have the same preferences?

MODELO: E1: *Frecuentemente como ensaladas y bebo cerveza. ¿Y tú?*
         E2: *Yo frecuentemente como hamburguesas con papas fritas y bebo refrescos.*

3-7 Las comidas. Tell a classmate what you usually have for breakfast, lunch, and dinner. Then find out what he/she usually eats for those meals.

MODELO: *En el desayuno, como tostadas y bebo café. ¿Y tú?*

3-8 Dietas especiales. Which is the best option from this menu for the following people?

1. Su amiga Luisa está un poco delgada y desea subir de peso (*gain weight*). ¿Qué va a comer de este menú?
2. Su mamá es alérgica a los mariscos (*seafood*). ¿Cuál de las ensaladas va a comer?
3. Su amigo José está un poco gordo y quiere bajar de peso (*lose weight*). ¿Cuál de los platos principales no debe comer?
4. El profesor/La profesora de español está enfermo/a (*sick*) del estómago hoy. ¿Qué debe comer?

Cultura

Fast food is popular among young Hispanics, and American-style hamburger places may be found in Hispanic countries. They often adapt to local tastes, and it is not unusual to have hamburgers served with rice and black beans instead of fries. Beer and wine may also be sold in addition to soft drinks.

MENÚ

SOPAS

Sopa de pollo	S/. 9
Sopa de tomate	S/. 7
Sopa de vegetales	S/. 7
Sopa de pescado	S/. 12

ENSALADAS

Ensalada de lechuga y tomate	S/. 8
Ensalada de pollo	S/. 14
Ensalada de atún	S/. 12

PLATOS PRINCIPALES

Bistec con papas y vegetales	S/. 20
Hamburguesa con papas fritas	S/. 16
Pescado con papas fritas	S/. 18
Arroz con vegetales	S/. 15

3-9 ¿Qué te gusta más? Using the words below, ask what your partner prefers to drink **por las mañanas, para el almuerzo, por las noches**. Alternate asking questions and taking notes. Then explain your partner's preferences to the class.

MODELO: E1: *¿Qué te gusta beber por las mañanas, té o café?*
          E2: *Me gusta más el café.*

el agua mineral con gas	una copa de vino	un refresco
el agua mineral sin gas	una cerveza	el té (helado)
un batido (*shake*) de yogur y fruta	un chocolate caliente	un vaso (*glass*) de leche
	el jugo de naranja	

3-10 En el café. It is 9:00 on Saturday morning, and you and a friend are in a café in Lima. Ask what your friend wants to order. Then say what you are going to order.

MODELO: E1: *El desayuno es muy bueno aquí. ¿Qué deseas comer?*
          E2: _____ *¿Y tú?*
          E1: _____ *¿Y qué vas a tomar?*
          E2: _____

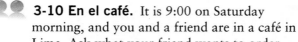

DESAYUNOS	
café	S/.3
té	S/.3
café con leche	S/.5
jugo de naranja	S/.5
chocolate	S/.6
tostadas	S/.5
pan con mantequilla	S/.5
pan dulce	S/.6
cereal	S/.8
huevos fritos	S/.10

3-11 Un viaje (*trip*). You are in Peru and are planning a day trip to Machu Picchu. Arrange to take some food and beverages with you.

1. Make a list of the food and beverages that you need to take.
2. Talk about the things that you are going to do.

3-12 Nuestro menú. You and your roommate want to have guests over for dinner tonight. Decide whom each of you is going to invite and what you are going to serve. Finally, compare your menu with that of another pair of classmates.

■ Vamos a invitar a _____ .

■ Vamos a servir _____ .

3-13 ¿Qué hacen estos estudiantes? PRIMERA FASE. You will listen to two students, Rafael and Miguel, talk about their activities and weekend plans. Before you listen, write down three activities you normally do during the week, and three that you plan for this weekend.

CD 2
Track 5

actividades de la semana: _____

planes para el fin de semana: _____

SEGUNDA FASE. Now, listen to Rafael and Miguel and pay attention to the general idea of what they say. Then check (✓) the activities they mention they will do during the weekend.

1. —— estudiar para los exámenes
2. ___ comer en un restaurante
3. ___ descansar y tomar el sol
4. ___ trabajar en la librería
5. ___ celebrar el cumpleaños de Rafael

EN ACCIÓN

Diarios de bicicleta: La invitación

Antes de ver

3-14 In this video segment, Javier is at a restaurant. Based on your knowledge of Mexican restaurants in the United States, mark (✓) the sentences that you think describe restaurants in Mexico.

1. ___ Hay muchos colores.
2. ___ Hay música de mariachis.
3. ___ La comida cuesta mucho dinero.
4. ___ Muchos platos tienen chile.

Mientras ve

3-15 Mark (✓) the correct answer according to the information provided.

1. Javier va al restaurante para...
   - a. ___ desayunar
   - b. ___ almorzar
   - c. ___ cenar

2. Para comer, Javier pide...
   - a. ___ pollo con papas fritas y chile habanero.
   - b. ___ pollo con papas fritas y chile verde.
   - c. ___ sopa azteca.

3. Para beber, Javier pide...
   - a. ___ agua mineral bien fría.
   - b. ___ un té frío con limón.
   - c. ___ una limonada bien fría.

Después de ver

3-16 PRIMERA FASE. Mark (✓) the statement that describes the problem that Javier has in this segment.

1. ___ Javier no tiene dinero para pagar la cuenta (*bill*).
2. ___ Gabi no puede almorzar con Javier.
3. ___ A Javier no le gusta la comida del restaurante.

SEGUNDA FASE. Write a sentence indicating how Javier's problem is solved.

FUNCIONES Y FORMAS

1. Talking about daily activities: Present tense of *hacer*, *poner*, *salir*, *traer*, and *oír*

Unos amigos nuevos conversan sobre sus actividades

CAROLINA: Bueno, para conocernos mejor, ¿por qué no jugamos a *Decir la verdad*? José Manuel, la primera pregunta es para ti. ¿Qué **haces** cuando estás aburrido?

JOSÉ MANUEL: **Pongo** la tele para ver películas. Ahora, Tomás, ¿adónde **sales** cuando tienes tiempo? ¿Y con quién?

TOMÁS: Bueno, **salgo a comer** con mi novia Pilar. Pero cuando tengo exámenes, debo **salir para** la biblioteca. Carolina, cuando **oyes** música salsa, ¿qué **haces**?

CAROLINA: Eso es muy fácil. Siempre bailo cuando **oigo** música salsa. Mi pregunta es para los dos. ¿Qué **hacen** ustedes en casa que no les gusta **hacer**?

TOMÁS: Yo **hago** mi cama porque me gusta el orden.

JOSÉ MANUEL: Mis hermanitos me **traen** su ropa y lavo ropa sucia (*dirty*) todo el fin de semana. La ropa sucia de ellos es repugnante. ¡Qué asco! ¿Y tú, Carolina?

CAROLINA: ¿Yo? Pues, **pongo la mesa** todos los días. ¡Qué lata!

José Manuel   Carolina   Tomás

Piénselo. Match each idea on the left with a logical ending on the right. More than one answer may be possible.

1. ____ **Pongo** la tele…
2. ____ **Pongo la mesa**…
3. ____ **Oigo** música…
4. ____ Debo **salir para** la biblioteca…
5. ____ **Hago** mi cama…
6. ____ Lavo la ropa que **traen** mis hermanos…

a. porque me gusta el orden.
b. cuando **salgo** con mis amigos.
c. para pasarlo bien (*have a good time*).
d. para ayudar (*help*) con el trabajo de casa.
e. porque me gusta ver películas.
f. porque deseo aprender mucho.

■ In the present tense, the verbs **hacer**, **poner**, **salir**, **traer**, and **oír** have irregular **yo** forms, but are regular in all other forms.

HACER (*to make, to do*)			
yo	**hago**	nosotros/as	**hacemos**
tú	**haces**	vosotros/as	**hacéis**
Ud., él, ella	**hace**	Uds., ellos/as	**hacen**

■ **Hacer** means *to do* or *to make*. It is used frequently in questions to ask in a general sense what someone does, is doing, or likes to do.

¿Qué **haces** para sacar buenas notas?	*What do you do to get good grades?*
Hago la tarea para mis clases todos los días.	*I do the homework for my classes every day.*

PONER (*to put*)			
yo	**pongo**	nosotros/as	**ponemos**
tú	**pones**	vosotros/as	**ponéis**
Ud., él, ella	**pone**	Uds., ellos/as	**ponen**

■ **Poner** means *to put*. When used with some electrical appliances, **poner** means *to turn on*; **poner la mesa** means *to set the table*.

Por la mañana **pongo** mis libros en mi mochila.	*In the morning I put my books in my backpack.*
Mi abuelo **pone** la televisión después de la cena.	*My grandfather turns on the TV after dinner.*
Yo **pongo** la mesa a la hora de la cena.	*I set the table at dinner time.*

SALIR (*to leave*)			
yo	**salgo**	nosotros/as	**salimos**
tú	**sales**	vosotros/as	**salís**
Ud., él, ella	**sale**	Uds., ellos/as	**salen**

■ **Salir** can be used with several different prepositions. To express that you are leaving a place, use **salir de**; to express your destination, use **salir para**; to express with whom you go out or the person you date, use **salir con**; to express what you are going to do, use **salir a**.

Yo **salgo de** mi cuarto a las 7:15 de la mañana.	*I leave my room at 7:15 in the morning.*
Salgo para la cafetería.	*I am leaving for the cafeteria.*
Mi mejor amiga **sale con** Mauricio.	*My best friend is dating Mauricio.*
Ellos **salen** a bailar los sábados.	*They go out dancing on Saturdays.*

TRAER (*to bring*)			
yo	**traigo**	nosotros/as	**traemos**
tú	**traes**	vosotros/as	**traéis**
Ud., él, ella	**trae**	Uds., ellos/as	**traen**

Yo siempre **traigo** un postre a estas fiestas.	*I always bring a dessert to these parties.*

OÍR (to hear)			
yo	**oigo**	nosotros/as	**oímos**
tú	**oyes**	vosotros/as	**oís**
Ud., él, ella	**oye**	Uds., ellos/as	**oyen**

■ **Oír** means *to hear* in the sense of *to perceive sounds*. Note the spelling and the accent marks in the infinitive, **nosotros/as**, and **vosotros/as** forms.

Yo **oigo** música.	*I hear music.*
— ¿**Oyes** la alarma?	— *Do you hear the alarm?*
— No, no **oigo** nada.	— *No, I don't hear anything.*

3-17 La perfección andante (*Perfection in motion*). PRIMERA FASE. Are you organized, considerate, studious, and/or punctual? Check (✔) the statements that refer to things you do or don't do regularly.

1. _____ Yo **hago** mi cama temprano por la mañana.
2. _____ Cuando **oigo** que un amigo está triste, lo invito a salir.
3. _____ Siempre **pongo** música rock cuando estudio.
4. _____ Generalmente, **traigo** el periódico a la mesa para leer las noticias mientras desayuno.
5. _____ En general, no **traigo** el periódico a la mesa mientras desayuno porque prefiero conversar con mi familia.
6. _____ Por las mañanas, **hago** ejercicio y luego **salgo** para la universidad.

 SEGUNDA FASE. Take turns talking about the activities you both do that show off your best qualities.

MODELO: E1: *Yo soy organizado. Siempre hago mi cama temprano. ¿Y tú?*
E2: *Pues, yo también... /No, yo no...*

3-18 ¿Usa usted bien su tiempo libre? PRIMERA FASE. Check (✔) the version of each activity that best describes your habits.

1. _____ Pongo la mesa para cenar.   _____ Como en cualquier lugar de la casa.
2. _____ Hago el desayuno.   _____ Salgo a desayunar fuera de casa.
3. _____ Hago la cama cada día.   _____ Hago la cama una vez por semana.
4. _____ Oigo las noticias en la radio.   _____ Veo las noticias en la televisión.
5. _____ Traigo el periódico a la casa.   _____ Leo el periódico en el cibercafé.
6. _____ Pongo la televisión para ver películas.   _____ Salgo al cine para ver películas.

SEGUNDA FASE. Working with a partner, compare your answers and determine which of you has more fun doing these things. Explain why.

3-19 Mi rutina. PRIMERA FASE. Talk about the activities that you routinely do. Then ask your classmate about his/her activities.

MODELO: tener clases por la mañana/por la tarde
   E1:   *Yo tengo clases por la mañana. ¿Y tú?*
   E2:   *Yo tengo clases por la mañana y por la tarde./Yo también tengo clases por la mañana.*

1. normalmente salir de su casa temprano/tarde por la mañana
2. generalmente poner la radio/tele para escuchar su música favorita por la mañana
3. hacer la tarea en casa/en la biblioteca
4. frecuentemente salir a comer/ver películas con su familia por la noche
5. con frecuencia traer muchos libros a casa después de las clases

SEGUNDA FASE. Write a brief paragraph comparing your routine with that of your classmate. In your opinion, who has a more interesting routine, and why? Provide a few reasons.

3-20 Para pasarlo bien. PRIMERA FASE. Write a check (✓) next to the activities that, in your opinion, your classmates probably do to have fun.

1. _____ Ponen películas los fines de semana.
2. _____ Oyen música y bailan mientras estudian para los exámenes.
3. _____ Frecuentemente hacen fiestas con sus amigos.
4. _____ Asisten a conciertos y exposiciones de arte.
5. _____ Hacen ejercicio en el gimnasio o en el parque.
6. _____ Escuchan programas en la radio pública.
7. _____ Salen a comer en grupo.
8. _____ …

SEGUNDA FASE. Using the activities you marked in the *Primera fase* as a starting point, ask if your instructor does the same activities to have fun. Refer to *En directo* to help you express your reactions to your instructor's responses.

MODELO: PAREJA: *Para pasarlo bien, nosotros asistimos a conciertos de música rock. ¿Asiste a conciertos de música rock para pasarlo bien?*
   PROFESOR/A: *No asisto a conciertos de música rock. Para pasarlo bien escucho conciertos de música clásica en la radio pública.*
   PAREJA: *¡Qué aburrido!*

En directo

To react to what someone has said:

¡Qué interesante!

¡Qué divertido!
How funny!

¡Qué aburrido!

SITUACIONES

1. **Role A.** You are interviewing a potential roommate for your two-bedroom apartment. Find out a) if he/she likes things to be neat (**si le gusta el orden**); b) what household chores he/she likes to do and does not like to do; and c) what he/she likes to do at home in his/her free time. Your interviewee will have questions for you also. At the end of the conversation, decide whether to accept this person as a roommate.

   Role B. You are new in town and are being interviewed by someone who has a room to rent in his/her apartment. Answer the questions in as much detail as possible and ask some questions of your own. At the end of the conversation, decide whether you are interested in the room.

2. **Role A.** You have just been hired to take care of a five-year-old boy for the summer. Ask what time the parent leaves the house in the morning and find out a) what the child eats and drinks for breakfast and lunch; b) whether he has to make his bed or set the table; and c) what his favorite activities are.

   Role B. You have just hired a college student to take care of your five-year-old son for the summer. Answer his/her questions. To get to know him/her better, ask a) what he/she studies at school and b) what he/she likes to do in his/her free time.

2. Expressing movement and plans: Present tense of *ir* and *ir a + infinitive*

Elena, la chica en el centro, habla de sus amigos

Mis amigos y yo somos diferentes, pero somos muy unidos. Para mi cumpleaños, nosotros **vamos a** un restaurante todos los años. Los sábados, yo **voy a** la casa de mi amiga Estela, y luego ella **va** conmigo **al** gimnasio para hacer ejercicio. A veces Rafael, Humberto y Rodrigo también **van al** gimnasio con nosotras. Mi amiga Teresa, no sale mucho porque prefiere estudiar. Yo siempre bromeo (*joke*) con ella: "Tere, ¿**vas a** la biblioteca a pasarlo bien?" Fernando, es muy tranquilo y artístico y le fascina el silencio. Con frecuencia él y Estela **van a** la librería a comprar libros.

Piénselo. Read the following statements about Elena and her friends. Then indicate (✔) if the statement is **probable** or **improbable**, based on the information Elena provides.

	PROBABLE	IMPROBABLE
1. Elena y sus amigos **van a** lugares juntos para celebrar su cumpleaños.	——	——
2. Fernando **va a** los conciertos de música rock.	——	——
3. Estela afirma: "Frecuentemente, yo **voy a** la librería a comprar libros".	——	——
4. Teresa comenta: "Fernando y yo **vamos al** museo de arte esta tarde".	——	——
5. Elena no **va a** las fiestas de cumpleaños de sus amigos.	——	——

■ After the verb **ir**, use **a** to introduce a noun that refers to a place. When **a** is followed by the article **el**, the two words contract to form **al**.

Voy **a la** fiesta de María.	*I am going to María's party.*
Vamos **al** gimnasio.	*We are going to the gym.*

■ Use **¿adónde?** when asking *where (to)?* with the verb **ir**.

¿**Adónde** vas ahora?	*Where are you going now?*

IR (*to go*)			
yo	**voy**	nosotros/as	**vamos**
tú	**vas**	vosotros/as	**vais**
Ud., él, ella	**va**	Uds., ellos/as	**van**

■ To express a future action or condition, use the present tense of **ir a +** the infinitive form of the verb.

Mis amigos **van a nadar** después.	*My friends are going to swim later.*
¿**Vas a ir** a la fiesta?	*Are you going to go to the party?*

■ The expression **vamos a +** *infinitive* can mean *let's*.

Vamos a cenar en mi casa.	*Let's have dinner at my house.*
Vamos a bailar después.	*Let's go dancing afterward.*

Lengua

The following expressions denote future time:

después, más tarde, esta noche, mañana, pasado mañana, la próxima semana, el próximo mes/año.

3-21 ¿Adónde van? PRIMERA FASE. Josh and Steve are North American students visiting Peru for their summer vacation. Match the descriptions on the left with the places they plan to see on the right.

1. ____ Steve estudia historia. Por eso, desea ver la universidad prestigiosa y más antigua de América de Sur. Está en Lima. Él va a…

2. ____ Los dos amigos van a visitar uno de los lugares más misteriosos del planeta. Allí hay enormes figuras geométricas trazadas (*drawn*) en la tierra que son visibles solamente desde el aire. Ellos van a…

3. ____ Josh conoce (*meets*) a Susana en Perú. Ella lo invita a un evento folclórico donde las personas oyen poesía, música tradicional y comen y bailan también. Josh y Susana van a…

4. ____ Steve y Josh van a un lugar histórico imposible de ignorar. Es considerado el símbolo del imperio inca. Está cerca de Cuzco. Steve y Josh van a…

a. Machu Picchu

b. las líneas de Nazca

SEGUNDA FASE. Now indicate where you will go to do the following in Peru.

1. Para hacer amigos, conversar y bailar ritmos peruanos, yo voy a

_____ .

2. Voy a _____ para tomar fotos de los alumnos y el edificio de una universidad muy antigua.

3. Para escalar unas montañas altas de mucha importancia histórica, voy a

_____ .

c. la Universidad de San Marcos

3-22 Intercambio. PRIMERA FASE. Your classmate's friends are busy today. Find out when each friend is leaving the place listed and where he/she is going afterward.

MODELO: E1: *¿A qué hora sale del trabajo tu amigo Armando?*
E2: *(Sale) a las seis de la tarde.*
E1: *¿Adónde va después?*
E2: *Va al cine.*

d. una peña

NOMBRE	HORA	LUGAR
Juan	8:00 a.m.	gimnasio
Alicia	9:30 a.m.	laboratorio de computadoras
Sofía	8:30 p.m.	oficina
Tú	…	…

SEGUNDA FASE. Exchange information with your partner about what each of you does at the times listed in the *Primera fase.*

MODELO: E1: *¿Qué haces a las 8:00 de la mañana?*
E2: *Salgo de mi casa para la universidad.*
E1: *¿Adónde vas cuando llegas a la universidad?*
E2: *Voy a mi clase de español. ¿Qué haces tú a las 8:00 de la mañana?*

3-23 ¡Qué lío! (*What a mess!*) PRIMERA FASE. Cristina had a party at her house while her parents were out of town, and now her friends are helping her clean up. Match each situation on the left with its probable solution.

1. ____ Hay muchos platos sucios.
2. ____ Cristina ve mucha comida en la mesa.
3. ____ La casa está desordenada.
4. ____ Cristina y sus amigos necesitan energía para limpiar la casa.
5. ____ Los amigos de Cristina están cansados después de la fiesta.

a. Dos chicos van a ordenar todo.
b. Algunos amigos van a recoger (*pick up*) los platos.
c. Una amiga va a refrigerar la comida.
d. Una amiga va a preparar café.
e. Van a descansar.

 SEGUNDA FASE. Brainstorm how Cristina's parents are going to react when they find out about her party. Some suggestions may include: *cancelar las tarjetas de crédito, prohibir fiestas/amigos, conversar seriamente, ...*

SITUACIONES

1. Role A. Your friend has invited you to a concert. Call him/her to find out a) where and when the concert is going to be; b) who is going to sing; c) who is going to introduce (**presentar**) the group; and d) how much the ticket (**el boleto/el billete/la entrada**) costs.

Role B. Your friend calls to find out about a concert you invited him/her to. Answer all the questions with as much information as possible.

2. Role A. You call to invite a friend to a café tonight where a mutual friend is going to sing. After your friend responds, ask about his/her plans for later in the evening: a) where he/she is going; b) with whom; and c) what time, etc.

Role B. A friend calls to invite you to a café tonight where a mutual friend is going to sing. Inquire about the event to find out a) what time and where it will be and b) if other friends are going to go. Accept the invitation and mention your plans for later in the evening.

3-24 Mi agenda para la semana. Invite six classmates individually to do the following activities with you. Each will accept or reject your invitation according to his/her schedule for the week. Indicate the day, the activity and the name of the classmate who accepted your invitation.

MODELO: estudiar en la biblioteca el lunes
E1: *¿Vamos a estudiar en la biblioteca el lunes?*
E2: *Lo siento, Miguel, el lunes voy a ir al cine con David. Pero, ¿por qué no salimos a comer el martes?*
E3: *Buena idea. Vamos a salir el martes.*

1. ir a un concierto
2. mirar televisión en casa
3. tomar algo en un café
4. estudiar para un examen difícil
5. bailar en la discoteca
6. hacer ejercicio

DÍA	¿QUÉ VA A HACER?	¿CON QUIÉN?
martes	comer en un restaurante peruano	Miguel

3-25 Los planes de Maribel. PRIMERA FASE. Take turns saying what Maribel is going to do at the times indicated.

SEGUNDA FASE. Tell your classmate what you are going to do at those times on Friday.

3. Talking about quantity: Numbers 100 to 2.000.000

Piénselo. Your instructor will say a number from each of the following series. Identify each number you hear. The numbers in the last row are dates.

1. 114	360	850	524
2. 213	330	490	919
3. 818	625	723	513
4. 667	777	984	534
5. 1.310	1.420	3.640	6.860
6. 10.467	50.312	100.000	2.000.000
7. 1492	1776	1890	2001

■ You have already learned the numbers up to 99. In this section you will learn numbers to use to talk about larger quantities.

100	cien/ciento	1.000	mil
200	doscientos/as	1.100	mil cien
300	trescientos/as	2.000	dos mil
400	cuatrocientos/as	10.000	diez mil
500	quinientos/as	100.000	cien mil
600	seiscientos/as	150.000	ciento cincuenta mil
700	setecientos/as	500.000	quinientos mil
800	ochocientos/as	1.000.000	un millón (de)
900	novecientos/as	2.000.000	dos millones (de)

■ Use **cien** to say 100 when used alone or when followed by a noun. Use **ciento** for numbers from 101 to 199.

100	**cien**
100 chicos	**cien** chicos
120 profesoras	**ciento** veinte profesoras
177 libros	**ciento** setenta y siete libros

■ Multiples of 100 agree in gender with the noun they modify.

200 periódicos	**doscientos** periódicos
1.400 revistas	**mil cuatrocientas** revistas

■ Use **mil** for *one thousand*. Multiples of 1,000 are also **mil**.

1.000	**mil** alumnos, **mil** alumnas
12.000	**doce mil** residentes

■ Use **un millón** to say *one million*. Use **un millón de** when a noun follows.

1.000.000	**un millón**
1.000.000 de personas	**un millón de personas**
12.000.000 de dólares	**doce millones de dólares**

■ In many Spanish-speaking countries, a period is used to separate thousands, and a comma is used to separate decimals.

$1.000	$19,50

 3-26 ¿Cuándo va a ocurrir? Exchange opinions with a classmate about when each of the following events will occur.

MODELO: Todos los libros van a ser electrónicos.
   E1: *En el año 2020.*
   E2: *Estoy de acuerdo.* Or
      No estoy de acuerdo. Todos los libros van a ser electrónicos en 2050.

1. Los adultos van a trabajar sólo 20 horas por semana.
2. Los estudiantes no van a ir a clases. Van a estudiar en universidades virtuales.
3. Todos los autos van a ser eléctricos y van a ser muy rápidos.
4. Los turistas van a ir de un país a otro sin pasaporte.
5. La contaminación va a ser muy grande, y las personas van a usar máscaras (*masks*) en los parques y en las calles.
6. Los robots, y no las personas, van a servir la comida en los restaurantes.
7. Las personas van a comunicarse por telepatía.
8. Muchas personas van a comer solamente la comida artificial.
9. Muchos turistas van a viajar (*travel*) al espacio interplanetario.
10. Los viajes en avión van a ser más rápidos y van a costar poco.

3-27 Unas vacaciones. PRIMERA FASE. Your classmate has chosen one of the destinations in the ad for an upcoming vacation. To find out where he/she is going, ask the following questions. Then switch roles.

1. ¿Adónde vas?
2. ¿Qué lugares vas a ver?
3. ¿Cuántos días vas a estar allí?
4. ¿Cuánto cuesta la excursión?

SEGUNDA FASE. Based on your classmate's answers, fill in the information and share it with the class.

1. planes que su compañero/a necesita hacer (sacar un pasaporte, obtener una visa, hacer reservaciones, etc.):
   _____

2. lugar(es) que va a visitar: _____

3. tiempo que va a estar allí: _____

4. costo de la excursión: _____

5. dinero extra que usted cree que su compañero/a va a necesitar: _____

AGENCIA MUNDIAL

A SU SERVICIO SIEMPRE 20 años de experiencia, responsabilidad y profesionalidad.

TODOS LOS PRECIOS INCLUYEN PASAJES AÉREOS Y SERVICIOS TERRESTRES POR PERSONA

PERÚ Y BOLIVIA

LIMA, AREQUIPA, CUZCO, MACHU PICCHU, PUNO, LA PAZ, 15 días. La Ruta del Inca. Hoteles de 3 y 4 estrellas. Desayuno incluido.
$2.760

PERÚ

LIMA, CUZCO, MACHU PICCHU, NAZCA, 12 días. Visite fortalezas incas. Vea las misteriosas líneas de Nazca desde el aire. Hoteles de primera. Desayuno y cena incluidos.
$3.150

LIMA, NAZCA, AREQUIPA, LAGO TITICACA, 10 días. Admire la arquitectura colonial de Lima y Arequipa. Vea las líneas de Nazca desde el aire. Navegue en el lago más alto del mundo. Hoteles de primera.
$2.620

ARGENTINA

BUENOS AIRES, BARILOCHE, MENDOZA, 12 días. Disfrute de una gran metrópoli. Esquíe en uno de los lugares más bellos del mundo. Hoteles de 4 y 5 estrellas. Desayuno y cena.
$3.590

CHILE Y ARGENTINA

SANTIAGO, PUERTO MONTT, BARILOCHE, BUENOS AIRES, 12 días. Excursión a Viña del Mar y Valparaíso. Cruce de los Andes en minibús y barco. Hoteles de 3 y 4 estrellas.
$4.075

CARIBE

JAMAICA, 7 días. Happy Inn, todo incluido. Exclusivo para parejas.
$2.480

PUERTO RICO

SAN JUAN, 5 días. Hotel de 5 estrellas. Excursión a Ponce. Visita con guía al Viejo San Juan. Desayuno incluido.
$1.995

MÉXICO

MÉXICO, TAXCO, ACAPULCO, 7 días. Hoteles de 3 y 4 estrellas. Excursión a Teotihuacán. Desayuno bufet incluido.
$1.800

CANCÚN, 5 días. Hotel de 4 estrellas. Excursión a Cozumel. Visita a ruinas mayas. Las mejores playas.
$1.510

Solicite los programas detallados con variantes de hoteles e itinerarios a su agente de viajes.

Tel. 312-785-4455   Fax: 312-785-4456

SITUACIONES

1. **Role A.** You have been saving up for a special trip (**viaje**) during the next school vacation, and you are now making plans. Call a friend to explain a) where you plan to go; b) who will travel with you; and c) what you plan to do.

   Role B. Your friend calls to tell you about his/her travel plans for the next school break. Ask a) with whom he/she is planning to go; and b) what places he/she is going to visit. You are curious about the cost of the trip (**viaje**), so you inquire about the cost of the flight (**el vuelo**), the hotel, and the activities your friend plans to do.

2. **Role A.** You have been working hard, and you would like to splurge on a weekend trip to do some special (but expensive) activities, like rent a car, go to a professional sports event or rock concert, eat in good restaurants, and shop (**ir de compras**). Call and invite your friend to go. Explain your plan and be prepared to answer questions about the cost of this weekend adventure.

   Role B. Your friend calls to invite you on an exciting (but expensive) weekend trip. After your friend explains the plan, ask questions to get an idea of the cost. Decide whether you can afford it, and either accept or decline the invitation.

4. Stating what you know: *Saber* and *conocer*

ALFREDO: Me gustan mucho los músicos y ella **sabe** cantar muy bien.

ELENA: Sí, es una cantante fabulosa.

MARIO: Luisa, **conoces** a Liliana, ¿no?

LUISA: Sí, las dos estamos en la clase de arte de la profesora Ruiz.

Piénselo. Indicate (✓) in the appropriate box whether each sentence refers to knowing a fact, knowing how to do something, knowing a person, or being familiar with a place, an event, or a thing.

	KNOWING A FACT	KNOWING HOW TO DO SOMETHING	KNOWING A PERSON	BEING FAMILIAR WITH A PLACE, EVENT, ETC.
1. ¿**Conoces** la música afro-peruana?	——	——	——	——
2. Me gusta mucho la música, pero no **sé** bailar.	——	——	——	——
3. ¿**Sabes** los nombres de esos grupos musicales?	——	——	——	——
4. ¿**Conoces** a Alfredo Roncal? Toca la guitarra.	——	——	——	——
5. ¿**Sabes** si hay un club de música hispana en la ciudad?	——	——	——	——
6. Alfredo **conoce** todos los clubes de música en la ciudad.	——	——	——	——

■ Both *saber* and *conocer* mean *to know*, but they are not used interchangeably.

	SABER	CONOCER
yo	sé	conozco
tú	sabes	conoces
Ud., él, ella	sabe	conoce
nosotros/as	sabemos	conocemos
vosotros/as	sabéis	conocéis
Uds., ellos/as	saben	conocen

■ Use **saber** to express knowledge of facts or pieces of information.
Él **sabe** dónde está el club.   *He knows where the club is.*

■ Use **saber +** *infinitive* to express knowing how to do something.
  Yo **sé** tocar la guitarra.   *I know how to play the guitar.*

■ Use **conocer** to express familiarity with someone or something. **Conocer** also means *to meet.* Remember to use the *personal **a*** when referring to people.
  Conozco a los músicos.   *I know the musicians.*
  Conozco bien ese club.   *I am very familiar with that club.*
  Ella va a **conocer a** Luis.   *She is going to meet Luis.*

> ### Lengua
>
> **Sé**, the **yo** form of the verb **saber**, has a written accent to distinguish it from the pronoun **se**.
>
> Yo **sé** que su hermano **se** llama José.

3-28 Un encuentro entre dos estudiantes. Raúl just arrived on campus, and he asks Sergio some questions. Select the correct words to complete their conversation.

RAÚL: Soy un estudiante nuevo y no (1) _____ dónde está la biblioteca.	a. sé	b. conozco
SERGIO: Es muy fácil. Tú (2) _____ dónde está la cafetería, ¿no? Pues, está al lado.	a. sabes	b. conoces
RAÚL: Gracias. ¿Y (3) _____ si hay un club de español?	a. sabes	b. conoces
SERGIO: Sí, claro, y (4) _____ que esta noche tiene una reunión.	a. sé	b. conozco
RAÚL: Magnífico. Sólo (5) _____ a dos o tres personas en la universidad.	a. sé	b. conozco
SERGIO: Pues allí vas a (6) _____ a muchos estudiantes.	a. saber	b. conocer

3-29 ¿Sabes quién es...? Ask your partner if he/she knows who is being referred to and if he/she knows that person. Take turns asking questions.

MODELO: el actor principal de *El ultimátum de Bourne*
  E1: *¿Sabes quién es el actor principal de* El ultimátum de Bourne?
  E2: *Sí, sé quién es. Es Matt Damon.*
  E1: *¿Conoces a Matt Damon en persona?*
  E2: *No, no conozco a Matt Damon./Sí, conozco a Matt Damon, pero solamente en fotografías.*

1. el/la representante de la Cámara de Representantes (*Congress*) de su distrito
2. el decano/la decana de la facultad
3. su profesor/a de español
4. el rey de España
5. el gobernador de su estado
6. el vicepresidente de Estados Unidos

3-30 Adivina, adivinador. In small groups, take turns reading the descriptions and guessing who is being described.

MODELO: E1: *Es una chica muy pobre que va a un baile. Allí conoce a un príncipe, pero a las 12:00 de la noche ella debe volver a su casa.*
            E2: *Sé quién es. Es Cenicienta* (Cinderella).

1. Es un gorila gigante con sentimientos (*feelings*) humanos. En una película aparece en el edificio Empire State de Nueva York.
2. Fue (*She was*) una mujer muy importante en Argentina. Su esposo gobernó (*governed*) ese país por varios años. Hay un musical con su nombre y también una película donde Madonna la representa.
3. Es una diseñadora de ropa y joyas, hija de un famoso pintor cubista español. Su perfume más famoso lleva su nombre.
4. Es un hombre de otro planeta con doble personalidad. Trabaja en un periódico, pero cuando se pone una ropa azul especial, puede volar (*fly*).

SITUACIONES

1. **Role A.** If you have not already done so, make a list of five people, at least some of whom you think your partner knows personally. Choose three of them and ask a) if your partner knows them and b) what your partner knows about them. Be ready to answer similar questions.

   Role B. If you have not already done so, make a list of five people, at least some of whom you think your partner knows personally. Your partner will tell you the names of three people on his/her list and will ask a) if you know them and b) what you know about them. Answer and then ask your partner the same questions about three of the people on your list.

2. **Role A.** You are looking for a third roommate for your apartment. Your partner knows a student from Peru who is looking for a place to live. Ask your partner a) the Peruvian student's name; b) where in Peru he/she is from; and c) if your partner knows the Peruvian student well. Also find out if the Peruvian student knows how to cook Peruvian dishes and how to play soccer (**fútbol**).

   Role B. Your partner is looking for a third roommate for his/her apartment. Mention that you know a student from Peru who is looking for a place to live. Answer your partner's questions about that person.

3-31 ¿Qué sabes hacer? Ask your partner if he/she knows how to do the following things. If your partner says yes, ask more questions to get additional information.

MODELO: bailar salsa y merengue
    E1: *¿Sabes bailar salsa y merengue?*
    E2: *Sí, sé bailar salsa y merengue./No, no sé bailar salsa y merengue. ¿Y tú?*

1. tocar un instrumento musical
2. cantar bien
3. preparar ceviche
4. manejar (*drive*) un autobús
5. cocinar platos muy elaborados
6. sacar (*take*) fotos con una cámara digital
7. hablar muchas lenguas
8. …

3-32 Bingo. To win this game of bingo, you have to fill in three boxes (horizontal, vertical, or diagonal) with the names of classmates who answer the answers correctly.

¿Quién sabe dónde está la ciudad de Cuzco?	¿Quién sabe cuál es la capital de Perú?	¿Quién sabe qué es Machu Picchu?
¿Quién conoce al presidente de Perú?	¿Quién sabe cuál es la unidad monetaria de Perú?	¿Quién sabe el nombre de un lago importante que está entre Perú y Bolivia?
¿Quién conoce unos platos típicos de la cocina (*cuisine*) peruana?	¿Quién conoce algún país hispanoamericano?	¿Quién sabe cómo se llaman las montañas de Perú?

3-33 Saber y conocer. Complete the conversation with the correct forms of **saber** and **conocer**. Review your answers with a partner.

PACO: ¿ _____ (1) a esa chica?
AUGUSTO: Sí, yo _____ (2) a todas las chicas aquí.
PACO: Entonces, ¿ _____ (3) dónde vive?
AUGUSTO: No, no _____ (4) dónde vive.
PACO: ¿ _____ (5) cómo se llama?
AUGUSTO: Lo siento, pero no _____ (6).
PACO: Pero ¿cómo dices que _____ (7) a la chica? Tú no _____ (8) dónde vive y tú no _____ (9) su nombre.

5. Expressing intention, means, movement, and duration: Some uses of *por* and *para*

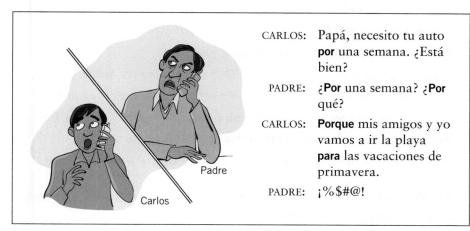

CARLOS: Papá, necesito tu auto **por** una semana. ¿Está bien?

PADRE: ¿**Por** una semana? ¿**Por** qué?

CARLOS: **Porque** mis amigos y yo vamos a ir la playa **para** las vacaciones de primavera.

PADRE: ¡%$#@!

Padre

Carlos

Piénselo. Indicate whether the following statements are true (**Cierto**) or false (**Falso**) according to the conversation.

1. ____ Carlos necesita el auto de su padre **por** una semana.
2. ____ El padre pregunta **por qué** Carlos desea el auto.
3. ____ Carlos desea ir a la playa **para** las vacaciones de primavera.
4. ____ Los amigos de Carlos necesitan el auto **para** trabajar.
5. ____ El padre está alegre **porque** Carlos necesita su auto.

■ **Por** and **para** have different meanings in Spanish, though sometimes they are both translated into English as *for*. The uses presented here include some you have already seen, as well as some new ones.

■ **Para** expresses *for* when you mean *intended for* or *to be used for*. It can refer to a person, an event, or a purpose.

Necesito un diccionario **para** la clase.	*I need a dictionary for the class.*
Este diccionario es **para** David.	*This dictionary is for David.*

■ **Para +** *infinitive* means *in order to.*

Uso el autobús **para** ir a la universidad.	*I use the bus (in order) to go to the university.*
El restaurante hace publicidad **para** traer clientes.	*The restaurant does advertising (in order) to bring in customers.*

■ **Por** appears in expressions such as **por favor**, **por teléfono**, and **por la mañana/tarde/noche**. Other expressions with **por** that you will find useful include the following:

por ciento	*percent*	**por fin**	*finally, at last*
por ejemplo	*for example*	**por lo menos**	*at least*
por eso	*that is why*	**por supuesto**	*of course*

■ **Por** and **para** can also be used to express movement in space and time.

Para indicates movement toward a destination.

Caminan **para** la playa.	*They walk toward the beach.*
Vamos **para** el túnel.	*We are going toward the tunnel.*

Por indicates movement through or by a place.

Caminan **por** la playa.	*They walk along the beach.*
Vamos **por** el túnel.	*We are going through the tunnel.*

You may also use **por** to indicate length of time or duration of an action.
Many Spanish speakers omit **por** in this case, or they use **durante**.

Necesito el auto (**por**) tres días.	*I need the car for three days.*

3-34 ¿Por o para? Match each use of **por** and **para** in the following text with the letter of its appropriate meaning from the list on the right.

Mis amigos y yo siempre estamos ocupados los fines de semana. Los viernes **por**[1] la noche, siempre vamos a un cine cerca de nuestro barrio. Cuando vamos **para**[2] el cine, caminamos **por**[3] el parque. Después del cine, a veces hacemos fiestas en casa. Yo compro una pizza y papas fritas **para**[4] comer con ellos. Si es una fiesta de cumpleaños, compro un regalo especial **para**[5] mi amigo. **Para**[6] celebrar, también invito a todos los miembros del grupo. A veces lo pasamos bien **por**[7] largas horas.

1. ____	**a.** intended for (person)
2. ____	**b.** used for (purpose)
3. ____	**c.** in order to
4. ____	**d.** length of time
5. ____	**e.** movement toward a destination
6. ____	**f.** movement through or by a place
7. ____	

3-35 ¿Para dónde van? Guess where these people are going, and compare your guesses with your classmate's. Then find out where your classmate is going after class, and why.

MODELO: Jorge busca su uniforme de fútbol.
Va para el estadio.

1. Es la una de la tarde y Pedro desea comer.
2. Sebastián lleva una mochila con sus libros de química y una calculadora.
3. Magdalena y Roberto van a consultar unos libros porque tienen un examen.
4. Gregorio va a comprar un libro para su clase de español.
5. Ana María va a ver una película de su actor favorito.
6. Amanda y Clara están muy elegantes y contentas. En este momento llegan Arturo y Felipe en su auto.

3-36 Caminante. Your classmate likes to walk. Ask him/her the following questions. Then switch roles.

1. ¿Te gusta caminar con amigos o solo/a? ¿Por qué?
2. ¿Por dónde caminas cuando quieres estar solo/a?
3. ¿Te gusta caminar por la playa o por un parque?
4. ¿Caminas por la mañana o por la tarde?
5. Cuando sales a caminar, ¿caminas por media hora o por más tiempo?

 3-37 ¿Para quiénes son los regalos (*gifts*)? You are very generous and have bought the following gifts. Your partner asks whom they are for.

MODELO: un disco compacto
         E1: *¿Para quién es el disco compacto?*
         E2: *Es para mi hermana.*

1. tres libros de español
2. dos billetes de avión
3. una revista de deportes
4. cuatro refrescos dietéticos
5. una guitarra española
6. un kilo de helado
7. una computadora portátil
8. un teléfono celular
9. un buen vino chileno
10. una colección de DVDs

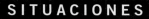

SITUACIONES

1. **Role A.** You run into a friend on the street who is carrying a large, gift-wrapped box. You are curious about the box, so you ask what it is and whom it is for.

   Role B. You are walking home from the store carrying a large, gift-wrapped package. You run into a friend on the way. Answer your friend's questions and explain why you are giving the gift.

2. **Role A.** You see your neighbor leaving his/her apartment, dragging a big suitcase. You are curious, so you ask a) where he/she is going; b) if the plane leaves in the afternoon or evening; c) how long he/she will be there; and d) why he/she is going.

   Role B. You are about to go on a long international trip, and as you are leaving your apartment with your suitcase you see your nosy neighbor. He/She asks a lot of questions. Answer in as much detail as possible.

MOSAICOS

A escuchar

CD 2
Track 6

Antes de escuchar

3-38 Preparación. You will listen to an ad for *ViajaMás*, a travel agency, which mentions several destinations in Latin America, the days of the flights, the flight numbers, and the price of a round-trip ticket from Miami. Before you listen, use your knowledge of Latin America and ticket prices to write down the name of one large city in each of the countries below that you think the ad may mention and the likely cost of each ticket.

CIUDADES LATINOAMERICANAS	PRECIO DEL BOLETO DE IDA Y VUELTA DESDE MIAMI
Perú:	
Argentina:	
Venezuela:	

Escuchar

3-39 ¿Comprende usted? Now listen to the ad and complete the chart with the information you hear.

CIUDAD	VUELO #	DÍAS	PRECIO DEL BOLETO
		sábados y domingos	
Buenos Aires	479		
			$250
Bogotá			

Después de escuchar

3-40 Ahora usted. A friend who is studying Spanish wants to visit a capital city in Latin America but is unsure where to go. After listening to the ad, write an e-mail to your friend to suggest a city to visit.

De: _____

Para: _____

Asunto: Una ciudad interesante en América Latina

Hola _____

¡Tengo una información excelente para ti! Hay tarifas (*fares*) fantásticas para visitar _____! ¡Es una ciudad _____! Los vuelos salen los _____. Los boletos cuestan _____.

¿Por qué no hablamos por teléfono este fin de semana? _____

114

A conversar

Organize information for a presentation

When preparing for an oral presentation, it is helpful to decide on a plan and then organize your information accordingly. In this section, you will make a presentation on students' food preferences. Organizing your information by meal (i.e., foods students would like to have available for breakfast, for lunch, etc.) is one approach; another is to start with categories of food that students like (e.g., **carnes**, **cereales**) and then list specific items in each category that students would like to see on the cafeteria menus. Both organizational plans will result in effective presentations.

Antes de conversar

3-41 Preparación. A new cafeteria is going to open on campus. You have been hired to survey students' food preferences so that the cafeteria menu will feature the most popular foods. Find out what your classmates like to eat and drink. Write down the names of students who answer **Sí** or **No** in the appropriate column.

MODELO: E1: *Susana, ¿comes cereal en el desayuno?*
         E2: *Sí, como cereal en el desayuno./No, no como cereal.*

	DESAYUNO		ALMUERZO		CENA	
	SÍ	NO	SÍ	NO	SÍ	NO
cereal con leche						
café/chocolate caliente						
jugo de naranja/tomate/manzana						
hamburguesas						
ensalada de frutas						
vino						
pan						
…						
…						

Conversar

3-42 Entre nosotros. Analyze the information you collected and write down a proposed menu. Present it to the new cafeteria supervisor (your classmate). Explain what most students (**la mayor parte de los estudiantes**) eat and drink. Be prepared to answer the supervisor's questions.

Después de conversar

3-43 Un poco más. Compare your menu with those of other classmates. Then vote on which menu is the most healthful and the most complete, and explain why.

Cultura

Despite differences from country to country, mealtimes in Hispanic countries generally differ from those in the United States. People typically eat breakfast at 7:00 or 8:00 a.m. It normally consists of **café**, **café con leche** (hot milk with strong coffee), **té**, or **chocolate caliente** with bread, a sweet roll, and sometimes juice or fruit. As this is a light breakfast, people sometimes have a snack in the late morning. Cereals are becoming more popular, especially among children and young adults.

In some countries, the main meal of the day is lunch (**el almuerzo** or **la comida**), eaten between 12:30 and 3:00 p.m. Supper (**la cena** or **la comida**) is served after 7:00 or 8:00 p.m., and sometimes as late as 10:00 p.m.

A leer

1.

NIÑOS

CORPORACIÓN CULTURAL DE LIMA. Santa María y Gálvez. 2209451. A las 12 y 16 horas. Bagdhadas. S/. 12.

TEATRO INFANTIL A DOMICILIO. 2390176. El patito feo. Adaptación del cuento de Andersen. Compañía Arcoiris.

CENTRO LIMA. Av. Grau y Velásquez. A las 12, show especial de Navidad.

FANTASÍA DISNEY. Desde las 15. Niños, S/. 8; adultos, S/. 14. Parque de entretenimientos.

EL MUNDO FANTÁSTICO DE MAFALDA. Desde las 10. Entrada general a todos los juegos. Niños, S/. 12. Calle Domingo Sarmiento 358.

PLANETARIO DEL MORRO SOLAR. A las 12, 17 y 19. Gratis para niños; adultos, S/. 15. Circunvalación, Nuevo Perú. Tel. 5620841.

PARQUE DE LAS LEYENDAS (ZOO). De 9 a 19 hrs. Niños y 3ra edad, S/. 5; S/. 10, otro público. Cerro Tongoy, 3701725.

Antes de leer

3-44 Preparación. PRIMERA FASE. The three ads in activity **3-45** come from a newspaper in Lima, Peru. Look them over quickly without reading them. Then mark which ad goes with each of the following descriptions.

1. ____ un restaurante de comida china
2. ____ actividades para niños
3. ____ un restaurante de comida tradicional peruana

SEGUNDA FASE. What word(s) in each ad helped you answer the questions in the *Primera fase*?

Leer

3-45 Primera mirada. Read the ads and offer a solution for the following choices that have to be made. Be prepared to explain your solutions to the class.

1. El señor y la señora Molina tienen cuatro hijos entre tres y ocho años. A los niños les fascinan los animales. ¿Adónde van a ir probablemente? ¿Por qué?
2. Carlos está triste porque se fracturó una pierna y no puede (*he can't*) salir de la casa. Su mamá tiene una sorpresa para él. ¿Qué es?
3. Cuatro médicos franceses visitan el Hospital Central. El Dr. Moreira, director del hospital, desea invitar a sus colegas a cenar en un restaurante cómodo, con comida tradicional peruana. ¿A qué restaurante va a invitarlos? ¿Por qué?

2.

Costa Verde

Sabrosa comida tradicional peruana
Menú especial los fines de semana

■ Aperitivo
■ Entrada
■ Segundo
■ Postre
■ Café y plus café (crema de café, crema de menta, anisado)

Valor: S/. 75

Carnes, pescados y mariscos preparados por los mejores cocineros del país

Avenida Arequipa 357
Reservas: 428 9654
Fax: 428 9655

3-46 Segunda mirada. Reread the ads (**3-45**) to answer the following questions.

Anuncio 1: ¿Qué palabras, indican que las actividades son para los niños? ¿Qué significa *3ra edad*? ¿Qué significa *otro público*?

Anuncio 2: Identifique qué expresión indica que este restaurante prepara comida nacional. ¿Cuánto cuesta el menú especial de los fines de semana?

Anuncio 3: ¿Qué expresiones se refieren a la buena calidad del restaurante? ¿Qué palabra significa *reservation*?

Después de leer

3-47 Ampliación. With a classmate, answer the following questions about the four ads from Peru.

1. ¿Cuál de las siguientes actividades desean hacer ustedes en Lima: ir a un parque de entretenimiento (*amusement park*), comer comida tradicional peruana, ver teatro o comer comida china? ¿Por qué?
2. ¿Cuál de los dos restaurantes sirve comida que a ustedes les gusta más, Costa Verde o Chifa Lungfung?

3.

El Chifa Lungfung

La más exquisita, variada y exótica carta de comida cantonesa-peruana: finas carnes, pescados y todo tipo de mariscos.

SÁBADOS Y DOMINGOS:

Almuerzos y cenas familiares

...los esperamos

AIRE ACONDICIONADO
MÚSICA AMBIENTAL
CAMAREROS PROFESIONALES
AV. REPÚBLICA DE PANAMÁ 8720
RESERVAS 3817543, 3816532, 3814241

A escribir

Use appropriate conventions in letter-writing

Writing a casual or formal letter requires observing certain basic conventions, such as including the date, a salutation, an introduction, a body, and a closing, as well as carefully selecting information that will interest your reader. Formalities of writing also require developing one idea per paragraph. Remember to follow these conventions even when writing to a friend.

Antes de escribir

3-48 Preparación. You are visiting a great vacation spot and want to write your friend a letter about it. To prepare to write the letter, do the following:

1. Write a tentative date for the letter: _____ (date) de _____ (month), 20____
2. Choose a salutation and a closing from the *En directo* box.
3. Prepare some information for the introduction. Mention the place where you are: Is it a beach, a park, a city, a historical landmark (**lugar histórico**)?
4. Decide on the information for the body of the letter:

   a. Make a list of words (adjectives) that describe the place: Is it small, big, beautiful, fun, interesting, historical?
   b. Write down some enjoyable activities (verbs) that people do there. Are they outdoor activities, sports (**deportes**), culturally oriented activities such as going to museums (**museos**), excursions (**excursiones**), fairs (**ferias**)?
   c. Indicate some of the activities that others do that you also like.

En directo
Salutations for casual correspondence:
Querido/a...
Estimado/a...
Hola...
Closings for casual correspondence:
Tu amigo/a,
Hasta pronto,
Cariños,
Love

Escribir

3-49 Manos a la obra. Now write the letter to your friend, telling about your vacation. Use the information you prepared in activity **3-48** and any other that you think may be of interest to your friend.

Después de escribir

3-50 Revisión. After completing your letter, read it at least twice with your friend in mind. Check the following:

1. Did you include the date in your letter?
2. Are your salutation and closing appropriate?
3. Did you include a brief introduction and enough information in the body of the letter to achieve your purpose?
4. Did you check for spelling or grammatical errors?
5. Finally, discuss your letter with one of your peers.

ENFOQUE CULTURAL

Breve perfil de Perú

Perú es un país extraordinario por su diversidad y riqueza histórica, geográfica y cultural. En efecto, Perú y México son las dos regiones más importantes durante la época colonial de América Latina. Pero antes de los españoles, en Perú ya existe uno de los imperios indígenas más interesantes del continente. Y, finalmente, en Perú encontramos ruinas espectaculares de las culturas indígenas y de la época colonial, y también ciudades modernas con una mezcla de razas y una diversidad étnica muy grande.

Antes de la llegada de los conquistadores españoles, el imperio de los incas es una de las principales civilizaciones nativas de América. Esta civilización es famosa por su compleja organización social, su avanzada arquitectura y sus sistemas de comunicación. Muchas ciudades conservan restos de esta cultura. Por ejemplo, en Cuzco, la capital del imperio inca, hay espectaculares construcciones, como la gran fortaleza de Sacsayhuamán. Y, naturalmente, una de las ciudades incas más prestigiosas es Machu Picchu.

El Conde de Nieva, virrey de Perú entre 1561 y 1584, depende del rey Felipe II.

La fortaleza de Sacsayhuamán cerca de Cuzco

Cuando los españoles conquistan América, dividen el territorio en tres tipos diferentes de administración. El tipo más importante de administración en el imperio español es el *virreinato*. Esta palabra "vir**rei**nato" se relaciona con "rey", porque la autoridad más importante es el virrey. El segundo tipo más importante de administración es la *gobernación*, bajo la autoridad del gobernador. Y el tercer tipo es la *capitanía general*, bajo la autoridad principal del capitán general. México, Perú y la Nueva Granada (la actual Colombia) son los tres virreinatos españoles en el continente americano durante la colonia.

La geografía de Perú es variada y compleja. Tiene una multitud de sistemas ecológicos que forman el hábitat de una infinidad de plantas y animales. Hay tres regiones

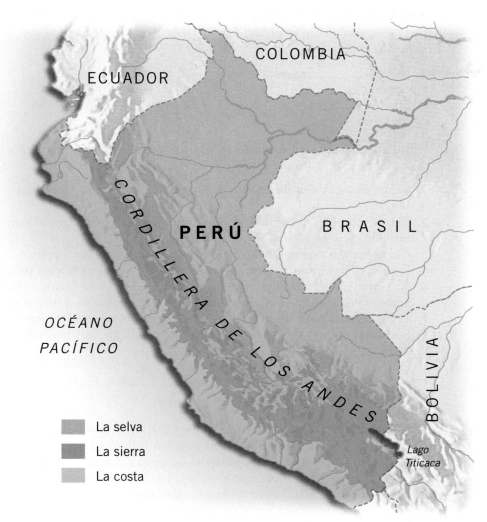

La geografía de Perú presenta tres regiones diferentes.

La selva

La sierra

La costa

geográficas principales en Perú. La costa del Pacífico es muy rica en una gran variedad de peces y productos agrícolas. Una de las atracciones más famosas de esta región son las misteriosas líneas de Nazca. La segunda región es la sierra, que está formada por los Andes y que tiene algunas montañas muy altas, tales como el Nevado de Huascarán, el pico más alto de Perú, de aproximadamente 6.700 metros. La tercera región es la selva del Amazonas, al oriente de los Andes. Las grandes selvas tropicales de esta región son una de las fuentes principales de oxígeno en el planeta.

Finalmente, la cultura peruana es el resultado de la mezcla de la cultura indígena de los incas con la cultura española. Muchos peruanos, especialmente entre los habitantes de la sierra, hablan quechua, la lengua original de los incas. Pero Perú también tiene una gran influencia de culturas de origen africano y asiático. En resumen, la comida, el arte, la literatura, y todas las manifestaciones culturales peruanas son realmente únicas.

En otras palabras

Expresiones peruanas

Me conseguí una **chamba**.
I found a job.

José y yo somos **patas**.
José and I are buddies.

¡Juanita es una **chancona**!
Juanita is a nerd!

119

3-51 Comprensión. PRIMERA FASE. **Reconocimiento de palabras clave.** Find in the text the Spanish word or phrase that best expresses the meaning of the following concepts:

1. profile _____
2. empire _____
3. rain forest _____
4. fort, fortress _____
5. fish, fishes _____
6. snow-capped peak _____
7. east _____

SEGUNDA FASE. **Oraciones importantes.** Underline the statements that contain ideas found in the text. Then indicate where in the text those ideas appear.

1. Before the arrival of the Spaniards, Cuzco was the capital of the Inca Empire.
2. The viceroyalties of Mexico and Peru were the most important colonies of Spain in the New World.
3. Colombia was one of the three viceroyalties in the Spanish Empire.
4. Peru has some beautiful modern cities, but they are all somewhat run down.
5. The mysterious Nazca drawings are located in the coastal region of Peru.
6. Some mountains, like Peru's highest peak, for example, are capped with snow.
7. A few mountains in the Peruvian Andes are very close to 8,000 meters high.
8. Spanish is not just the main language of Peru; it is the only language spoken there.

TERCERA FASE. **Ideas principales.** Write a brief paragraph in English summarizing the main ideas expressed in the text.

3-52 Use la información. You are visiting Peru, and you will spend tomorrow visiting Cuzco and its surroundings. Although it is late and you are tired, you take a few minutes to write a postcard to someone you really care about. Explain your plans for tomorrow: a) mention at least one place you plan to visit; b) if the place is in Cuzco or near/far (**cerca/lejos**); c) how you are going to get there; and d) what you are going to see. For help with this activity, go to the web page of *Mosaicos* and use the links provided there to write your postcard.

De..............................
....
....
....
....

Para............................
....
....
....
....

VOCABULARIO

CD 2
Tracks 7–14

Las diversiones y las celebraciones	**Leisure activities and celebrations**
la boda	wedding
la canción	song
el cumpleaños	birthday
la fiesta	party
la guitarra	guitar
la música	music
la película	film
la reunión	meeting, gathering
el tiempo libre	free time
las vacaciones	vacation

Las personas	**People**
el camarero/la camarera	server, waiter/waitress (restaurant)
el hombre	man
el/la joven	young man/woman
la mujer	woman

En un café o restaurante	**In a coffee shop or restaurant**
el agua	water
el almuerzo	lunch
el arroz	rice
la bebida	drink
el bistec	steak
el café	coffee
la cena	dinner, supper
el cereal	cereal
la cerveza	beer
el ceviche	dish of marinated raw fish
la comida	food; meal; dinner, supper
el desayuno	breakfast
la ensalada	salad
los espaguetis	spaghetti
el frijol	bean
la fruta	fruit
la hamburguesa	hamburger
el helado	ice cream
el huevo	egg
el jamón	ham
el jugo	juice
la leche	milk
la lechuga	lettuce
la naranja	orange
el pan	bread
el pan tostado/la tostada	toast
la papa	potato
las papas fritas	French fries
el pescado	fish
el pollo	chicken
el queso	cheese
el refresco	soda, soft drink
el sándwich	sandwich
la sopa	soup

el té	tea
el tomate	tomato
el vegetal/la verdura	vegetable
el vino	wine

La comunicación	**Communication**
el periódico	newspaper
la revista	magazine
el teléfono	telephone

Los lugares	**Places**
el cine	movies
la ciudad	city
el mar	sea
el país	country, nation

Las descripciones	**Descriptions**
caliente	hot
fabuloso/a	fabulous, great
frío/a	cold
frito/a	fried
rápido/a	fast
típico/a	typical

Verbos	**Verbs**
alquilar	to rent
cantar	to sing
celebrar	to celebrate
cenar	to have dinner
descansar	to rest
hacer la cama	to make the bed
nadar	to swim
poner la mesa	to set the table
tocar (un instrumento)	to play (an instrument)
tomar el sol	to sunbathe

Palabras y expresiones útiles	**Useful words and expressions**
¿adónde?	where (to)?
al	to the (contraction of **a** + **el**)
al aire libre	outdoors
¡claro!	of course!
cerca de	close to, near
después, luego	after, later
durante	during
¡estupendo!	fabulous!
felicidades	congratulations
mientras	while
otro/a	other, another
¿qué te parece?	what do you think?
si	if

See *Lengua* box on page 102 for expressions that denote future time.
See page 106 for numbers from 100 to 2.000.000.
See page 111 for expressions with *por*.

En familia

Fernando Botero, uno de los pintores contemporáneos más famosos de Colombia, pinta a unos padres con sus hijos en este cuadro titulado *En familia*.

Source: © Fernando Botero, courtesy of Marlborough Gallery, New York.

In this chapter you will learn how to:

- talk about family

- discuss what you have to do

- describe daily routines

Las calles de Cartagena de Indias

Mar Caribe

Barranquilla

Cartagena de Indias

PANAMÁ

VENEZUELA

Medellín

Bucaramanga

Pereira

Pieza antigua del Museo del Oro de Bogotá

El Parque Nacional del café, Departamento El Quindío

Cali

⊛ Bogotá

Río Magdalena

COLOMBIA

Popayán

OCÉANO

PACÍFICO

ECUADOR

CORDILLERA DE LOS ANDES

Arepas de queso

BRASIL

BRASIL

Cordillera de Los Andes

 A vista de pájaro. Complete las siguientes oraciones (*the following sentences*) con la información correcta.

1. Ecuador, _____ y Brasil están al sur de Colombia.
2. _____ es la capital de Colombia.
3. El _____ es el mayor producto de exportación de Colombia.
4. Fernando Botero es un_____ colombiano.

A PRIMERA VISTA

🔊 Los miembros de la familia

CD 2
Track 15

Una familia colombiana de tres generaciones: **abuelos, hijos** y **nietos**. ¿Cuántos **niños** hay? ¿Hay muchos niños en la familia de usted?

Estos tres niños son **hermanos**. A ellos les gusta **jugar** con el gato. El niño de la **izquierda** se llama Juan y es **el mayor**. La niña se llama Julia y es la segunda. El pequeño, a la **derecha**, se llama Roberto.

En esta foto vemos un **bautizo**. En estas ceremonias participan los **padres**, los **padrinos** y los **ahijados**. Para muchas familias hispanas, el bautizo es un día muy especial.

El árbol familiar de Pablo

don José   doña Olga

María   Jorge   Osvaldo   Lola   Elena   Jaime

Elenita   Ana   Jorgito   Sofía   Inés   Pablo

Lengua

Use your knowledge of gender and number in Spanish words to understand some variations that are not presented in *A primera vista*. If you know **esposa**, what do you think **esposo** means? If you know **padres**, what to you think **padre** means? Can you guess what **madrina** means? And **novia**?

124

Pablo habla de su familia

CD 2
Track 16

Me llamo Pablo Méndez Sánchez y vivo con mis padres, mi **hermana** y mis **abuelos** en un apartamento en Bogotá, la capital de Colombia.

Mi **madre** tiene un **hermano**, mi **tío** Jorge. Su **esposa** es mi **tía** María. Tienen tres hijos y viven también en Bogotá. Mi **primo** Jorgito es el **menor**. Mis **primas** Elenita y Ana son **gemelas**. Mis primos son muy simpáticos y **pasamos** mucho tiempo **juntos**.

Mis tíos tienen sólo dos **sobrinos** en Bogotá, mi hermana Inés y yo. Su otra **sobrina**, la hija de mi tía Lola, vive en Cartagena, al norte del país.

La **nieta** favorita de mis abuelos es mi hermanita Inés. Tiene sólo tres años y es la menor de todos sus **nietos**.

4-1 Asociación. Asocie la descripción en la columna izquierda con la expresión correcta en la columna derecha.

1. ___ la esposa de mi padre	a. mi primo
2. ___ el hermano de mi prima	b. mi nieto
3. ___ los padres de mi padre	c. mi madre
4. ___ el hijo de mi hijo	d. mis abuelos
5. ___ el hermano de mi madre	e. mi tío

4-2 La familia de Pablo. Complete las siguientes oraciones (*following sentences*) de acuerdo con (*according to*) la información que usted tiene sobre la familia de Pablo.

1. La hermana de Pablo se llama _____ .
2. Don José y doña Olga son los _____ de Pablo.
3. Pablo es el _____ de Jaime.
4. Jaime es el _____ de Pablo, y Elena es su _____ .
5. Inés y Ana son _____ . Elenita y Ana son _____ .
6. Elena es la _____ de Jorgito, Elenita y Ana.
7. Lola es la _____ de Jorge y Elena.

Otros miembros de la familia de Pablo

CD 2
Track 17

La única hermana de mi **mamá** es mi tía Lola. Lola y Sergio están **divorciados** y tienen una hija, mi prima Sofía. Ahora la tía Lola está casada con Osvaldo, el **padrastro** de Sofía. Sergio está casado con Paula y tienen un hijo, Roberto. Paula es la **madrastra** de Sofía, y Roberto es su **medio hermano**.

4-3 ¿Cierto o falso? Marque (✔) la columna adecuada de acuerdo con la información sobre la familia de Lola.

	CIERTO	FALSO
1. La tía Lola está casada con Sergio.	——	——
2. Osvaldo es el papá de Roberto.	——	——
3. Paula es la madrastra de Roberto.	——	——
4. Lola es la madre de Sofía.	——	——
5. Sofía tiene un medio hermano.	——	——

 4-4 ¿Quién es y cómo es? PRIMERA FASE. Escojan (*Choose*) un miembro de una familia famosa (la familia real [*royal*] española, los Jackson, los Kennedy, los Bush, etc.). Preparen su árbol familiar.

SEGUNDA FASE. Túrnese (*Take turns*) con su compañero/a de clase (*classmate*) para describir el árbol familiar de esta persona.

MODELO: el príncipe Felipe
E1: *Su padre es el rey de España. Su madre es la reina Sofía. Felipe tiene dos hermanas. Está casado con la princesa Letizia.*
E2: *Tiene dos hijas y seis sobrinos. Su hermana Elena tiene un hijo y una hija. Su hermana Cristina tiene tres hijos y una hija.*

4-5 El arte de preguntar. PRIMERA FASE. Prepare las preguntas (*questions*) necesarias para obtener la siguiente información.

1. Tengo cuatro abuelos vivos (*alive*).
2. No, no soy hijo único/hija única.
3. Tengo dos hermanos.
4. Vivo con mi madre y mi padrastro.
5. Mis abuelos no viven con nosotros.
6. Tengo muchos primos.
7. Tengo una media hermana, pero no vive con nosotros.
8. Mi media hermana vive con su madre.

 SEGUNDA FASE. Ahora háganse preguntas (*ask each other questions*) para obtener información sobre la familia de su compañero/a. Después, compartan (*share*) esta información con la clase.

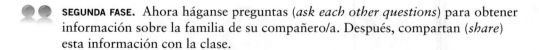 **4-6 Mi familia. PRIMERA FASE.** Preparen su árbol familiar individualmente. Luego, intercambien (*exchange*) su árbol.

SEGUNDA FASE. Háganse preguntas sobre su familia para obtener la siguiente información.

1. nombre de los abuelos vivos
2. nombre de los padres (padrastro/madrastra)
3. número y nombre de los hermanos (medios hermanos, hermanastros)
4. número y nombre de los primos
5. descripción de dos parientes (*relatives*)

♪) ¿Qué hacen los parientes?

CD 2
Track 18

Mis abuelos viven en una casa al lado del parque. Normalmente, ellos **pasean** por las mañanas y **almuerzan** muy temprano. Después, **duermen la siesta** y por la tarde **visitan** a sus **parientes**.

Jorgito es mi primo favorito. Es un poco menor que yo. Nosotros corremos y jugamos mucho **juntos**. También nos gusta ver el fútbol en la televisión y montar en bicicleta los domingos.

Hace dos años que mi prima Ana tiene **novio**, y **frecuentemente dice** que **quiere casarse** muy pronto. Elenita, su hermana gemela, **piensa** que Ana no debe casarse porque es muy joven.

Mi tío Jorge es un hombre muy **ocupado**. Sale de casa muy **temprano** y **vuelve tarde** todos los días. Mi tía María, su esposa, dice que él **prefiere** el trabajo a su familia. Pienso que en todas las familias hay problemas. En la mía también, pero me gusta mi familia.

> ### Lengua
>
> In Spanish, the direct object of a verb is normally introduced without a preposition. However, the preposition **a** is required when the direct object is a person or a specific animal: **los abuelos visitan a los parientes**; **la hija pasea al perro**.

4-7 ¿Cierto o falso? Conteste (*Answer*) de acuerdo con la información adicional sobre la familia de Pablo.

	CIERTO	FALSO
1. Normalmente los abuelos están muy ocupados.	——	——
2. Jorgito y Pablo montan en bicicleta frecuentemente.	——	——
3. Elenita piensa que su hermana es muy joven para casarse.	——	——
4. El tío Jorge cree que Elenita tiene problemas.	——	——
5. El tío Jorge trabaja mucho.	——	——
6. El tío Jorge llega temprano a su casa.	——	——

4-8 ¿Y qué hace su familia? Hágale preguntas a su compañero/a para obtener más información sobre su familia. Use la siguiente guía (*guide*).

1. número de personas en la casa, edad (*age*) y relación de parentesco (*kinship*)
2. ocupación y descripción (física y de personalidad) de algunos (*some*) miembros de la familia
3. actividades de estas personas en su tiempo libre
4. nombre del pariente favorito, relación familiar y razón (*reason*) de su preferencia

·)) **Las rutinas familiares**

CD 2
Track 19

En casa de Pablo hay mucha actividad por la mañana. Los niños **se despiertan** a las siete. **Se levantan, se lavan** y luego **desayunan** en la cocina con sus padres. Después salen para la escuela.

Poco después, la madre **se ducha, se seca, se viste** y **se maquilla.**

Más tarde, el padre **se afeita**, **se baña** y **se pone la ropa,** pero no sale de casa hasta las nueve.

4-9 Cada cosa a su tiempo. Ponga (*Put*) en orden cronológico las siguientes oraciones según (*according to*) las escenas.

____ La madre se maquilla.
____ Los niños se despiertan a las siete.
____ El padre se baña y luego se pone la ropa.
____ La madre se ducha.
____ El padre sale de casa a las nueve.
____ Los niños desayunan y después salen para la escuela.

4-10 Las rutinas diarias. Conteste las siguientes preguntas sobre la rutina diaria de la familia de Pablo:

1. ¿Con quién desayunan los niños?
2. ¿Quién se maquilla por las mañanas?
3. ¿A qué hora se despiertan los niños?
4. ¿Quién sale de casa a las nueve?
5. ¿Quién se afeita por las mañanas?
6. ¿Qué hace la madre después de ducharse?

4-11 Mañanas ocupadas (*busy*). Marque (✓) las acciones diarias de los miembros de su familia.

	SE DESPIERTA TEMPRANO	SE DUCHA POR LA MAÑANA	SE PONE ROPA ELEGANTE	DESAYUNA CON LA FAMILIA
Mi padre (padrastro)				
Mi madre (madrastra)				
Mi hermano/a				
Mi abuelo/a				
Mi tío/a				

> ### Lengua
> The following are expressions to organize time sequentially: **Primero, luego, poco después, más tarde,** and **por último.**

4-12 ¿Y usted? Complete el siguiente párrafo indicando el orden de las acciones en la rutina diaria de usted. Use las expresiones siguientes:

me ducho
me despierto
me levanto
salgo para la universidad
desayuno

Primero _____, luego _____. Poco después _____, más tarde _____. Por último _____.

 4-13 ¿A qué hora? Túrnense para hacerse las siguientes preguntas sobre la rutina diaria.

1. ¿A qué hora se levanta tu madre/padre/hermano?
2. ¿Te duchas por la mañana o por la noche?
3. ¿Quién se levanta temprano en tu familia?
4. ¿Te vistes antes o después de desayunar?
5. ¿Te pones ropa elegante o informal para ir a clase?
6. ¿A qué hora te acuestas durante la semana?
7. ¿A qué hora te acuestas durante los fines de semana?
8. ¿A qué hora te levantas durante los fines de semana?
9. ¿A qué hora tienes la clase de español?
10. ¿Quién se despierta antes los domingos en tu familia?

4-14 Algunas familias hispanas. You will listen to descriptions of four Hispanic families. Before you listen, answer these questions: Is your family large or small? How many brothers and sisters, cousins, aunts, and uncles do you have?

CD 2
Track 20

Now pay attention to the general idea of what is said. As you hear each description, write a check mark (✓) in the corresponding column.

	TIENE UNA FAMILIA GRANDE	TIENE HERMANOS	TIENE MUCHOS TÍOS	TIENE PRIMOS
Pedro				
Alicia				
Magdalena				
Alberto				

EN ACCIÓN

Diarios de bicicleta: Nada de bromas

Antes de ver

4-15 En este segmento, Javier se encuentra con Luciana y su familia en el parque. Marque (✓) las actividades que las personas hacen normalmente cuando están en un parque.

1. ___ Juegan con una pelota (*ball*).
2. ___ Comen sándwiches y beben refrescos.
3. ___ Leen el periódico.
4. ___ Buscan trabajo.
5. ___ Escuchan música.

Mientras ve

4-16 Ponga en orden cronológico las acciones de Javier cuando la familia de Luciana le hace una broma (*plays a joke*).

___ Cierra los ojos.   ___ Se levanta y se va enojado.
___ Se pone el sombrero.   ___ Levanta los brazos y los mueve.
___ Se sienta.   ___ Abre los ojos.

Después de ver

4-17 ¿Qué ocurre después de esta escena? Marque (✓) todas las actividades que usted cree que son posibles.

1. ___ Javier come con la familia de Luciana.
2. ___ Javier sale del parque sin despedirse de (*without saying good-bye*) Luciana.
3. ___ La abuela habla con Javier.
4. ___ El padre de Luciana duerme una siesta después del almuerzo.
5. ___ Marcos está enojado y sale del parque.

FUNCIONES Y FORMAS

1. Expressing opinions, plans, preferences, and feelings: Present tense of stem-changing verbs: *e → ie*, *o → ue*, and *e → i*

Carmen habla

Quiero conversar seriamente con ustedes y les **pido** su ayuda. **Pienso** que mamá y papá **quieren** algunos cambios en casa. Ellos no **pueden** hacer todo. El día **empieza** muy temprano para ellos y **duermen** muy poco. Con frecuencia, **almuerzan** en la oficina, aunque **prefieren** comer en casa. Nosotros necesitamos ayudar. Luis y Ximena, ustedes **vuelven** a casa a las 2:00. Si ustedes le **sirven** el almuerzo a Juanito y **juegan** con él, nuestros padres van a estar muy contentos. **Cuesta** mucho dinero pagar los servicios de una niñera (*babysitter*). ¿**Piensan** ustedes que mis ideas son buenas o **tienen** otras?

Piénselo. Identifique a la(s) persona(s) que probablemente hace(n) estas actividades en la familia del texto anterior: Los padres (**P**), Luis y Ximena (**LX**), Juanito (**J**) o Carmen (**C**). A veces hay más de una respuesta correcta.

1. ____ **Almuerzan** fuera de casa.
2. ____ **Necesita** ayuda para almorzar.
3. ____ **Prefieren** almorzar en casa.
4. ____ **Vuelven** a casa a las 2:00.
5. ____ **Sirven** el almuerzo a su hermanito.
6. ____ **Pide** la colaboración de sus hermanos.

■ Some common verbs in Spanish undergo a vowel change in all forms of the present tense except **nosotros/as** and **vosotros/as**.

PENSAR (e → ie) (*to think*)			
yo	pienso	nosotros/as	pensamos
tú	piensas	vosotros/as	pensáis
Ud., él, ella	piensa	Uds., ellos/as	piensan

VOLVER (o → ue) (*to return*)			
yo	vuelvo	nosotros/as	volvemos
tú	vuelves	vosotros/as	volvéis
Ud., él, ella	vuelve	Uds., ellos/as	vuelven

PEDIR (e → i) (*to ask for*)			
yo	pido	nosotros/as	pedimos
tú	pides	vosotros/as	pedís
Ud., él, ella	pide	Uds., ellos/as	piden

■ Other common verbs that have vowel changes in the stem are:

e → ie	o → ue	e → i
cerrar (*to close*)	**almorzar** (*to have lunch*)	**repetir** (*to repeat*)
empezar (*to begin*)	**costar** (*to cost*)	**servir** (*to serve*)
entender (*to understand*)	**dormir** (*to sleep*)	
preferir (*to prefer*)	**encontrar** (*to meet*)	
querer (*to want; to love*)	**poder** (*to be able to, can*)	

■ Use **pensar** + *infinitive* to express what you or someone else is planning to do.

Pienso estudiar esta noche.	*I plan to study tonight.*
Pensamos comer a las ocho.	*We are planning to eat at 8:00.*

■ Note the irregular **yo** form in the following **e → ie** and **e → i** stem-changing verbs.

tener (*to have*)	**tengo**, tienes, tiene, tenemos, tenéis, tienen
venir (*to come*)	**vengo**, vienes, viene, venimos, venís, vienen
decir (*to say, to tell*)	**digo**, dices, dice, decimos, decís, dicen
seguir (*to follow*)	**sigo**, sigues, sigue, seguimos, seguís, siguen

■ In the verb *jugar* (*to play a game or sport*) **u** changes to **ue**.

Mario **ju**ega muy bien al tenis, pero nosotros jugamos regular.	*Mario plays tennis very well, but we play so-so.*

4-18 Planes para la boda. Beatriz y Miguel se casan en un mes. Complete la descripción de los planes para la boda con la forma correcta de un verbo apropiado.

empezar   poder   querer   servir
entender   preferir   seguir   volver

Beatriz y Miguel (1) _____ tener una boda pequeña, pero elegante. La ceremonia (2) _____ a las 7:00. Los sobrinos y primos jóvenes de los novios no asisten a la ceremonia. Ellos no (3) _____ la ceremonia, y (4) _____ jugar con una niñera en otra parte de la iglesia. Después de la ceremonia, todos van a un restaurante, donde los invitados (5) _____ bailar y cenar. Los camareros (6) _____ una cena italiana, porque los padres de Miguel son de Italia. Después de la cena, la familia (7) _____ a la casa de los padres de la novia. Los invitados (8) _____ en la celebración, pero Beatriz y Miguel salen para su luna de miel (*honeymoon*) a Colombia.

4-19 ¿Qué piensan hacer? Túrnense para decir qué piensa hacer cada (*each*) miembro de la familia en las situaciones siguientes.

MODELO: Mi hermano quiere estar delgado.
      E1:   *Tu hermano probablemente piensa correr mucho.*
      E2:   *Él probablemente piensa empezar una dieta.*
      E3:   *Y probablemente piensa ir al gimnasio todos los días.*

1. Mi hermana tiene un examen de matemáticas mañana.
2. Mi hermana estudia bastante, pero no entiende muchos de los problemas.
3. Mi tía está enferma, por eso se siente muy débil y cansada.
4. Mis abuelos están de vacaciones en Colombia.
5. Mis primos quieren ir a Cartagena para visitar a los abuelos.
6. Mi tío lee y escucha comentarios contradictorios sobre Colombia, por eso, quiere aprender más sobre el país.

4-20 ¿Qué pasa en las reuniones familiares? PRIMERA FASE. Muchas familias se reúnen (*get together*) para las fiestas, los eventos especiales o sólo para reunirse. Describan las reuniones de su familia a su compañero/a. Tomen nota de las semejanzas (*similarities*) y las diferencias.

MODELO: preparar la comida
      E1:   *En las reuniones de mi familia, mi abuela prepara mucha comida.*
      E2:   *En las reuniones de mi familia, tenemos mucha comida también. Pero mi madre y mi tía preparan la comida.*

1. venir
2. jugar con los niños
3. servir la comida
4. dormir en el sofá
5. preferir hablar de temas políticos
6. volver a casa

SEGUNDA FASE. Hablen de una semejanza y una diferencia entre las reuniones de su familia. Estén listos (*Be ready*) para compartir la información con la clase.

Lengua

■ **Pensar en** is the Spanish equivalent of *to think of/about someone or something.*

¿Piensas en tu familia cuando estás fuera de casa?
Do you think of/about your family when you are away from home?

Sí, **pienso** mucho **en** ellos.
Yes, I think of/about them a lot.

■ **Pensar de** is used to ask for an opinion. **Pensar que** is normally used in the answer.

¿Qué **piensas de** los planes de ayuda familiar?
What do you think of the plans to help families?

Pienso que son excelentes.
I think they are excellent.

4-21 Entrevista. Túrnense para entrevistarse (*interview each other*). Hablen sobre los siguientes temas (*topics*) y después compartan la información con otro compañero/otra compañera.

1. la hora del almuerzo, qué prefiere comer y dónde
2. los deportes que prefiere practicar o mirar en la televisión
3. a qué hora empieza a hacer la tarea generalmente
4. si duerme una siesta durante el día
5. si vuelve a la casa de sus padres para las vacaciones
6. qué piensa hacer después de la universidad

 4-22 ¿Cuándo y con quién? PRIMERA FASE. Háganse preguntas para obtener la siguiente información.

1. quiénes son sus amigos y qué actividades hacen juntos durante el año académico, durante la semana y los fines de semana
2. actividades de diversión (o deportivas) que hacen juntos, cuándo y dónde
3. actividades preferidas del fin de semana

SEGUNDA FASE. Preparen una lista de sus actividades semejantes o diferentes. Comparen su lista con la de otra pareja (*pair*).

MODELO: *Durante la semana, nosotros almorzamos en la cafetería de la universidad. ¿Y ustedes?*

4-23 Una reunión. En su universidad hay un fin de semana cuando los padres visitan a sus hijos en el campus. Ustedes quieren organizar una reunión para las familias de los miembros de su grupo. Decidan lo siguiente:

1. lugar y hora de la reunión
2. número de niños y adultos que van a participar (especifiquen la relación familiar)
3. comida y bebida que piensan servir
4. actividades y diversiones para los niños y para los adultos

---

En directo

These expressions help maintain the flow of conversation:

¡Cuánto me alegro!
I am so happy for you!

Claro, claro...
Of course . . .

¡Qué bien/bueno!
That's great!

SITUACIONES

1. **Role A.** You and a member of your family are planning to visit Latin America. Your friend has heard about your plans and calls with some questions. Answer your friend's questions in as much detail as possible.

   Role B. Your friend is planning to go to Latin America with a relative. Call to find out a) when he/she is planning to go; b) with whom; c) what country and cities he/she wants to visit and why; d) if his/her relative prefers to go to other places; and e) when they are returning.

2. **Role A.** The entire family has gathered for a party for the holidays. An elderly aunt/uncle is very curious about your life in college. After commenting on the party and several family members, answer her/his questions politely.

   Role B. You are at a family holiday gathering and you are very happy to see your young nephew/niece who is in college. After commenting on the party and several family members, ask about these aspects of college life: a) his/her classes; b) which class(es) he/she prefers; c) if the food is good; d) when vacation (**vacaciones**) starts; and e) what he/she plans to do after college.

2. Expressing obligation: *Tener que + infinitive*

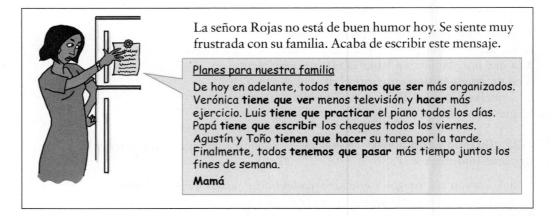

La señora Rojas no está de buen humor hoy. Se siente muy frustrada con su familia. Acaba de escribir este mensaje.

Planes para nuestra familia

De hoy en adelante, todos **tenemos que ser** más organizados. Verónica **tiene que ver** menos televisión y **hacer** más ejercicio. Luis **tiene que practicar** el piano todos los días. Papá **tiene que escribir** los cheques todos los viernes. Agustín y Toño **tienen que hacer** su tarea por la tarde. Finalmente, todos **tenemos que pasar** más tiempo juntos los fines de semana.

Mamá

Piénselo. Según el texto anterior, asocie la situación de la columna izquierda con la obligación de cada persona en la columna derecha.

1. _____ Verónica mira mucha televisión.
2. _____ La madre tiene planes para todos.
3. _____ El padre no se preocupa de los cheques.
4. _____ Luis no es muy constante con la música.
5. _____ Agustín y Toño probablemente prefieren practicar deportes y no estudian.
6. _____ Cada miembro de la familia hace sus actividades independientemente.

a. Todos **tienen que pensar** en la importancia de hacer actividades en familia.
b. **Tienen que dedicar** suficiente tiempo a sus estudios.
c. **Tiene que hacer** más actividades físicas.
d. **Tiene que colaborar** con su esposa.
e. **Tiene que practicar** regularmente.
f. La familia **tiene que organizar** sus actividades.

■ **Tener que +** *infinitive*. Use **tener que** to express what someone *has to*, *needs to*, or *must* do.

Eliana, **tienes que estudiar** más.　　　　*Eliana, you have to study more.*

Tengo que visitar a mis abuelos este fin de semana.　　*I have to visit my grandparents this weekend.*

4-24 Mis obligaciones. PRIMERA FASE. Marque (✓) las tareas que usted tiene que hacer regularmente. Luego compare sus obligaciones con las de otro compañero/otra compañera.

___ sacar a caminar al perro　　　　___ poner los platos sucios en el lavaplatos (*dishwasher*)
___ hacer ejercicio　　　　___ escuchar los mensajes (*messages*) telefónicos
___ comprar comida　　　　___ ir a la universidad
___ hacer la tarea para sus clases　　　　___ trabajar por las tardes
___ revisar el aceite (*oil*) del carro　　　　___ visitar a mis parientes

SEGUNDA FASE. Ahora dígale (*tell*) a su compañero/a cuándo usted tiene que hacer cada tarea. Luego compare sus obligaciones con las de él/ella.

MODELO:　E1: *Tengo que poner la mesa todos los días. ¿Y tú?*
　　　　　E2: *Yo no tengo que poner la mesa, pero tengo que*
　　　　　　　preparar la comida los domingos.

4-25 Un viaje (*trip*) a Colombia. PRIMERA FASE. Su familia va a viajar a Colombia. Escoja la mejor recomendación para cada persona.

1. ___ Mariela quiere visitar un lugar interesante para una persona religiosa.
2. ___ A mis padres les gustaría ver el trabajo que se hace con metales preciosos en Colombia.
3. ___ Mi prima Mónica quiere escuchar música colombiana.
4. ___ Mis abuelitos prefieren las actividades al aire libre.

a. Tiene que asistir a un concierto de Los Príncipes del Vallenato.
b. Tiene que ir a la Catedral de Sal.
c. Tienen que ir al Museo del Oro.
d. Tienen que conocer el Parque Ecológico El Portal.

> ### *Cultura*
>
> El Portal is an ecological park near Bucaramanga, in the northeastern part of Colombia. With its natural springs and wooded trails, it is a well-known destination for ecotourism. Guests may visit a working sugar mill, and they may also enjoy activities such as horseback riding and mountain biking.

SEGUNDA FASE. Preparen una breve descripción de uno de los lugares o eventos mencionados en la *Primera fase*. Incluyan la localización y las actividades que las personas hacen allí. Luego, compartan la información con la clase.

1. los Príncipes de Vallenato
2. la Catedral de Sal
3. el Museo del Oro
4. el Parque Ecológico El Portal

4-26 Sugerencias. PRIMERA FASE. ¿Qué tienen que hacer (o no) las personas en estas circunstancias?

MODELO: Luis no tiene dinero (*money*).
 E1: *¿Qué tiene que hacer Luis?*
 E2: *Tiene que leer el periódico para encontrar trabajo.*

1. Mi amigo Juan tiene un examen el lunes.
2. Francisco siempre está cansado.
3. Manuel y Victoria no tienen una buena relación de pareja (*couple*).
4. Mi hermana Marta ve televisión todos los días y saca malas notas en sus clases.
5. Luis y Emilia quieren aprender español.
6. Isabel y Lucía desean visitar un país hispano, pero no hablan español.

SEGUNDA FASE. Escriban individualmente tres circunstancias. Cada persona explica sus circunstancias y su compañero/a dice qué tiene que hacer.

3. Expressing when, where, or how an action occurs: Adverbs

Sierra de Santa
Marta, Colombia

Los senderistas (*hikers*) siguen una ruta difícil y tienen que caminar **lentamente**. Si van **rápidamente** van a estar cansados. Cruzan el riachuelo (*creek*) **cuidadosamente**. Hay animales peligrosos en la sierra, pero **afortunadamente** es otoño y **seguramente** no encuentran serpientes.

Piénselo. Asocie la expresión en negrita (*bold*) en la columna izquierda con su significado (*meaning*) en la columna derecha.

1. ___ Los senderistas piensan escalar **poco a poco**.
2. ___ Si los senderistas suben la montaña **con rapidez**, ellos van a estar cansados.
3. ___ **Por suerte**, ahora es otoño.
4. ___ Los senderistas **saben que** no van a encontrar serpientes.
5. ___ Cruzan el riachuelo **con mucha atención**.

a. rápidamente
b. afortunadamente
c. seguramente
d. cuidadosamente
e. lentamente

■ Adverbs are used to describe when, where, and how an action/event takes place. You may already be familiar with adverbs referring to time (**mañana, siempre, después**) and place (**allí, abajo, afuera**), and you have used adverbs to express how you feel (**bien, muy mal, regular**). These adverbs can also be used to express how things are done.

Diego nada **bien**, pero yo nado muy **mal**.   *Diego swims well, but I swim badly.*

■ Many Spanish adverbs end in **-mente**, an ending that corresponds to the English *-ly*. To form these adverbs, add **-mente** to the feminine singular form of the adjective. With adjectives that do not have a separate feminine form, simply add **-mente** to the singular form.

Abuelita camina **lentamente**.   *Grandma walks slowly.*

Mis tíos cantan **alegremente** en las fiestas.   *My aunts and uncles sing happily at parties.*

■ When two or more adverbs are used in a series, only the last one has the **-mente** ending. The other adverbs in the series have the same form as the feminine singular form of the adjective.

La profesora habla **clara** y **lentamente**.   *The professor speaks clearly and slowly.*

Siempre ganan **rápida** y **fácilmente** el partido.   *They always win the game quickly and easily.*

■ Some commonly used adverbs ending in **-mente** are:

básicamente	**lógicamente**	**realmente**	**simplemente**
frecuentemente	**normalmente**	**regularmente**	**tradicionalmente**
generalmente	**perfectamente**	**relativamente**	**tranquilamente**

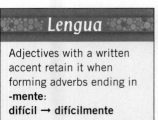

Lengua

Adjectives with a written accent retain it when forming adverbs ending in **-mente**:
difícil → difícilmente

4-27 ¿Está de acuerdo o no? PRIMERA FASE. Las características de la familia pueden variar entre una comunidad y otra. Indique si usted está de acuerdo (**Sí** o **No**) con las siguientes afirmaciones.

En mi comunidad...

1. _____ los padres frecuentemente hablan con los hijos adolescentes sobre temas importantes.
2. _____ los nietos regularmente visitan a sus abuelos.
3. _____ generalmente los hijos solteros viven con sus padres.
4. _____ los padres siempre hablan lentamente cuando están enojados con sus hijos.
5. _____ idealmente el padre trabaja fuera de casa y la madre trabaja en casa.
6. _____ los hijos adolescentes siempre tratan a sus padres cortésmente.

SEGUNDA FASE. Comparen sus respuestas y digan por qué están de acuerdo.

MODELO: E1: *Estoy de acuerdo con el número uno. Generalmente los padres hablan sobre temas importantes con sus hijos.*
E2: *No estoy de acuerdo. Los padres generalmente hablan sobre educación o dinero, pero no hablan de drogas.*

4-28 ¿Lenta o rápidamente? Escriba tres actividades de la siguiente lista que usted hace rápidamente y tres que hace lentamente. Indique el lugar y/o las circunstancias.

almorzar	escribir composiciones	hablar español	pasear
beber	estudiar	leer el periódico	tomar apuntes

MODELO: *Como rápidamente cuando tengo poco tiempo.*

4-29 ¿Cómo lo hace usted? Primero, individualmente escriba cómo o cuándo usted hace las siguientes actividades. Usando las palabras en la lista u otras, forme adverbios para escribir sus frases. Luego, comparen sus respuestas.

difícil	frecuente	lógico	perfecto
fácil	lento	ocasional	rápido

1. caminar cuando usted está muy cansado/a
2. pensar en la clase de matemáticas
3. respirar (*breathe*) después de una hora de ejercicio en el gimnasio
4. responder en un examen fácil

4-30 Actividades frecuentes. PRIMERA FASE. Hágale estas preguntas a su compañero/a. Después él/ella tiene que hacerle las mismas (*same*) preguntas a usted. Tome apuntes sobre las respuestas de su compañero/a.

1. ¿Qué haces normalmente con tu familia?
2. ¿A qué lugares vas regularmente con tu familia? ¿Y con tus amigos?
3. Generalmente, ¿sales por las noches? ¿Adónde vas y con quién?
4. ¿A quiénes llamas por teléfono más frecuentemente, a tus amigos o a tu familia?

SEGUNDA FASE. Ahora escriba una breve comparación entre usted y su compañero/a con respecto a cada pregunta en la *Primera fase*. ¿Hacen ustedes actividades semejantes o diferentes?

En directo

To express surprise at what you hear:

¡Qué increíble!
Incredible!

¡No me diga(s)!
Really!

SITUACIONES

1. **Role A.** Your class is conducting a survey regarding students' movie habits. Ask a classmate a) when and with whom he/she generally goes to the movies; b) the type of movies he/she normally prefers (**románticas, dramáticas, de ciencia ficción**, etc.); c) what he/she often eats or drinks at the movies; and d) the name of his/her favorite movie.

   Role B. Answer the questions a classmate will ask about your movie preferences.

2. **Role A.** In your Sociology and the Family course, you are helping to conduct a survey about family traditions and activities. Ask a classmate a) if the members of his/her immediate family generally eat together; b) if they visit other family members frequently; and c) which family member normally organizes family gatherings.

   Role B. First answer your classmate's questions about your family. Then ask him/her these questions for the survey: a) Who is generally more organized (**organizado/a**) at home, men or women?; b) Do family members frequently do activities together?; c) Who prepares dinner well in the family?; d) Who talks calmly when angry, your father or your mother?

4. Expressing how long something has been going on: *Hace* with expressions of time

PATRICIA: Señora, **¿cuánto tiempo hace que** practico esta sonata? ¡Estoy muy cansada!

SRA. ESCOBEDO: **Hace dos horas que** trabajas en ella. Pero una vez más, por favor, Patricia. El recital es en dos días.

Sra. Escobedo   Patricia

SRA. ESCOBEDO: Les presento a Patricia Suárez. Estudia el violín conmigo **hace cinco años.** Ahora va a tocar la Sonata N° 4 de Mozart.

Piénselo. Diga si las siguientes afirmaciones son lógicas (**L**) o ilógicas (**I**).

1. ＿＿ **Hace mucho tiempo que** Patricia toca el violín perfectamente.
2. ＿＿ **Hace cinco años que** Patricia no pasa mucho tiempo con sus amigos porque tiene que practicar la sonata.
3. ＿＿ Patricia conoce a la profesora de violín **hace cinco años.**
4. ＿＿ **Hace sólo un día que** Patricia trabaja en la sonata de Mozart.
5. ＿＿ **Hace poco tiempo que** la señora Escobedo toca el violín.
6. ＿＿ Los padres de Patricia no le pagan a la profesora por las clases de violín **hace un año.**

■ To say that an action/state began in the past and continues into the present, use **hace +** *length of time* **+ que +** *present tense.*

Hace dos horas que juegan.   *They have been playing for two hours.*

■ If you begin the sentence with the present tense of the verb, do not use **que.**

Juegan **hace dos horas.**   *They've been playing for two hours.*

■ To find out how long an action/state has been taking place, use **cuánto tiempo + hace que +** *present tense.*

¿Cuánto tiempo hace que juegan?   *How long have they been playing?*

¿Cuántas horas hace que los niños juegan al fútbol?   *How many hours have the children been playing soccer?*

4-31 Este soy yo. PRIMERA FASE. Lea esta descripción y conteste las preguntas.

Me llamo Jaime Caicedo y soy de Cali, Colombia. Quiero aprender inglés para poder trabajar en una compañía internacional. Estudio inglés **hace dos años**, pero tengo que estudiar más para hablar correctamente. Siempre miro programas de televisión en inglés. Mis favoritos son *American Idol* y *Grey's Anatomy*. **Hace dos años que** miro estos programas y me gustan mucho. Tengo un auto **hace un año**, y salgo en él con mis amigos y también con mi novia. **Hace seis meses que** somos novios. Somos muy felices.

1. Jaime Caicedo es de...
   a. Estados Unidos. b. Cali. c. *Grey's Anatomy*.
2. Hace dos años que Jaime...
   a. tiene novia. b. va al cine. c. mira televisión en inglés.
3. Hace seis meses que Jaime...
   a. va a fiestas. b. estudia inglés. c. tiene novia.

SEGUNDA FASE. Ahora escriba su propia descripción, siguiendo el modelo en la *Primera fase*. Luego, comparta su descripción con un compañero/una compañera.

Me llamo (1) _____ . Soy de (2) _____ ,
(3) _____ (ciudad y país). Quiero aprender (4) _____
(lengua extranjera) porque (5) _____ . Estudio
(6) _____ (lengua extranjera) hace (7) _____ (período
de tiempo), pero tengo que estudiar más para hablar
correctamente. Miro (8) _____ películas como _____
(películas en español) y escucho la música de (9) _____
(cantante o grupo español) para aprender más.
Mi programa favorito es (10) _____ . Hace
(11) _____ (período de tiempo) que (12) _____
el programa y me gusta mucho. En mi tiempo libre,
(13) _____ . Tengo (14) _____ (vehículo/objeto o
animal) hace (15) _____ . Hace (16) _____ (período
de tiempo) que estudio en (17) _____ (nombre de la
universidad). Espero ser (18) _____ (profesión)
(19) _____ en el futuro.

4-32 ¿Cuánto tiempo hace que...? Túrnense para hacerse las siguientes preguntas. Después compartan la información con otra pareja.

1. ¿Dónde vive tu familia? ¿Cuánto tiempo hace que viven allí?
2. ¿Dónde trabajas? ¿Cuánto tiempo hace que trabajas allí?
3. ¿Cuánto tiempo hace que estudias en esta universidad? ¿Y por qué estudias español?
4. ¿Practicas algún deporte? ¿Cuánto tiempo hace que juegas al...? ¿Juegas bien?

SITUACIONES

1. **Role A.** You live in Queens, New York, and a friend has come to visit. Explain that there are many Hispanic restaurants in this neighborhood (**barrio**). You suggest your favorite Colombian restaurant for dinner. When your friend asks about the Colombian food that they serve, you may want to mention **ajiaco de pollo** (a chicken stew made with potatoes, corn, and cream), **papas chorreadas** (potatoes covered with a sauce made with onions, tomatoes and milk), and **arroz con coco** (rice cooked in coconut milk).

   Role B. You are visiting a friend in Queens, New York. He/She suggests a Colombian restaurant for dinner. Ask a) how long he/she has been living in Queens; b) if he/she knows the restaurant well; c) what Colombian dishes they serve, and what they are like; and d) how much they cost.

2. **Role A.** You go to see your counselor (**consejero/a**) to talk about a personal problem (**un problema**). Greet the counselor and explain your problem. Answer the counselor's questions in as much detail as possible. When the session is over, thank the counselor.

   Role B. You are a student counselor (**consejero/a**). A student comes to you with a problem (**un problema**). Exchange greetings and ask a) how long the student has been at the university; b) how long he/she has been having the problem; and c) what he/she is doing to solve (**resolver**) the problem and for how long. Finally, suggest several things he/she has to do to improve (**mejorar**) the situation.

5. Talking about daily routine: Reflexive verbs and pronouns

Yo **me llamo** Óscar Torres. Mi esposa Rosa y yo tenemos una vida muy ocupada. Nosotros **nos levantamos** a las seis todos los días. Yo **me ducho** mientras Rosa se viste rápidamente. Después, Rosa **despierta** a Carlitos y a Roberto, nuestros hijos. Roberto **se viste**, y Rosa **viste** a Carlitos. Desayunamos y luego todos **nos lavamos** los dientes y a las siete salimos de la casa.

Piénselo. Para cada acción, indique si cada persona hace la acción a sí misma(s) (*him/her/themselves*) o a otra persona.

ACCIÓN	A SÍ MISMO/A	A OTRA PERSONA
1. Óscar **se ducha** por la mañana.	——	——
2. Rosa **despierta** a Carlitos.	——	——
3. La madre **viste** al niño porque es muy pequeño.	——	——
4. Roberto **se viste** rápidamente.	——	——
5. Nosotros **nos lavamos** los dientes después de desayunar.	——	——
6. Rosa probablemente **se baña** por la noche, porque no tiene tiempo por la mañana.	——	——

■ Reflexive verbs express what people do to or for themselves.

REFLEXIVE: Mi hermana **se lava**.   *My sister washes (herself).*

NONREFLEXIVE: Mi hermana **lava** el auto.   *My sister washes the car.*

LAVARSE (*to wash oneself*)	
yo **me lavo**	nosotros/as **nos lavamos**
tú **te lavas**	vosotros/as **os laváis**
Ud., él, ella **se lava**	Uds., ellos/as **se lavan**

■ A reflexive pronoun refers back to the subject of the sentence. English sometimes uses the pronouns ending in *-self/-selves* to express reflexive meaning. In many cases, Spanish uses reflexives where English does not.

Yo **me levanto, me ducho, me seco** y   *I get up, take a shower, dry*
   me visto rápidamente.   *myself, and get dressed quickly.*

■ Place reflexive pronouns after the word **no** in negative constructions.

Rosa **no se ducha** por la mañana.   *Rosa does not take a shower in the morning.*

■ The pronoun **se** attached to the end of an infinitive indicates the verb is reflexive.

vestir	*to dress (someone else)*
vestirse	*to get dressed (oneself)*

■ With a conjugated verb followed by an infinitive, place the reflexive pronoun before the conjugated verb or attach it to the infinitive.

Yo **me** voy a levantar a las siete. ⎫
Yo voy a levantar**me** a las siete. ⎬ *I am going to get up at seven.*

■ When referring to parts of the body and articles of clothing, use definite articles rather than possessives with reflexive verbs.

Me lavo **los** dientes.	*I brush my teeth.*
Roberto se pone **la** chaqueta.	*Roberto puts on his jacket.*

■ Some verbs change meaning when used reflexively.

acostar	*to put to bed*	**acostarse**	*to go to bed, to lie down*
dormir	*to sleep*	**dormirse**	*to fall asleep*
levantar	*to raise, to lift*	**levantarse**	*to get up*
llamar	*to call*	**llamarse**	*to be called*
poner	*to put, to place*	**ponerse**	*to put on*
quitar	*to take away*	**quitarse**	*to take off*

4-33 ¿Qué hacemos todos los días? Ponga estas actividades en el orden más lógico.

____ Me duermo.   ____ Salgo para mis clases. ____ Me lavo la cara (*face*).
____ Me levanto.   ____ Me acuesto.   ____ Desayuno.

4-34 ¿Tenemos las mismas rutinas? Hablen sobre sus actividades diarias.

MODELO: despertarse
          E1: *Yo me despierto a las siete. ¿Y tú?*
          E2: *Generalmente, me despierto a las ocho.*

1. levantarse   3. vestirse   5. acostarse
2. ducharse   4. desayunar   6. dormirse

4-35 Los horarios. PRIMERA FASE. Usen la información en la tabla para escribir un párrafo sobre el horario de las hermanas gemelas (*twins*) Alicia y Blanca y su hermanito Carlitos.

	CARLITOS	ALICIA Y BLANCA	YO
despertarse	8:00	7:00	
levantarse	8:15	7:05	
bañarse	8:20	7:10	
vestirse	8:30	7:20	

SEGUNDA FASE. Ahora escriba individualmente sus actividades en la tabla. Luego, hablen de su horario y hagan comparaciones entre su horario y el de las personas de la *Primera fase*.

SITUACIONES

1. **Role A.** A young person in your family has to do a report for school based on an interview of a family member. That person is going to interview you. Exchange greetings and answer his/her questions as completely as possible.

   Role B. You are a middle school student who has to write a report about a family member (your classmate). Greet him/her and explain the purpose of the interview. Then find out a) where he/she lives and for how long he/she has lived there; b) what his/her daily routine is; and c) some differences between the routine of a college student and that of a middle school student.

2. **Role A.** You live in Bogota, and you would like your niece to attend a summer camp (**campamento de verano**) in the United States so she will learn English. Ask the camp director questions to find out a) how many children there are per counselor (**por consejero/a**); b) what time the children get up; c) what sports they play; d) what they eat; e) what they do in the evenings; and f) what time they go to bed.

   Role B. You are the director of the summer camp (**campamento de verano**). Answer the questions of the aunt/uncle of a prospective camper. Add as much information as possible.

MOSAICOS

A escuchar

Antes de escuchar

4-36 Preparación. Usted va a escuchar el mensaje de Pedro para Julio sobre una fiesta sorpresa (*surprise*) que está organizando Pedro. Antes de escuchar, escriba el propósito (*purpose*) posible de un mensaje como este. ¿A qué información específica es importante poner atención?

propósito posible: _____

información específica: _____

Escuchar

4-37 ¿Comprende usted? First read the information you will need to have in order to attend the party Pedro is organizing. Then, as you listen, complete the sentences with the rest of the information. Don't worry if you do not understand every word.

CD 2
Track 21

1. La fiesta es para…
2. La fiesta va a ser en la casa de…
3. El día de la fiesta es…
4. Julio debe llevar (*take*)…
5. Julio tiene que llegar a la casa a las…
6. La dirección es…

Después de escuchar

4-38 Ahora usted. Usted va a dar una fiesta sorpresa para un amigo/una amiga en la clase de español y desea invitar a su profesor/a de español. Complete la nota que usted va a poner en el buzón (*mailbox*) de su profesor/a.

> Estimado/a profesor/a _____:
>
> Este fin de semana, pienso dar una fiesta sorpresa para _____.
>
> ¿Le gustaría venir? Vamos a comer _____ y _____. Vamos a tener refrescos para todos.
>
> La fiesta va a ser el _____ en mi casa a las _____ de la noche. Mi dirección es _____.
>
> Lo/La espero el _____.
>
> Hasta pronto.
>
> _____

ESTRATEGIA

Listen for a purpose

Listening with a purpose in mind will help you focus your attention on what is important and relevant to meet your goal. As you focus your attention, you screen what you hear and select only the information you need, letting go of what seems irrelevant to your purpose.

A conversar

Antes de conversar

4-39 Preparación. Complete las siguientes afirmaciones con los nombres de sus parientes, la relación de parentesco y sus actividades.

MODELO: *Mi primo David come* en restaurantes los fines de semana.

1. ... cerveza frecuentemente cuando mira(n) fútbol en la televisión.
2. ... mucho y con frecuencia está(n) cansado/a(s).
3. ... a conciertos de música popular.
4. ... en casa los fines de semana. Descansan, leen, escuchan música, etc.
5. ... ejercicio físico tres o cuatro veces por semana.
6. ... con amigos o con la familia en casa el día de su cumpleaños.
7. ... música romántica a todas horas.
8. ... por el teléfono celular. Llama(n) a sus amigos día y noche.

Conversar

4-40 Entre nosotros. Conteste las preguntas de sus compañeros/as con los nombres de los miembros de su familia para comparar las dos categorías.

MODELO: E1: *¿Quiénes son las personas artísticas en tu familia, las mujeres o los hombres?*
E2: *En mi familia, las mujeres son muy artísticas. Por ejemplo, mi hermana Carlota pinta y escribe poemas. En contraste con las mujeres, los hombres son deportistas. Mi primo Alberto, por ejemplo, practica tenis y fútbol.*

1. ¿Quiénes son las personas activas en tu familia, las mujeres o los hombres?
2. ¿Qué miembros de la familia pasan mucho tiempo en casa, los jóvenes o los mayores?
3. ¿Quiénes son muy sociables, las mujeres o los hombres, los jóvenes o los mayores? ¿Por qué?

Después de conversar

4-41 Un poco más. Completen un pequeño informe (*report*) con la información de su grupo de la actividad **4-40**. Luego compartan la información con el resto de la clase.

1. En nuestras familias (los hombres/las mujeres) _____ son muy activos/as. Por ejemplo, _____. Por otro lado, _____ no son muy activos. Por ejemplo, _____.
2. (Los jóvenes/Los mayores) _____ pasan mucho tiempo en casa porque _____. Por ejemplo, _____ . En cambio, _____ no pasan mucho tiempo en casa porque _____. Por ejemplo, _____ .
3. (Las mujeres/Los hombres/Los jóvenes/Los mayores) _____ son muy sociables. Por ejemplo, _____ . En contraste, _____ no son muy sociables. Por ejemplo, _____ .

Use title and illustrations to anticipate content

Before you start to read, it is important to gather as much information about the text as possible. The title, section headings, and illustrations can help you anticipate content, so pay special attention to them before you start to read. Verbalize to yourself (aloud or by writing notes) what you think the text is about, and refer to your notes as you are reading, correcting them as necessary. This will help you focus on understanding each section of the text as you read it.

A leer

Antes de leer

4-42 Preparación. Lea el título y los subtítulos del artículo a continuación y observe las fotos. Luego, use la información del título, los subtítulos y las fotos para contestar las siguientes preguntas.

1. Basándose en el título del artículo, los subtítulos, las fotos y sus leyendas (*captions*), adivine el tema del artículo.
   a. la comunicación entre amigos
   b. la comunicación entre los miembros de una familia
   c. la comunicación con los colegas en el trabajo

2. En su opinión, ¿cuáles de las siguientes ideas va a incluir el artículo? (Hay más de una respuesta correcta.)
   a. Hoy en día la comunicación entre padres e hijos es mejor que (*better than*) en el pasado.
   b. Los jóvenes no hablan con sus padres sobre sus problemas porque los padres siempre están ocupados.
   c. La vida moderna afecta la comunicación entre padres e hijos.
   d. La tecnología tiende a reducir la comunicación sobre temas importantes.

3. Marque (✓) las actividades de la siguiente lista que usted asocia usted con una buena relación entre padres e hijos.

   a. ___ conversar
   b. ___ pasar tiempo juntos
   c. ___ hablar por teléfono
   d. ___ pelear (*argue*)
   e. ___ escribir correos electrónicos a un miembro de la familia que vive lejos (*far*)

   f. ___ comprar regalos con frecuencia
   g. ___ expresar cariño (*affection*) verbalmente
   h. ___ no hablar de sus problemas con los padres

Leer

4-43 Primera mirada. Lea los dos primeros párrafos del texto y siga las instrucciones.

Subraye (*Underline*)…

1. las palabras en el título que probablemente indican el tema del artículo.
2. una palabra que describe la condición de la familia de hoy.
3. una palabra que indica la importancia de la comunicación dentro de la familia.

Escriba…

4. una causa de los problemas de comunicación en la familia.
5. dos necesidades de los hijos que tienen padres que trabajan fuera de casa.
6. dos efectos de la ausencia de los padres de la casa.

La importancia de la comunicación familiar

La familia en crisis

Los expertos afirman que la familia de hoy está en crisis por la falta[1] de comunicación entre sus miembros o por la mala comunicación que existe entre ellos. También dicen que la comunicación es vital en todas las relaciones, especialmente en las relaciones familiares.

La comunicación entre padres e hijos sobre temas importantes forma relaciones familiares fuertes y cariñosas.

Ausencia de los padres

¿Por qué hay problemas de comunicación en las familias? Hay varias razones. Una razón es que la madre y el padre trabajan largas horas fuera de casa y los hijos están solos mucho tiempo, sin la compañía y la supervisión de sus mayores. La ausencia casi todos los días de los padres puede crear cierta independencia en los hijos y una distancia emocional que causa dificultades en la comunicación entre padres e hijos.

La tecnología

Un segundo factor es la tecnología. Nuestro mundo está controlado por la tecnología en casa, en el trabajo, etc. Evidentemente la tecnología facilita muchas cosas, pero su uso excesivo puede complicar la vida. Un gran número de hogares[2] están conectados a Internet, así que muchos jóvenes tienen acceso ilimitado al correo electrónico y a la Red, sobre todo a los sitios web de comunicación social y entretenimiento, como MySpace y YouTube. Idealmente, el bajo costo de la conexión debería afectar positivamente la comunicación en la familia, pero la realidad indica que la comunicación moderna (e.g., correo electrónico, mensajes de texto) tiende a ser más breve y más superficial. Los hijos prefieren no discutir sus problemas por correo electrónico o mensajes de texto. Prefieren hablar directamente con sus padres, si es que sus padres tienen el tiempo. Lo mismo ocurre con el teléfono celular. Es cierto que muchos jóvenes usan celulares para llamar a sus padres, pero no muchos usan el celular para conversar largamente con sus padres sobre temas personales importantes. ¡Muy pocos!

La tecnología puede facilitar la comunicación familiar.

Conclusión

En conclusión, el tiempo limitado que los padres pueden dar a sus hijos y la tendencia a usar la tecnología para comunicaciones muy breves pueden afectar negativamente las relaciones familiares. Por eso es importante crear oportunidades para una comunicación real y profunda dentro de la familia. Si usted usa la tecnología de manera positiva para pasar tiempo con sus familiares y para expresar el amor y el cariño que siente por ellos, su familia va a ser más fuerte y unida.

[1]lack   [2]homes

4-44 Segunda mirada. Ahora lea el resto del artículo y siga las indicaciones.

En el párrafo sobre la tecnología, el artículo presenta otra razón de la mala comunicación entre padres e hijos.

Indique...

1. una palabra asociada con los problemas de comunicación familiares.
2. por qué la tecnología probablemente afecta las relaciones de la familia.
3. dos ejemplos de cómo la tecnología puede causar problemas en la familia.
4. dos palabras que indican la calidad de la comunicación cuando usamos el correo electrónico o los mensajes de texto.
5. dos formas de usar la tecnología positivamente en la comunicación con la familia.

Después de leer

4-45 Ampliación. Se pueden aplicar las ideas del artículo a la situación de los estudiantes que viven en la universidad y ya no viven en casa con su familia. Hable con su compañero/a sobre el impacto en la comunicación familiar entre los estudiantes universitarios y sus padres. Enfóquese (*Focus*) en los dos temas principales del artículo:

■ la separación física entre los padres y los hijos
■ el uso de la tecnología como medio de comunicación

A escribir

En directo

To write a salutation:

Querido papá/abuelo:
Dear ...,

Querida mamá/abuelita:
Dear ...,

To close correspondence:

Con cariño,
Affectionately,

Con mucho cariño,
With much love,

Abrazos y besos,
Hugs and kisses,

Te recuerdo con cariño,
I remember you
(familiar) *with affection,*

ESTRATEGIA

Choose between informal and formal language to express the desired tone

Choosing the appropriate level of formality when you write to someone depends on your relationship to that person. When writing to elders in your family, such as parents or grandparents, a more formal tone may be needed than when writing to friends. The abbreviated format and casual language of computer-based communication may not be the best choice to show your elders love and respect. When you write to them, either in letters or on the computer, choose your language more carefully and write about issues more seriously than you would when corresponding with friends.

The salutation, closing, and forms of address used in letter writing also reflect your degree of closeness and formality. The expressions in *En directo* include some common salutations and forms of address that are appropriate to use when you write to elders in your family.

Antes de escribir

4-46 Preparación. **PRIMERA FASE.** La madre de Julián, un alumno universitario colombiano, está triste y preocupada porque su hijo estudia en la Universidad de los Andes y vive lejos de casa. Ella le escribe la siguiente carta a su hijo. Lea la carta.

Querido Julián:

¿Qué tal estás? ¿Cómo van tus clases? Hace un mes que no tenemos información sobre ti. ¡No escribes correos electrónicos, no llamas por teléfono! ¿Qué ocurre?

Bueno, es el fin del semestre y debes tener mucho trabajo. ¿Estás muy estresado? ¿Duermes suficiente? ¿Comes bien en la universidad? En tu próxima visita, pienso preparar tus platos favoritos. Tu hermana Mariela, tus abuelos y tíos van a estar con nosotros y vamos a conversar largas horas.

Tengo una sorpresa para ti. Gustavo tiene novia. Se llama Alicia. Pasan mucho tiempo juntos; van al cine, salen a comer por las noches, etc. La semana próxima ambos tienen vacaciones y, para conocerla un poco más, Gustavo piensa ir a Cartagena con ella. Las temperaturas allí están perfectas para nadar y descansar un poco.

Tengo que confesarte que tu padre y yo pensamos mucho en ti. ¿Por qué no escribes? ¿Tienes problemas en tus clases? ¿Trabajas mucho? ¿Estás desconectado de Internet? Por favor, escribe o llama pronto.

Un beso de papá, Mariela y toda la familia.

Abrazos,

Tu madre

SEGUNDA FASE. Usted es Julián. Prepárese para responder a la carta de su madre. Haga lo siguiente:

1. Identifique las preguntas de su madre que usted quiere contestar y escriba algunas ideas que piensa incluir. Seleccione las palabras adecuadas para lograr (*achieve*) el tono adecuado.
2. Escriba algunas preguntas que usted quiere hacerle a su madre: sobre su padre, sus hermanos, sus abuelos, su perro o gato, etc.

Escribir

4-47 Manos a la obra. Ahora responda a la carta de su madre. Use la información de la *Segunda fase* de la actividad **4-46**. Seleccione cuidadosamente las palabras para mostrar respeto a su madre. Recuerde incluir la fecha, un saludo y una despedida (*closing*) apropiados.

Querida madre:

Después de escribir

4-48 Revisión. Revise los siguientes aspectos de su carta.

1. Primero, el grado de intimidad (*intimacy*) y formalidad para comunicarse con su madre. ¿Incluye usted un saludo y una despedida apropiados en la carta? ¿Usa usted el vocabulario adecuado para dirigirse (*address*) a su madre?
2. La coherencia de sus ideas y la cantidad de información que su madre probablemente desea
3. Luego, la precisión gramatical: la estructura de las oraciones, la concordancia, etc.
4. Finalmente, la ortografía, la acentuación

ENFOQUE CULTURAL

La riqueza de Colombia

Normalmente asociamos a Colombia con el café de Juan Valdez, un personaje inventado por las agencias de publicidad, como el representante de Colombia ante el mundo. En realidad, Colombia se conoce en todas partes por la calidad suave de su café y el símbolo de Juan Valdez es una de las imágenes corporativas más famosas del mundo. Sin embargo, Colombia es mucho más que su café. Su diversidad geográfica y climática, y la variedad natural, étnica y cultural de sus regiones hacen de Colombia un país con un inmenso potencial.

Para empezar, Colombia es el único país de América del Sur que tiene costas en los dos mares. La costa Atlántica, que es la región caribeña, tiene playas espectaculares, montañas impresionantes en la Sierra Nevada de Santa Marta, selvas tropicales en el Urabá y un desierto en La Guajira.

Las cinco regiones de Colombia continental

Los habitantes de la costa Atlántica tienen fama de tener un carácter alegre y festivo. La costa Pacífica es la región con mayor biodiversidad del mundo y es la región más lluviosa del planeta. Una gran parte de la población afro-colombiana habita en las dos costas.

En contraste, la Amazonía colombiana forma parte de la zona de selvas tropicales que se extienden a Perú, Brasil y Venezuela para formar el "pulmón del mundo". Se llama así porque es la zona donde se produce la mayor cantidad del oxígeno que respiramos. En esta región se hablan más de cien idiomas indígenas, y hay una gran variedad de animales y plantas. Los indígenas de la región usan muchas de estas plantas como medicinas y muchos científicos investigan los beneficios de estas plantas para la medicina. En la Amazonía, por ejemplo, hay una estación científica para el estudio de la malaria, donde el Dr. Manuel Patarroyo hace investigación para encontrar una vacuna contra esta enfermedad.

La región de los Llanos Orientales está formada por grandes praderas que se extienden a Venezuela. Colombia y Venezuela son dos países hermanos que están unidos por su historia y geografía. La ganadería y la agricultura son las actividades más importantes de esta región. En efecto, los llaneros o habitantes de esta región, son muy aficionados a los caballos y en las fiestas populares practican un deporte similar al rodeo para demostrar sus destrezas. Además, los Llanos Orientales son el hábitat de una gran variedad de aves, reptiles, mamíferos y peces. Esta es la única región de Colombia donde habita el oso hormiguero, un bello animal que come hormigas.

El oso hormiguero habita en los Llanos Orientales de Colombia.

Medellín, conocida como "la capital de la montaña"

La región andina de Colombia es la zona central del país. Precisamente en esta región, cerca de la ciudad de Armenia, se produce el mejor café de Colombia. Está formada por la Cordillera de los Andes y es el lugar donde vive la gran mayoría de los colombianos. Aquí están las ciudades más grandes del país: Bogotá, la capital; Medellín, la ciudad más industrial; Cali, la tercera ciudad más grande de Colombia. La mayoría de la clase media de Colombia vive en las ciudades de la zona central y aquí se encuentran también las universidades más importantes del país, que atraen a jóvenes de todas las regiones colombianas.

Además de las cinco regiones continentales, Colombia tiene una región insular. Las Islas de San Andrés y Providencia están en el Caribe y son un verdadero paraíso tropical. Sus playas blancas, las aguas cristalinas y tranquilas del mar, sus bellas palmeras y sus excelentes restaurantes hacen de estas islas un lugar ideal para el turismo. Las otras islas colombianas están en el Océano Pacífico y son una reserva natural y ecológica. Cerca de la Isla Gorgona se pueden ver ballenas durante gran parte del año.

En otras palabras

Expresiones colombianas

Sacar una A en español es difícil. Eso no es como **soplar y hacer botellas**.
To get an A in Spanish is hard. It is not as easy as it looks.

No puedo ir al cine. Tengo mucho **camello**.
I can't go to the movies. I have a lot of work.

Te llamo más tarde. Ahora **estoy de afán**.
I'll call you later. I'm in a hurry now.

151

4-49 Comprensión. PRIMERA FASE. **Reconocimiento de palabras clave.** Encuentre en el texto la palabra o expresión que mejor expresa el significado de las siguientes ideas.

1. mild, soft   _____
2. to begin with   _____
3. rainy   _____
4. lung   _____
5. research   _____
6. vaccine   _____
7. ant   _____

SEGUNDA FASE. **Oraciones importantes.** Subraye las afirmaciones que contienen ideas que se encuentran en el texto. Luego indique en qué parte del texto están.

1. Juan Valdez was created by a marketing agency.
2. The Pacific coast of Colombia is the rainiest region in the world.
3. Most of the oxygen in the Earth's atmosphere is produced in the Amazon region.
4. Manuel Patarroyo is a Colombian who is searching for a cure for HIV.
5. Spanish is the only language spoken in the Amazonian region of Colombia.
6. The Eastern Prairies (*Llanos Orientales*) of Colombia extend into Venezuela, giving these sister countries a common geography.
7. Different varieties of anteaters can be found all over Colombia.
8. Most Colombians live in the Andean region.

TERCERA FASE. **Ideas principales.** Escriba un párrafo breve en inglés resumiendo (*summarizing*) las ideas principales expresadas en el texto.

 4-50 Use la información. Prepare un afiche (*poster*) para hacer una presentación sobre dos colombianos famosos. Elija personas que representen áreas diferentes de la vida colombiana, como la política, las artes, la música, los deportes, etc. Incluya fotos y la siguiente información: lugar donde viven, el trabajo que hacen y otra información de interés. Para preparar esta actividad visite la página web de *Mosaicos* y siga los enlaces útiles.

VOCABULARIO

La familia	The family
la abuela	grandmother
el abuelo	grandfather
el ahijado/la ahijada	godchild
la esposa	wife
el esposo	husband
la hermana	sister
el hermano	brother
el hermanastro	stepbrother
la hermanastra	stepsister
la hija	daughter
el hijo	son
el hijo único/la hija única	only child
la madrastra	stepmother
la madre	mother
la madrina	godmother
la mamá	mom
la media hermana	half-sister
el medio hermano	half-brother
la nieta	granddaughter
el nieto	grandson
el niño/la niña	child
la novia	fiancée, girlfriend
el novio	fiancé, boyfriend
el padrastro	stepfather
el padre	father
los padres	parents
el padrino	godfather
el papá	dad
el pariente	relative
el primo/la prima	cousin
la sobrina	niece
el sobrino	nephew
la tía	aunt
el tío	uncle

Verbos	Verbs
acostar(se) (ue)	to put to bed; to go to bed
afeitar(se)	to shave; to shave (oneself)
almorzar (ue)	to have lunch
bañar(se)	to bathe; to take a bath
casar(se)	to get married
cerrar(ie)	to close
costar (ue)	to cost
decir (g, i)	to say, to tell
desayunar	to have breakfast
despertar(se) (ie)	to wake (someone up); to wake up
dormir(se) (ue)	to sleep; to fall asleep
dormir (ue) la siesta	to take a nap
duchar(se)	to give a shower to; to take a shower
empezar (ie)	to begin, to start

entender (ie)	to understand
jugar (ue)	to play (a game, sport)
lavar(se)	to wash (oneself)
levantar(se)	to raise; to get up
maquillar(se)	to put makeup on (someone); to put makeup on (oneself)
pasar	to spend (time)
pasear	to take a walk, to stroll
pedir (i)	to ask for; to order
peinar(se)	to comb (someone's hair); to comb (one's hair)
pensar (ie)	to think
pensar (ie) + infinitive	to plan to + verb
poder (ue)	to be able to, can
poner(se) (g) la ropa	to put one's clothes on
preferir (ie)	to prefer
querer (ie)	to want
quitar(se)	to take away; to take off
secar(se)	to dry (oneself)
seguir (i)	to follow, to go on
sentarse (ie)	to sit down
sentir(se) (ie)	to feel
servir (i)	to serve
tener (g, ie)	to have
venir (g, ie)	to come
vestir(se) (i)	to dress; to get dressed
visitar	to visit
volver (ue)	to return

Las descripciones	Descriptions
divorciado/a	divorced
gemelo/a	twin
ocupado/a	busy

Palabras y expresiones útiles	Useful words and expressions
el bautizo	baptism, christening
la derecha	right
la foto(grafía)	photo(graph)
la izquierda	left
juntos/as	together
el/la mayor	the oldest
el/la menor	the youngest
la noticia	news
tarde	late
temprano	early
un poco	a little

See *Lengua* box on page 129 for time expressions.
See *Lengua* box on page 134 for other expressions with *pensar*.
See page 138 for a list of adverbs.
See page 140 for time expressions with *hacer*.

Mi casa es su casa

Cuadro de un pueblo hondureño, Jorge Fermán, pintor de Honduras

In this chapter you will learn how to:

- discuss housing, furnishings, and architecture
- talk about daily chores and household activities
- talk about activities in progress
- describe physical and emotional states

Cultural focus: Nicaragua, El Salvador, Honduras

Mar Caribe

BELICE

MÉXICO

Ruinas mayas

HONDURAS

GUATEMALA

Copán   Tegucigalpa

El café

EL SALVADOR
San Salvador

NICARAGUA

Mango verde
con limón y sal

León

Managua

Un edificio de arquitectura colonial

Granada

El Volcán de Izalco

OCÉANO PACÍFICO

COSTA
RICA

PANAMÁ

 A vista de pájaro. Mire el mapa y después asocie la información de las dos columnas.

1. ___ Tegucigalpa…
2. ___ El mango verde con limón y sal…
3. ___ Al oeste de El Salvador…
4. ___ Las ruinas de Copán…
5. ___ El café…
6. ___ Granada y otras ciudades de Nicaragua…

a. es un plato típico de El Salvador.
b. es un producto de exportación de los tres países.
c. es la capital de Honduras.
d. tienen arquitectura colonial.
e. son de la civilización maya.
f. está el volcán de Izalco.

•)) En casa

CD 2
Track 26
or CD 3
Track 1

En las ciudades de Nicaragua, El Salvador y Honduras, hay **viviendas** de diferentes **estilos.** La ciudad de Granada, en Nicaragua, tiene **calles** y plazas como esta, con casas coloniales de colores alegres. En Tegucigalpa, la capital de Honduras, hay **edificios** de **apartamentos.** Algunas personas prefieren vivir **cerca** del **centro. Creen** que los **barrios** de las **afueras** están muy **lejos** del **trabajo** y de los centros de diversión.

Alquileres	
Categoría:	Alquiler Apartamentos
Ciudad:	Tegucigalpa
Ubicación:	Palmira
Descripción:	PALMIRA ALQUILER DE APARTAMENTO MUY AMPLIO, CÉNTRICO Y ACCESIBLE, 2 HABITACIONES, SALA–COMEDOR, COCINA, 1 BAÑO, ÁREA DE LAVANDERÍA, ESTACIONAMIENTO, TELÉFONO.
Precio:	$ 450,00

En otras palabras

Some words for the parts of a house vary from one region to another in the Spanish-speaking world. Here are some examples:

habitación, dormitorio, cuarto, alcoba, recámara

sala, salón, living

planta, piso

piscina, pileta, alberca

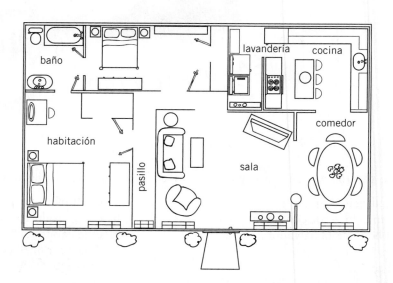

El apartamento del anuncio

CD 2
Track 27
and
CD 3
Track 2

MARTA DÍAZ: Hola, buenos días. Me llamo Marta Díaz. ¿Es posible visitar el apartamento del anuncio?

DIEGO LÓPEZ: Sí, claro. Mucho gusto, señorita Díaz. Yo soy Diego López. Pase, pase. Como usted puede ver, el apartamento es muy alegre.

MARTA DÍAZ: ¡Ah, sí! Tiene muchas ventanas.

DIEGO LÓPEZ: Esta es la **sala**. Es muy grande. Junto a la sala hay un **comedor** pequeño y al lado está la **cocina**.

MARTA DÍAZ: ¡La cocina es lindísima!

DIEGO LÓPEZ: Sí, todos los **electrodomésticos** son nuevos. A la izquierda del **pasillo** hay dos **habitaciones** y un **baño**.

MARTA DÍAZ: Esta habitación tiene muy buena **vista** al **jardín**. Además, los **muebles** son de buena calidad. Me gusta el apartamento. ¿Cuánto es el **alquiler**?

DIEGO LÓPEZ: 8.000 lempiras al mes.

MARTA DÍAZ: Pues, señor López, me encantan el apartamento y esta **zona** céntrica. Y el precio es muy bueno. Voy a decidir esta noche y lo llamo mañana.

DIEGO LÓPEZ: Perfecto, señorita Díaz. Hasta mañana.

En otras palabras

The Spanish word for *apartment* varies according to the country. **El apartamento** is used in Central America, Colombia, and Venezuela, while **el departamento** is common in Mexico, Argentina, Peru and Chile. The word used in Spain is **el piso**.

En otras palabras

The expressions **Pase(n)** and **Adelante** invite people to enter a room or a house in many Spanish-speaking countries. In others, like Colombia, the expression **Siga(n)** is preferred.

5-1 Asociación. Indique si las siguientes afirmaciones son ciertas (**C**) o falsas (**F**), según el diálogo anterior.

1. ___ Marta Díaz quiere comprar el apartamento.
2. ___ La sala es pequeña.
3. ___ El apartamento tiene dos baños.
4. ___ Los electrodomésticos son nuevos.
5. ___ Los muebles son de buena calidad.
6. ___ A Marta no le gusta la zona céntrica.

5-2 ¿En qué piso viven? Pregúntele a su compañero/a dónde viven las diferentes personas. Su compañero/a debe contestarle de acuerdo con el dibujo (*drawing*).

MODELO: E1: *¿Dónde viven los Girondo?*
E2: *Viven en el cuarto piso, en el apartamento 4-A.*

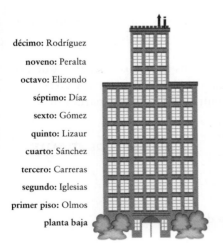

décimo: Rodríguez
noveno: Peralta
octavo: Elizondo
séptimo: Díaz
sexto: Gómez
quinto: Lizaur
cuarto: Sánchez
tercero: Carreras
segundo: Iglesias
primer piso: Olmos
planta baja

5-A López	5-B Alemán
4-A Girondo	4-B Mujica
3-A Ozollo	3-B Ponce
2-A Cárdenas	2-B García-Gil
1-A Jiménez	1-B Valbuena
PB-A Martínez	PB-B Casal

Lengua

Ordinal numbers are adjectives and agree in gender and number with the noun they modify (e.g., **la segunda casa**, **el cuarto edificio**). **Primero** and **tercero** drop the final **-o** when used before a masculine singular noun.

el **primer** apartamento
el **tercer** piso

Cultura

Notice that the first floor is normally called **la planta baja** in most Hispanic countries. The second floor is called **el primer piso**.

5-3 Un hotel de lujo. Ustedes van a gastar los millones que ganaron (*won*) en la lotería para construir un hotel de lujo en la Bahía de Jiquilisco, cerca de San Salvador. Decidan cómo distribuir los siguientes espacios del hotel.

MODELO: el restaurante
E1: *¿En qué piso vamos a poner el restaurante?*
E2: *Debe estar en la planta baja.*

1. la discoteca
2. la recepción
3. el gimnasio
4. la oficina de seguridad

5. las habitaciones
6. la piscina
7. la cafetería con vista a la playa
8. el salón de computadoras

 5-4 Agentes de bienes raíces (*real estate*). PRIMERA FASE. Los fines de semana ustedes trabajan en una agencia de bienes raíces. Para vender o alquilar la casa del dibujo escriban un anuncio similar al anuncio de la página 156.

Incluyan la siguiente información en su anuncio:

1. número de habitaciones
2. número de baños
3. distribución (*layout*) de los cuartos
4. color de la sala
5. otras características (garaje, jardín, sótano [*basement*], ático, etc.)

6. localización de la casa en relación al centro de la ciudad
7. localización de la casa en relación a la universidad
8. precio de la casa

SEGUNDA FASE. Presenten su anuncio al resto de la clase y contesten las preguntas de sus compañeros sobre la casa que quieren vender o alquilar.

 5-5 Ventajas y desventajas. Discutan los aspectos positivos y negativos de los siguientes temas relacionados con la vivienda. Escriban una ventaja y una desventaja para cada uno de los siguientes puntos. Después compartan sus opiniones con el resto de la clase.

	VENTAJAS	DESVENTAJAS
1. vivir en un apartamento		
2. vivir en una casa		
3. tener una piscina		
4. vivir con un compañero/una compañera de cuarto/casa		

La casa, los muebles y los electrodomésticos

CD 2
Track 28
or CD 3
Track 3

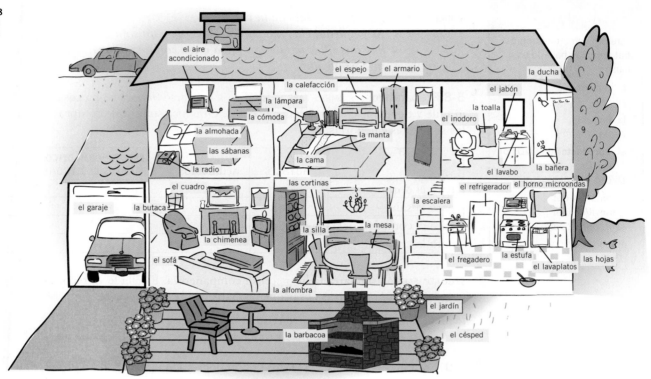

5-6 ¿Aparatos eléctricos, muebles o accesorios? PRIMERA FASE. Escriba cada una de las siguientes palabras en la columna apropiada.

la alfombra   el cuadro   el/la radio
el armario   la butaca   el refrigerador
la cómoda   el horno   las sábanas
las cortinas   el lavaplatos   la silla

APARATOS ELÉCTRICOS	MUEBLES	ACCESORIOS

En otras palabras

Words for household items often vary from one region to another, for example:

manta, cobija, frazada

armario, clóset

bañera, bañadera, tina

refrigerador, nevera

estufa, cocina

SEGUNDA FASE. Respondan a las siguientes preguntas relacionadas con la *Primera fase*.

1. Según ustedes, ¿qué aparato eléctrico cuesta más dinero?
2. ¿Qué muebles necesita todos los días un/a estudiante? ¿Necesita un aparato electrónico también? ¿Cuál?
3. ¿Qué accesorios tienen ustedes en su cuarto?
4. ¿En qué parte de la casa generalmente están estos objetos?

5-7 El curioso. Intercambien preguntas para describir los cuartos de la casa/el apartamento de cada uno/a. Traten (*Try*) de obtener la mayor información posible.

MODELO: E1: *¿Cómo es la sala de tu casa?*
E2: *Es pequeña. Hay una alfombra verde y un sofá grande. También hay dos sillas modernas y una mesa con una lámpara. ¿Y cómo es tu dormitorio?*

5-8 Preparativos. PRIMERA FASE. Usted va a mudarse (*move*) a una casa muy grande y tiene que comprar muchas cosas. Organice su lista de compras según las siguientes categorías.

	MUEBLES	ACCESORIOS	ELECTRODOMÉSTICOS/ APARATOS ELECTRÓNICOS
para el dormitorio			
para la sala			
para el comedor			
para la cocina			

SEGUNDA FASE. Comparta la lista con su compañero/a. Él/Ella le va recordar (*remind you about*) otras cosas que probablemente va a necesitar.

MODELO: E1: *Voy a comprar una cama nueva para el dormitorio.*
E2: *¿No vas a comprar sábanas y mantas?/¿Y no necesitas un sofá?*

5-9 Por catálogo. Miren las fotos del catálogo y elijan (*choose*) un producto de cada categoría. Intercambien sus preferencias y expliquen en qué lugar de la casa van a poner estos accesorios. Las palabras de la lista los/las pueden ayudar.

barato/a   caro/a   de buena calidad   grande   pequeño/a
bonito/a   confortable   de color...   lindo/a

MODELO: E1: *Me gusta la primera toalla porque no es cara y es muy linda. Es para el cuarto de baño.*
E2: *Yo prefiero la tercera porque es más grande.*

🔊 Las tareas domésticas

CD 2
Track 29
or CD 3
Track 4

Gustavo **lava** los **platos**.

Beatriz **seca** los platos.

Beatriz **cocina**. Ella usa mucho los electrodomésticos.

Gustavo **limpia** el baño y **pasa** la **aspiradora**.

Gustavo **saca** la **basura**.

Gustavo **barre** la terraza.

Beatriz **tiende** la **ropa**.

la lavadora   la secadora

Después la **dobla** cuando está **seca**.

Beatriz **plancha** la ropa.

5-10 Por la mañana. ¿En qué orden hace usted estas actividades por la mañana? Use las siguientes expresiones para indicar el orden: **primero, luego, más tarde, después, finalmente.** Compare sus respuestas con las de su compañero/a.

___ lavar los platos   ___ desayunar
___ preparar el café   ___ secar los platos
___ salir para la universidad   ___ hacer la cama

5-11 Actividades en la casa. Pregúntele a su compañero/a dónde hace estas cosas normalmente cuando está en casa.

MODELO: E1:   *¿Dónde ves televisión?*
              E2:   *Veo televisión en mi cuarto. ¿Y tú?* O
                    No veo televisión. ¿Y tú?

1. dormir la siesta   5. pasar la aspiradora
2. escuchar música   6. estudiar para un examen
3. planchar   7. tender la ropa
4. lavar la ropa   8. hablar por teléfono con amigos/as

5-12 ¡A compartir las tareas! PRIMERA FASE. Ustedes van a compartir una casa el próximo año académico. Preparen una lista de todas las tareas domésticas que van a hacer.

SEGUNDA FASE. Discutan qué tareas va a hacer cada uno/a de ustedes según sus gustos. Finalmente, hagan un calendario de tareas y compártanlo con el resto de la clase.

MODELO: *A mí me gusta planchar la ropa pero a mi compañero/a no le gusta. Por eso, yo voy a planchar la ropa los lunes por la tarde.*

CD 2
Track 30
or CD 3
Track 5

5-13 El agente de bienes raíces. PRIMERA FASE. Mr. and Mrs. Mena and their two children live in San Salvador. They have decided to move to a larger place and they are talking to a real estate agent. Before you listen, write down the kind of dwelling and the characteristics of the neighborhood they may be looking for.

SEGUNDA FASE. Now, as you listen, circle the letter next to the correct information.

1. Los señores Mena quieren comprar...
   a. una casa.
   b. un apartamento.

2. El señor y la señora Mena prefieren vivir...
   a. en una buena zona.
   b. lejos de un parque.

3. El agente de bienes raíces...
   a. no sabe cómo ayudarlos.
   b. tiene una casa buena para ellos.

4. El agente dice que la casa del barrio La Mascota...
   a. cuesta mucho.
   b. tiene un buen precio.

5. El señor Mena dice que...
   a. los niños necesitan estar al aire libre para jugar.
   b. los niños no necesitan jugar al aire libre.

EN ACCIÓN

Diarios de bicicleta: El apartamento

Antes de ver

5-14 **PRIMERA FASE.** En este segmento, Javier está buscando un lugar para vivir. Escriba cuatro muebles o accesorios que probablemente va a necesitar para su habitación o apartamento.

SEGUNDA FASE. ¿Qué características le parecen a usted más importantes cuando busca un apartamento o una habitación? Marque (✓) sus respuestas.

1. ___ Está cerca de la universidad o del trabajo.
2. ___ Es barato/a.
3. ___ Tiene mucha luz natural.
4. ___ Es grande.
5. ___ Está amueblado/a.

Mientras ve

5-15 Marque (✓) lo que Javier menciona cuando le describe un apartamento a Daniel.

En la sala:
___ la mesa
___ el sofá
___ la silla
___ el televisor
___ la lámpara

En la cocina:
___ el microondas
___ la estufa
___ el lavaplatos
___ el fregadero
___ el refrigerador

En el baño:
___ el inodoro
___ la ducha
___ la bañera
___ el lavabo
___ el jacuzzi

En el cuarto:
___ el clóset
___ la mesa de noche
___ la lámpara
___ la cama
___ la alfombra

Después de ver

5-16 Al final de este segmento, Javier decide compartir casa con Daniel. Imagine cómo es esta casa y escriba cinco oraciones para describirla.

FUNCIONES Y FORMAS

1. Expressing ongoing actions: Present progressive

ÓSCAR:	¿Aló?
CATALINA:	Hola, Óscar. Te habla Catalina. ¿Qué **estás haciendo**?
ÓSCAR:	Hola, Catalina. **¡Estoy trabajando** mucho!
CATALINA:	¿Por qué?
ÓSCAR:	Mis padres **están pasando** sus vacaciones en la playa y vuelven mañana. ¡La casa es un desastre total!
CATALINA:	¿Así que **estás limpiando**?
ÓSCAR:	¡Claro! **Estoy barriendo** el piso, **ordenando** la sala, **recogiendo** la ropa de mi cuarto…. Y tú, ¿qué **estás haciendo**?
CATALINA:	¿Yo?… Nada. **Estoy leyendo** el periódico y **tomando** un café.

Piénselo. Indique las oraciones que son **ciertas** (**C**) o **falsas** (**F**), de acuerdo con la conversación entre Catalina y Óscar.

1. ___ Catalina y Óscar **están trabajando** juntos.
2. ___ Óscar **está descansando**.
3. ___ Óscar **está pasando** sus vacaciones con sus padres en la playa.
4. ___ Óscar **está limpiando** la casa de sus padres.
5. ___ Óscar no está contento porque él **está trabajando** mucho en casa.

- Use the present progressive to emphasize that an action or event is in progress at the moment of speaking, rather than a habitual action.

Óscar **está limpiando** la casa.	*Oscar is cleaning the house.* (at this moment)
Óscar **limpia** la casa.	*Oscar cleans the house.* (habitually)

- Form the present progressive with the present tense of **estar** + *present participle*. To form the present participle, add **-ando** to the stem of **-ar** verbs and **-iendo** to the stem of **-er** and **-ir** verbs.

ESTAR		PRESENT PARTICIPLE
yo	**estoy**	
tú	**estás**	hablando
Ud., él, ella	**está**	comiendo
nosotros/as	**estamos**	escribiendo
vosotros/as	**estáis**	
Uds., ellos/as	**están**	

■ When the verb stem of an **-er** or an **-ir** verb ends in a vowel, add **-yendo**.

leer	→	le**yendo**
oír	→	o**yendo**

■ Stem-changing **-ir** verbs (**o → ue, e → ie, e → i**) change **o → u** and **e → i** in the present participle.

dormir (ue)	(**o → u**)	d<u>u</u>rm**iendo**
sentir (ie)	(**e → i**)	s<u>i</u>nt**iendo**
pedir (ie)	(**e → i**)	p<u>i</u>d**iendo**

■ Spanish does not use the present progressive to express future time, as English does; Spanish uses the present tense instead.

Salgo mañana.	*I am leaving tomorrow.*
¿**Te levantas** temprano mañana?	*Are you getting up early tomorrow?*

5-17 Un día ocupado. Hoy es un día muy ocupado para la familia Villa. Asocie las acciones de la columna de la izquierda con las explicaciones de la columna de la derecha para averiguar (*find out*) por qué.

1. ___ La Sra. Villa está preparando una cena deliciosa y un pastel (*cake*) especial.
2. ___ Su hijo Marcelo está barriendo la terraza.
3. ___ Su hija Ana está lavando los platos en el fregadero.
4. ___ Alicia está decorando la mesa.
5. ___ Pedro está hablando por teléfono.

a. Está llamando a su mejor amigo para invitarlo a la fiesta.
b. El lavaplatos no está funcionando.
c. Es una ocasión especial.
d. Es el cumpleaños de su esposo.
e. Está muy sucia (*dirty*) y unos amigos vienen a celebrar el cumpleaños.

Rodrigo   Soledad

5-18 La vida activa. Túrnense para describir lo que está haciendo cada persona en estas escenas. Indiquen en qué lugar de la casa está cada uno de ellos. Luego, imaginen lo que, según ustedes, cada persona va a hacer más tarde.

MODELO: E1: *Rodrigo y Soledad están cantando en una fiesta. Están en la terraza.*
E2: *Después van a bailar y conversar con sus amigos.*

Pepe   Catalina   Arturo   Gonzalo   Carlos

5-19 Lugares y actividades. PRIMERA FASE. Miren las siguientes fotografías de celebraciones y hagan lo siguiente:

1.

3.

2.

Asocien las fotos con el país/los países en que probablemente se realiza cada una: Foto **1.** ___, **2.** ___, **3.** ___

a. España   c. México   e. Uruguay
b. Estados Unidos d. Ecuador   f. en muchos países

SEGUNDA FASE. Descríbanle a otra pareja dos o tres actividades que las personas están haciendo en la escena de una de las fotos. La otra pareja debe adivinar el nombre del lugar. Luego, entre todos, escriban una descripción completa de una de las fotos. Incluyan el nombre de la fiesta o celebración, su significado cultural y las actividades de las personas en la foto.

SITUACIONES

1. **Role A.** Your best friend calls to invite you to go out. Respond that you and your housemates are busy cleaning the apartment. Explain the chores that each of you is doing.

   Role B. Call your best friend to invite her/him to go out with you. Ask what your friend and her/his roommates are doing. Ask if your friend can go out later (**más tarde**).

2. **Role A.** There is a big family gathering at your aunt's house today, but you are away at school. Call and greet the family member who answers the phone. Explain that you will not be attending, and excuse yourself for not being there. Ask how everyone is and what each family member is doing at the moment.

   Role B. You are at a big family gathering today. A family member calls to say he/she can't attend. Answer the phone. Greet the caller and answer his/her questions. Finally, mention that everyone says hello (**todos te mandan saludos**) and say good-bye.

2. Describing physical and emotional states:
Expressions with *tener*

Hoy es un día de verano y los Robledo se mudan. **Tienen prisa** porque ya son las tres de la tarde. El señor Robledo y su hija Isabel **tienen calor** porque hace cuatro horas que trabajan bajo (*under*) el sol. Ella **tiene mucha sed** y está bebiendo agua. El bebé, Nicolás, llora porque **tiene hambre**. La señora Robledo le da de comer mientras la abuelita Rosa duerme la siesta. Después de empacar su ropa y todas sus fotografías, libros y plantas, Rosa **tiene mucho sueño**. ¡Qué día para los Robledo!

Piénselo. Asocie la descripción del estado físico con la(s) persona(s) del dibujo. Escriba el nombre de la(s) persona(s) al lado de la descripción.

_____ 1. Va a comer porque **tiene hambre.**
_____ 2. Está tomando agua porque **tiene sed.**
_____ 3. No **tienen frío** porque es verano y hace calor.
_____ 4. Está cansada y **tiene sueño.**
_____ 5. **Tienen calor** porque están trabajando bajo el sol.
_____ 6. **Tienen prisa** porque quieren salir pronto.

■ Spanish uses **tener +** *noun* for many conditions and states where English uses *to be* + *adjective*. You have already seen the expression **tener... años: Eduardo tiene veinte años.** Here are some other useful expressions.

TENER + *NOUN*		
	hambre	*hungry*
	sed	*thirsty*
	sueño	*sleepy*
	miedo	*afraid*
	calor	*hot*
tener	cuidado	*to be* ⎨ careful
	frío	*cold*
	suerte	*lucky*
	prisa	*in a hurry/rush*
	razón	*right, correct*

■ With these expressions, use **mucho/a** to indicate *very.*

Tengo **mucho** calor (frío, miedo, sueño, cuidado).

I am very hot (cold, afraid, sleepy, careful).

Tienen **mucha** hambre (sed, suerte).

They are very hungry (thirsty, lucky).

5-20 Asociaciones. Lea las situaciones en que están usted y algunos miembros de su familia. Luego asocie las situaciones con las expresiones de la derecha.

1. Mi hermano siempre tiene _____ y, por eso, está comiendo ahora.
2. Mi hermana duerme a todas horas porque siempre tiene _____ .
3. En este momento mis primos están visitando la Antártida; probablemente tienen _____ .
4. Mis abuelos están bebiendo agua en la cocina porque tienen _____ .
5. Mi mamá tiene _____ ; siempre gana (*wins*) cuando juega a la lotería.
6. ¡Uf! Todavía estoy planchando mi blusa y mis amigos van a llegar en cinco minutos. Yo tengo _____ .

a. sed
b. prisa
c. suerte
d. sueño
e. mucho frío
f. hambre

5-21 ¿Qué están haciendo, dónde están y cómo se sienten? PRIMERA FASE. Observen a las personas en los dibujos y hagan lo siguiente.

1. Digan qué está(n) haciendo la(s) persona(s) y dónde está(n).
2. Describan su estado físico.

MODELO: *El padre y su hijo están durmiendo en el sofá. Tienen sueño.*

1.

2.

3.

4.

SEGUNDA FASE. Respondan a las siguientes preguntas sobre las escenas de la *Primera fase*. Expliquen.

1. ¿Cuál de los dibujos describe mejor cómo se sienten ustedes en este momento?
2. ¿Qué dibujo refleja (*reflects*) el clima de su región en diciembre?
3. ¿A qué hora se sienten ustedes como las personas del dibujo del modelo?

5-22 ¿Estados de ánimo (*moods*) semejantes o diferentes? PRIMERA FASE. Primero, termine las siguientes ideas y, luego, compare sus respuestas con las de su compañero/a. Tome apuntes de las respuestas de su compañero/a. Use expresiones con **tener**.

1. En las mañanas de invierno, yo siempre _____ .
2. Cuando mi madre pasa mucho tiempo limpiando nuestra casa, ella
   _____ .
3. Generalmente, cuando mis hermanos y yo hacemos barbacoa, nosotros
   _____ .
4. Cuando yo leo un libro aburrido, siempre _____ .
5. Inmediatamente yo _____ cuando llego a casa y mi esposo está preparando mi plato favorito.

SEGUNDA FASE. Usando sus apuntes de la *Primera fase*, escriba una semejanza y una diferencia entre usted y su compañero/a.

SITUACIONES

1. **Role A.** You share an apartment with a messy friend. Complain to him/her that a) his/her books, backpack, etc., are always all over the living room; b) he/she uses a lot of dishes, but never washes them; c) his/her bottles of soft drinks (**botellas de refrescos**) are always on the table; and d) he/she makes a lot of noise (**ruido**) during the night and you can't sleep.

   Role B. The friend with whom you share an apartment has some complaints about you. Apologize and explain that you a) don't pick up your books or wash the dishes because you are always in a rush to do homework; b) drink a lot of soft drinks because you are always thirsty; and c) go to bed late because you're not sleepy before midnight or later and also because you're scared at night. Say as convincingly as you can that you are going to be more careful in the future.

2. **Role A.** You are a young child. It is a busy Saturday morning at your house, and nobody is paying any attention to you. Go to your parent and say the following: a) You are hungry and want to eat; b) you are thirsty and want some juice; and c) you are bored and want to play outside. What you really want is your parent's attention, so you react negatively to suggestions that you entertain yourself.

   Role B. You are the parent of a young child. You are really busy, and you think your child is old enough to take care himself/herself for awhile. When your child makes demands, say that if he/she a) is hungry, there is fruit in the kitchen; b) is thirsty, there is orange juice in the refrigerator; c) is bored, he/she has a lot of toys (**juguetes**) in his/her room. Explain that you are in a hurry and cannot play outside. Suggest things your child can do while you are busy with your household tasks.

3. Avoiding repetition in speaking and writing: Direct object nouns and pronouns

A.

¿Qué hacen estas personas?

B.

C.

La abuela cuida (*takes care of*) a la niña.
La cuida todos los días.

El padre lava los platos y los niños **los** secan.

Las señoras preparan la comida en la cocina del restaurante y después **la** sirven.

Piénselo. Ponga la letra de la foto correcta al lado de la descripción.

1. ___ La niña está contenta porque su abuela **la** cuida.
2. ___ El padre trabaja y los niños **lo** ayudan.
3. ___ Las señoras tienen una parrilla (*grill*) enorme. Ellas **la** usan todos los días.
4. ___ Las cocineras (*cooks*) están preparando mucha carne en la parrilla. Después, los clientes van a comer**la**.
5. ___ La abuela está cuidando a la niña. La abuela **la** quiere mucho.
6. ___ El padre está en la cocina con sus hijos. Él **los** mira con cariño y habla con ellos mientras trabajan.

■ Direct objects answer the question *what?* or *whom?* in relation to the verb.

¿Qué dobla Pedro?	*What does Pedro fold?*
(Pedro dobla) **las toallas.**	*(Pedro folds) the towels.*

■ Direct objects may be nouns or pronouns. When direct object nouns refer to a specific person, a group of persons, or a pet, the word **a** precedes the direct object. This **a** is called the *personal a* and has no equivalent in English. The personal **a** followed by **el** contracts to **al**.

Amanda seca **los platos.**	*Amanda dries the dishes.*
Amanda seca **al perro.**	*Amanda dries off the dog.*
¿Ves la piscina?	*Do you see the swimming pool?*
¿Ves **al** niño en la piscina?	*Do you see the child in the swimming pool?*

■ With the verb *tener* the personal **a** is not needed.

María tiene un hijo.   *María has a child.*

■ Direct object pronouns replace direct object nouns and are used to avoid repeating the noun while speaking or writing. These pronouns may refer to people, animals, or things already mentioned.

DIRECT OBJECT PRONOUNS			
me	*me*	**nos**	*us*
te	*you* (familiar, singular)	**os**	*you* (familiar plural, Spain)
lo	*you* (formal, singular), *him, it* (masculine)	**los**	*you* (formal and familiar, plural), *them* (masculine)
la	*you* (formal, singular), *her, it* (feminine)	**las**	*you* (formal and familiar plural), *them* (feminine)

■ Place the direct object pronoun before the conjugated verb form.

¿Barre **la cocina** Mirta?   *Does Mirta sweep the kitchen?*

No, no **la** barre.   *No, she does not sweep it.*

¿Cuidas **a tu hermanito**?   *Do you take care of your little brother?*

Sí, **lo** cuido.   *Yes, I take care of him.*

■ With compound verb forms (a conjugated verb and an infinitive or present participle), a direct object pronoun may be placed before the conjugated verb, or may be attached to the accompanying infinitive or present participle.

¿Vas a ver **a Rafael**?   *Are you going to see Rafael?*

Sí, **lo** voy a ver mañana. ⎫
Sí, voy a ver**lo** mañana. ⎭   *Yes, I am going to see him tomorrow.*

¿Están limpiando **la casa**?   *Are they cleaning the house?*

Sí, **la** están limpiando. ⎫
Sí, están limpiándo**la**. ⎭   *Yes, they are cleaning it.*

■ Since the question word **quién(es)** refers to people, use the *personal* **a** when **quién(es)** is used as a direct object.

¿**A quién** vas a ayudar?   *Whom are you going to help?*

Voy a ayudar **a** Pedro.   *I am going to help Pedro.*

Lengua

You have seen that words that stress the next-to-the-last syllable do not have a written accent if they end in a vowel: **lav<u>a</u>ndo**. If we attach a direct object pronoun, we are adding a syllable, so the stress now falls on the third syllable from the end and a written accent is needed: **lav<u>á</u>ndol<u>o</u>**.

5-23 La división del trabajo. Sus compañeros Martín, Pedro y Julio comparten un apartamento y usted le hace las siguientes preguntas a Julio para saber cómo dividen las tareas domésticas entre ellos. Escriba la letra de la respuesta más apropiada de Julio.

1. ¿Quién limpia la nevera?
   a. Yo lo limpio.   **b.** Pedro la limpia.   **c.** Nosotros las limpiamos.
2. ¿Quién hace las camas?
   a. Pedro la hace.   **b.** Yo los hago.   **c.** Martín las hace.
3. ¿Quién tiende la ropa?
   a. Los tres lo tendemos.   **b.** Pedro los tiende.   **c.** Martín la tiende.
4. ¿Quién saca la basura?
   a. Martín lo saca.   **b.** Pedro las saca.   **c.** Yo la saco.
5. ¿Quién pasa la aspiradora?
   a. Martín y yo las pasamos.   **b.** Pedro la pasa.   **c.** Ellos lo pasan.

5-24 ¿Qué es lógico hacer? PRIMERA FASE. Las afirmaciones de la columna de la izquierda describen la situación doméstica de esta familia. Léalas y, luego, asocie cada afirmación con una acción lógica.

1. ___ Las camas están sin hacer.
2. ___ La ropa está seca.
3. ___ Los dormitorios están desordenados.
4. ___ El aire acondicionado no funciona.
5. ___ Las ventanas están sucias.
6. ___ No pueden poner el auto en el garaje porque hay muchos muebles viejos y cajas con libros.

a. Los hijos los van a ordenar.
b. La madre las hace después de leer el periódico.
c. El padre las va a limpiar.
d. La hija va a plancharla.
e. Los hijos lo van a organizar y limpiar.
f. El hijo mayor lo va a reparar (*fix*).

 SEGUNDA FASE. Dígale a su compañero/a cuál(es) de las afirmaciones de la *Primera fase* describe(n) mejor su apartamento o casa en este momento. Luego, explíquele qué va a hacer usted y cuándo.

5-25 Mis responsabilidades en casa. PRIMERA FASE. Averigüe (*Find out*) si su compañero/a es responsable de las siguientes tareas domésticas en su casa.

MODELO: sacar la basura
E1: *¿Sacas la basura?*
E2: *Sí, la saco. O No, no la saco. ¿Y tú?*

1. lavar los platos
2. ordenar el garaje
3. tender las cortinas después de lavarlas
4. limpiar la ducha y la bañera
5. lavar las sábanas
6. cortar el césped

SEGUNDA FASE. Ahora, comparen sus respuestas. Después díganle a otra pareja cuáles son las tareas domésticas que ustedes dos hacen y averigüen si ellos las hacen también.

MODELO: E1: *Nosotros no lavamos los platos en casa porque tenemos lavaplatos. ¿Y ustedes los lavan?*
E2: *Sí, nosotros los lavamos y hacemos las camas también.*

5-26 El apartamento de mi compañero/a. Usted va a cuidar el apartamento de su compañero/a por una semana, y quiere saber lo que debe hacer y lo que puede hacer allí.

MODELO: E1: *¿Debo sacar la basura?*
E2: *Sí, la debes sacar/debes sacarla todos los días.*

¿DEBO O NO DEBO?	SÍ	NO	¿PUEDO O NO PUEDO?	SÍ	NO
regar (*water*) las plantas	___	___	leer los libros	___	___
pasear al perro	___	___	usar los electrodomésticos	___	___
limpiar el apartamento	___	___	invitar a un amigo/una amiga	___	___
poner la alarma	___	___	hacer la tarea en la computadora	___	___
…	___	___	…	___	___

5-27 Los preparativos para la visita. La familia Granados está muy ocupada porque espera la visita de unos parientes. Conteste las preguntas de su compañero/a sobre lo que está haciendo cada miembro de la familia.

MODELO: E1: *¿Quién está preparando la comida?*
E2: *La abuela la está preparando/está preparándola.*

5-28 Una mano amiga. PRIMERA FASE. Su compañero/a le va a hacer preguntas sobre sus relaciones con otras personas. Conteste, escogiendo a una de las personas de la lista.

mi madre	mi novio/a	¿...?
mi mejor amigo/a	mi padre	

MODELO: ayudar económicamente
E1: *¿Quién te ayuda económicamente?*
E2: *Mis padres me ayudan económicamente.*

1. querer mucho
2. escuchar en todo momento
3. llamar por teléfono con frecuencia
4. ayudar con los problemas
5. aconsejar (*advise*) cuando estás indeciso/a
6. entender siempre

SEGUNDA FASE. Dígale a su compañero/a lo que usted hace por las siguientes personas. Indique en qué circunstancias lo hace.

MODELO: su esposo/a
E1: *Lo/La ayudo cuando está cansado/a.*
E2: *Y yo lo/la escucho cuando tiene problemas en el trabajo.*

1. su papá
2. su mamá
3. su mejor amigo/a
4. su novio/a
5. sus vecinos (*neighbors*)
6. su compañero/a de cuarto

SITUACIONES

1. **Role A.** You are at a furniture store buying a sofa. Tell the salesperson which sofa you want and ask when they can deliver (**entregar**) it. Explain that you are not going to be home at that time, but that you can be home in the afternoon. Agree to the time and thank the salesperson.

   Role B. You are a salesperson at a furniture store. Tell the customer that the sofa he/she wants is a very good one and that you can deliver (**entregar**) it next Monday morning. Mention that you can deliver it between three and five o'clock in the afternoon if the customer prefers.

2. **Role A.** You and your little brother/sister have to do some chores at home. Since you are older, you tell your sibling three or four things that he/she has to do. Be prepared to respond to complaints and questions.

   Role B. You and your older brother/sister have to do some chores at home. Because you are younger, you get some orders from your sibling about what you have to do. You do not feel like working, and you especially do not like being bossed around, so respond to everything you hear with a complaint or a question.

4. Pointing out and identifying people and things: Demonstrative adjectives and pronouns

AGENTE: **Esta** casa blanca es muy moderna y el precio es bueno.

CLIENTE: Pero **esa** tiene jardín y **esta** no tiene, ¿verdad?

AGENTE: No, **esta** casa y **aquella** no tienen jardín. Por eso, la casa amarilla es más cara.

Piénselo. En su presentación, el señor Mendoza describe algunos tipos de vivienda para un grupo de salvadoreños que desean comprar una casa. Indique si cada una de las siguientes descripciones se refiere a la vivienda que está cerca (**C**), un poco lejos (**P**) o lejos (**L**) del señor Mendoza.

1. ___ **Esta** casa de dos pisos está en una ciudad. Tiene muchas ventanas en cada piso, pero no tiene jardín.
2. ___ **Aquella** casa donde están la madre y su hija es de material sólido y de un color alegre.
3. ___ **Esa** casa es de construcción sólida y tiene dos pisos y un garaje. Tiene una pequeña área verde enfrente.

Demonstrative Adjectives

■ Demonstrative adjectives agree in gender and number with the noun they modify. English has two sets of demonstratives (*this, these* and *that, those*), but Spanish has three sets.

this	**este** cuadro **esta** butaca	*these*	**estos** cuadros **estas** butacas	
that	**ese** horno **esa** casa	*those*	**esos** hornos **esas** casas	
that (over there)	**aquel** camión **aquella** casa	*those (over there)*	**aquellos** camiones **aquellas** casas	

Lengua

Some Spanish speakers also use the words **este** and **pues** as pause fillers when trying to remember a word while speaking.

Voy a ver la película en el cine... este... Riviera.

What do English speakers do in this situation?

■ Use **este, esta, estos,** and **estas** when referring to people or things that are close to you in space or time.

Este escritorio es nuevo.   *This desk is new.*

Traen el sofá **esta** tarde.   *They will bring the sofa this afternoon.*

■ Use **ese**, **esa**, **esos**, and **esas** when referring to events, people, or things that are not relatively close to you. Sometimes they are close to the person you are addressing.

Esa lámpara es muy bonita.	*That lamp is very pretty.*
Ese amigo de Lola vende su auto, ¿verdad?	*That friend of Lola's is selling his car, isn't he?*

■ Use **aquel**, **aquella**, **aquellos**, and **aquellas** when referring to people or things that are more distant, or to events that are distant in time.

Aquel edificio es muy alto.	*That building (over there) is very tall.*
En **aquella** visita los niños jugaron en el parque.	*During that (long ago) visit, the children played in the park.*

Demonstrative pronouns

■ Demonstratives can be used as pronouns to mean *this one/these* or *that one/those*, thus avoiding repetition when speaking or writing.

Compran este espejo y **ese**.	*They are buying this mirror and that one.*
Estas lámparas y **aquellas** son mis favoritas.	*These lamps and those over there are my favorites.*

■ To refer to a general idea or concept, or to ask for the identification of an object, use **esto**, **eso**, or **aquello**. These forms are invariable.

Trabajan mucho y **eso** es muy bueno.	*They work a lot, and that is very good.*
¿Qué es **esto**?	*What is this?*
Es un espejo.	*It is a mirror.*
Aquello es un edificio de la universidad.	*That (over there) is a university building.*

5-29 Cerca, relativamente cerca o lejos. Decida qué adjetivo demostrativo debe usar de acuerdo con el lugar donde se encuentran los siguientes objetos.

Cerca de usted

1. ___ mesa es de Honduras.   a. Esta   b. Esa   c. Aquella
2. ___ cuadros también son de Honduras.   a. Estos   b. Esos   c. Aquellos

Relativamente cerca de usted

3. ___ sofá es muy grande.   a. Este   b. Ese   c. Aquel
4. ___ alfombra tiene unos colores muy alegres.   a. Esta   b. Esa   c. Aquella

Lejos de usted

5. ___ espejo es nuevo.   a. Este   b. Ese   c. Aquel
6. ___ lámparas son antiguas.   a. Estas   b. Esas   c. Aquellas

5-30 ¿Quién es? Coloque (*Place*) sus fotos en la clase de acuerdo con las instrucciones del profesor/de la profesora. Luego pregunte a un compañero/una compañera quién es el sujeto de cada foto.

MODELO: E1: *¿Quién es este/ese/aquel hombre?* (según la distancia de la foto de E1)

E2: *Este/Ese/Aquel hombre es Antonio Banderas.* (según la distancia de la foto de E2)

 5-31 En una mueblería en Managua. Usted y su compañero/a van a hacer los papeles de dos amigos/as nicaragüenses que deciden vivir juntos/as. Van a una mueblería para comprar muebles y accesorios. Usen las palabras y frases para hablar sobre lo que ven. Sigan el modelo.

bonito/a   feo/a   (no) me gusta(n)

caro/a   me encanta(n)

MODELO: E1: *¿Te gusta el sofá?*
E2: *¿Cuál? ¿Aquel sofá verde?*
E1: *No, ese sofá azul.*
E2: *Sí, me encanta.* O *No, es muy feo.*

5-32 Descripciones. Cada uno de ustedes va a pensar en tres objetos o muebles y va a decir en qué parte de la casa están. Su compañero/a va a hacerle preguntas para adivinar qué mueble u objeto es.

MODELO: E1: *Este mueble está generalmente en el comedor.*
E2: *¿Es grande?*
E1: *Puede ser grande o pequeño.*
E2: *¿Lo usamos para comer?*
E1: *Sí.*
E2: *Es la mesa.*

SITUACIONES

1. **Role A.** You have a good job and want to move to a nicer apartment. The property manager of several apartment complexes has already shown you pictures of one apartment (**ese apartamento**) and is now showing you pictures of a second one (**este apartamento**). Discuss with the property manager a) the rent (**el alquiler**); b) the number of rooms; and c) the facilities, such as laundry room (**lavandería**), garage, and pool, of both apartments. Say which of the two apartments you want to see and explain why.

   Role B. You are the property manager of several apartment complexes. You have already shown your client pictures of one apartment (**ese apartamento**) and now are showing pictures of a second one (**este apartamento**). Answer his/her questions by saying that a) the rent of the first apartment is $900 dollars per month and the second one is $1,100; b) both apartments have two bedrooms; and c) the first apartment comes with a one-car garage, while this one has a two-car garage. Also tell him/her the advantages of each of the two apartments.

2. **Role A.** You are in a car with a real estate agent, who is showing you some houses for sale in the neighborhood where you hope to live. You are interested in knowing more about one house on the side of the street closer to you (**esta casa**), another house on other side of the street (**esa casa**), and a third house (**aquella casa**) a couple of blocks away.

   Role B. You are a real estate agent driving with a client who is interested in three houses. Answer the client's questions about the three houses.

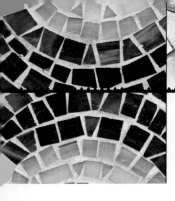

MOSAICOS

A escuchar

Antes de escuchar

ESTRATEGIA

Create mental images
You have already learned that visual cues can increase your listening comprehension. For example, seeing the pictures or objects that a speaker refers to can help you understand what is being said. Even when visuals are not present, you can form images in your mind by using your imagination or by making associations with experiences you have had. As you listen, practice creating mental images to help you develop your listening skills in Spanish.

5-33 Preparación. Usted va a escuchar la descripción de una casa. Antes de escuchar, piense en las casas que conoce y haga una lista de cuatro cuartos y de tres objetos (muebles, aparatos eléctricos o accesorios) que usted espera encontrar en cada uno de los cuartos.

Escuchar

5-34 ¿Comprende usted? Now, look at the following drawing, and as you hear the different statements about the location of pieces of furniture and objects, mark (✓) the appropriate column to indicate whether each of the statements is true (**Cierto**) or false (**Falso**).

CD 2
Track 31
or CD 3
Track 6

	CIERTO	FALSO
1.	——	——
2.	——	——
3.	——	——
4.	——	——
5.	——	——
6.	——	——
7.	——	——
8.	——	——

Después de escuchar

5-35 Ahora usted. Describa su vivienda (número de cuartos, colores, muebles, etc.) a un compañero/una compañera. Él/Ella va a tomar notas para describirle su casa a otra persona de la clase. Verifique si la información es correcta. Luego, intercambien roles.

A conversar

Antes de conversar

5-36 Preparación. Usted necesita alquilar un apartamento. Escriba algunas características esenciales y algunas secundarias del apartamento que usted necesita.

Conversar

5-37 Entre nosotros. Usted y su mejor amigo/a estudian en San Salvador este año y quieren alquilar un apartamento. Van a conversar por teléfono sobre unos apartamentos que se anuncian en el periódico.

PRIMERA FASE. Trabajando individualmente, piense en las características esenciales y secundarias de un buen apartamento. Lea los anuncios y decida qué apartamento prefiere. Organice mentalmente lo que va a decir. Luego, piense en el lenguaje que va a usar para expresarse y para negociar con su amigo/a, por ejemplo, *en mi opinión…, entiendo tu punto de vista pero…, (no) estoy de acuerdo porque…*

ALQUILERES

1. Se alquila condominio residencial privado, 3er nivel, 2 dormitorios, 1 baño, cuarto y baño empleada, cocina con despensa, sala y comedor separados, garaje 2 carros, área recreación niños. SVC 4.500 vigilancia incluida. 22 24 46 30.

2. Alquilo apartamento cerca de centro comercial. Transporte público a la puerta. Ideal para profesionales. 1 dormitorio, 1 baño con jacuzzi, con muebles y electrodomésticos, terraza, sistema de seguridad, garaje doble. SVC 7.500. Tfno. 22 65 16 92.

3. Alquilo apartamento, cerca zona universitaria. 3 dormitorios. 1ra planta. Ideal para estudiantes. (SVC 1.800) Contactar al 22 35 37 83.

4. Alquilo preciosa habitación en casa particular. Semi-amueblada. Amplia, enorme clóset, cable gratis. Alimentación opcional. Información al teléfono 22 63 28 07.

SEGUNDA FASE. Hable con su amigo/a por teléfono para llegar a un acuerdo sobre el apartamento que los/las dos quieren alquilar. En su conversación, pueden referirse a algunos de los siguientes temas: el alquiler, la localización, el número de habitaciones y baños, si tiene muebles o no, si tiene aire acondicionado/ calefacción.

Después de conversar

5-38 Un poco más. Ya que usted y su compañero/a saben qué apartamento les gusta más, tienen que dar el próximo paso (*next step*). Conversen para decidir lo siguiente:

1. ¿Por qué es este apartamento el favorito de ustedes?
2. ¿Qué preguntas quieren hacerle al dueño del apartamento para obtener más información?

Tomen apuntes, porque van a presentar sus ideas a la clase.

A leer

Antes de leer

5-39 Preparación. Muchas casas modernas tienen los aparatos que aparecen en la siguiente lista. Para cada función, escriba el/los aparato(s) correspondiente(s).

aire acondicionado central	red (*network*) inalámbrica
música ambiental en todos los cuartos	reproductor de DVD
computadora	sensor de temperatura
fotocopiadora	teléfono
lámpara	televisor
microondas	ventilador

FUNCIÓN   **APARATOS**

1. para trabajar desde (*from*) casa   _____
2. para hacer trabajos domésticos   _____
3. para controlar la temperatura de la casa   _____
4. para comunicarse con otras personas   _____
5. para entretenerse (*have fun*) en casa   _____

Leer

5-40 Primera mirada. El siguiente artículo describe la casa del futuro. Léalo y pase un marcador (*highlighter*) por las palabras en cada párrafo que se asocian con tecnología.

Segunda mirada. Lea el artículo otra vez y haga lo siguiente.

1. En el primer párrafo, el autor del artículo da una definición de una casa inteligente. Escriba la definición.
2. El segundo párrafo contrasta la casa inteligente con la casa tradicional. ¿Cuál es la diferencia? Escríbala.
3. El segundo párrafo también indica algunas formas en que la casa inteligente ayuda a las personas que viven en ella. Indique una función útil para una persona de su familia. ¿Por qué es útil?
4. En el tercer párrafo, se mencionan algunas de las funciones múltiples de los aparatos eléctricos y electrónicos. ¿Cuál de estas funciones múltiples es más beneficiosa para un/a estudiante? ¿Por qué?
5. En el cuarto párrafo se explica cómo la tecnología ayuda a los miembros de la familia a mantenerse en contacto (*to stay in touch*). ¿A su familia le gustaría (*would like*) usar esta tecnología?
6. En el quinto párrafo se mencionan algunos beneficios de la tecnología para divertirse en casa. ¿Cuál de las opciones le gusta más?
7. En el último párrafo, el autor introduce una duda sobre los beneficios de la casa del futuro. Subraye la frase donde se introduce la duda.

La casa inteligente del futuro

Las casas inteligentes o automatizadas ya existen en el presente. Tienen un gran número de aparatos eléctricos y electrónicos, controlados por una computadora, que se comunican entre ellos. Pero, ¿cuáles son las diferencias entre una casa tradicional y una inteligente?

Básicamente, la casa inteligente incorpora los últimos avances tecnológicos en beneficio de las personas que viven en ella. A través de complejos dispositivos[1] y sensores, estas casas facilitan el trabajo doméstico de sus dueños: abren y cierran cortinas y puertas, hacen funcionar electrodomésticos (microondas, ventiladores, etc.), el aire acondicionado y la calefacción central, por ejemplo. Los sensores también controlan el movimiento de unos robots móviles que limpian las alfombras y los pisos y, en el patio, limpian la piscina y cortan el césped.

Además, la casa inteligente ofrece un uso más eficiente y múltiple de los aparatos eléctricos y electrónicos en su interior. Un microondas se puede usar para calentar comida y también para ver televisión. De la misma manera, un refrigerador puede conectarse a Internet y permitir a una persona navegar por la Red o enviar mensajes electrónicos.

La casa inteligente del futuro facilita también las relaciones entre los miembros de la familia. Por ejemplo, cuando los miembros de la familia no están juntos, pueden reunirse para cenar o para pasar tiempo juntos, gracias a las tecnologías de videoconferencia en Internet. Con el video y la voz sobre IP, los miembros de la familia en todo el mundo pueden conversar, interactuar y cenar juntos de forma virtual.

La sala en la casa inteligente es el centro de entretenimiento, donde todos los dispositivos están conectados a la red inalámbrica central. Los juegos bajo demanda están disponibles[2] a través de la televisión de banda ancha[3] y satélite. Las películas de alta definición, la televisión sin anuncios y el contenido digital a petición[4] son normales. También es normal distribuir música y películas a cada habitación de la casa desde el servidor central.

En resumen, la casa del futuro es una versión técnicamente más sofisticada de la casa del presente. Es difícil predecir con exactitud cómo vamos a vivir dentro de 50 años. Sin embargo, muchos se preguntan si esta abundancia de tecnología va a afectar nuestra vida positiva o negativamente.

[1]*devices* [2]*available* [3]*broadband* [4]*on demand*

Después de leer

5-41 Ampliación. PRIMERA FASE. Lea la siguiente nota que el arquitecto de una casa inteligente le escribe a uno de sus colegas. Complete los espacios en blanco con la palabra adecuada.

funcionar	juegos bajo demanda	tecnológicos
funciones	películas de alta definición	urgentemente
inteligente	sensores	ventanas

Manolo,

¡Te tengo una gran sorpresa! El diseñador (*designer*) Óscar de la Renta necesita (1) _____ construir una casa (2) _____ en Managua. Como sabes, de la Renta es muy rico y quiere los últimos avances (3) _____ en ella. Desea una casa con dispositivos para abrir y cerrar puertas y (4) _____ . También quiere incorporar electrodomésticos con (5) _____ múltiples. Quiere calefacción controlada por (6) _____ . Desde luego (*Of course*) quiere un centro de entretenimiento que le permita mirar (7) _____ y recibir programación digital y (8) _____ . Tú sabes mucho de sistemas automatizados y yo de construcción, y pienso que eres la persona ideal para ayudarme en este proyecto. Vamos a darle una casa espectacular. Todo va a (9) _____ perfectamente.

Debemos responder pronto. Llámame.

Ricardo

 SEGUNDA FASE. Ahora comparen sus propias viviendas con la casa inteligente de la lectura. Hablen de la tecnología, los electrodomésticos y los aparatos electrónicos.

A escribir

Antes de escribir

5-42 Preparación. **PRIMERA FASE.** El periódico *La Prensa* de Tegucigalpa, Honduras, invita al público a participar en el concurso (*contest*) *La casa automatizada del futuro*. Uno de los requisitos del concurso es escribir un panfleto, según se explica en el anuncio del periódico.

El diario *La Prensa* invita al público a participar en el concurso *La casa automatizada del futuro*.

Bases del concurso:

Los participantes deben enviar la siguiente información por correo electrónico al Comité de Selección de *La casa automatizada del futuro*:

1. información personal: nombre completo, dirección, teléfono y dirección de correo electrónico
2. un panfleto descriptivo de la casa automatizada con la siguiente información:
   a. tamaño de la casa en pies (*feet*) o metros cuadrados (*square meters*)
   b. número y nombre de las habitaciones
   c. aparatos eléctricos y electrónicos de la casa y sus funciones
   d. dispositivos y sensores y su(s) función(es)
3. si es posible, un dibujo o foto digital de la casa automatizada

Fecha límite: el 30 de marzo
Premio: Una computadora portátil de último modelo y alta resolución, con programas de alta capacidad y funcionalidad.

SEGUNDA FASE. Usted decide participar en el concurso con un proyecto excepcional. Para preparar su proyecto para el comité que selecciona a los ganadores (*winners*), tenga en cuenta las bases del concurso y tome notas de los puntos 1, 2 y 3 que aparecen en el anuncio.

Escribir

5-43 Manos a la obra. Ahora prepare su panfleto. Para hacer la descripción de *La casa automatizada del futuro*, use sus ideas de la *Segunda fase* de la actividad **5-42**. Recuerde incluir toda la información que pide el concurso. Considere la cantidad de información necesaria y el tono apropiado para sus lectores, los miembros del Comité de Selección. ¡Buena suerte!

Después de escribir

5-44 Revisión. Antes de presentar su panfleto, revise:

1. primero, la claridad de sus ideas
2. la cantidad y la sofisticación de la información dada
3. lo apropiado del tono (impersonal, serio) para un comité de periodistas
4. la precisión gramatical (el vocabulario común y corriente y el vocabulario más técnico, las estructuras que utiliza para describir, la concordancia, etc.)
5. finalmente, la ortografía y la acentuación

ESTRATEGIA

Select the appropriate content and tone for a formal description

To write a description using a formal tone, you will need to do the following:

- Anticipate what your audience may know about the topic, including relevant details.
- Adapt the language of your text to the level of your readership. For example, if you are writing about technology for computer experts, you do not have to explain basic terms like *servidor* or *voz sobre IP*. Focus on the amount and kind of information your readers will need.
- Use an impersonal and formal tone. If you wish to address your reader(s) directly, use **usted/ustedes**.

ENFOQUE CULTURAL

La geografía espectacular de Nicaragua, El Salvador y Honduras

Una característica de la geografía de Nicaragua, El Salvador y Honduras es la gran cantidad de volcanes que hay en estos países. En realidad, toda la región centroamericana del Pacífico es rica en volcanes. Algunos son grandes montañas de una belleza impresionante; algunos están activos y producen explosiones de lava o ceniza; otros, en cambio, no tienen actividad volcánica notable. Algunos son muy viejos, otros, en cambio, como el Volcán de Cerro Negro, que nació en 1850, son relativamente jóvenes.

Muchos volcanes tienen una actividad constante que consiste en pequeñas explosiones internas, expulsión de gases y temblores de tierra que los humanos no perciben, pero que se pueden medir usando instrumentos científicos. Algunas veces, esa actividad normal aumenta sin presentar un peligro inmediato. Sin embargo, los científicos y el gobierno se preocupan cuando esto ocurre. El volcán de San Cristóbal, por ejemplo, tuvo un aumento importante (pero no peligroso) de su actividad normal en mayo de 2006.

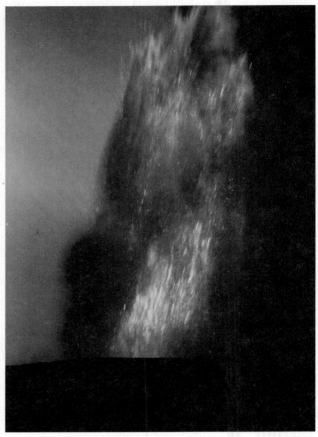

El volcán Cerro Negro de Nicaragua durante una explosión en 1995

Otra característica importante de toda la región centroamericana es la propensión a producir terremotos. Managua, la capital de Nicaragua, constantemente se ve afectada por grandes terremotos. En 1931, por ejemplo, un terremoto destruyó muchos edificios y causó la muerte de más de mil personas. También en 1972, un terremoto destruyó una gran parte del centro de esta ciudad, como muestra la foto. El 13 de enero de 2001, un violento terremoto mató a más de 700 personas y dejó a más de medio millón de personas sin casa en El Salvador. Y el 13 de febrero de 2001, un terremoto de 6,6 de intensidad destruyó en El Salvador más de 30.000 casas y dejó más de 300 muertos.

El terremoto de 1972 destruyó muchas casas del centro de Managua.

En otras palabras

Expresiones nicaragüenses

Él es **ñeque**.
He is strong/vigorous.

Ella **está jalando** con Luis.
She is Luis's girlfriend.

Ese **chavalo** es terrible.
That kid is terrible.

Finalmente, esta región también se caracteriza por ser muy montañosa y por tener selvas y playas espectaculares. El Salvador, por ejemplo, aunque es el país más densamente poblado de las Américas, tiene montañas, selvas y playas naturales de gran belleza. Las playas salvadoreñas del Pacífico son bellísimas y son un paraíso para los aficionados al surfing. Más del 80% del terreno de Honduras consiste de montañas, pero tiene también selvas. Honduras es uno de los países con mayor biodiversidad, porque tiene muchas especies diferentes de plantas y animales.

En otras palabras

Expresiones salvadoreñas

María **chinea** a su hijo.
María holds her child in her arms continuously.

Sólo es un **cipote**.
He is only a child.

—¿Vas a la playa mañana?
—Are you going to the beach tomorrow?

—**Primero** Dios.
—God willing.

Gustavo Estrasser en una competencia en La Libertad, El Salvador

En otras palabras

Expresiones hondureñas

Parece que José **me agarró de ojo de gallo**.
It looks like José has ill will towards me.

¿Qué está haciendo ese **güirro**?
What is that child doing?

185

5-45 Comprensión. PRIMERA FASE. **Reconocimiento de palabras clave.** Encuentre en el texto la palabra o expresión que mejor expresa el significado de las siguientes ideas.

1. ash _____
2. increases _____
3. danger _____
4. earthquakes _____
5. mountainous _____
6. jungles _____
7. paradise _____

SEGUNDA FASE. **Oraciones importantes.** Subraye las afirmaciones que contienen ideas que se encuentran en el texto. Luego indique en qué parte del texto están.

1. Many volcanoes in this region are located near the Pacific Ocean.
2. Some volcanoes are amazingly beautiful.
3. One can find some young volcanoes in this region.
4. Volcanoes are dangerous, and people are afraid of them.
5. Most volcanoes are always active, although people may not be able to feel it.
6. Although small increments in volcano activity are not dangerous, scientists usually worry about them.
7. Central America is prone to earthquakes.
8. Earthquakes and volcanoes have destroyed the biodiversity of the surrounding area.

TERCERA FASE. **Ideas principales.** Escriba un párrafo breve en inglés resumiendo las ideas principales expresadas en el texto.

 5-46 Use la información. Usted tiene $300.000 dólares y quiere comprar una casa en Nicaragua, Honduras o El Salvador. Siguiendo los enlaces, busque la mejor casa, apartamento o propiedad rural que puede comprar con ese dinero. Prepare un afiche (*poster*) para mostrar en la clase. Debe incluir: localización, tipo de propiedad, características más importantes de la propiedad y su precio. Incluya también información adicional de interés para usted. Para preparar esta actividad, visite la página web de *Mosaicos* y siga los enlaces útiles.

VOCABULARIO

La arquitectura — *Architecture*

el alquiler — *rent*
el apartamento — *apartment*
el edificio — *building*
el estilo — *style*
las ruinas — *ruins*
la vivienda — *housing*

En una casa — *In a home*

el aire acondicionado — *air conditioning*
el armario — *closet, armoire*
el baño — *bathroom*
la basura — *garbage, trash*
la calefacción — *heating*
la chimenea — *fireplace*
la cocina — *kitchen*
el comedor — *dining room*
el cuarto — *room; bedroom*
la escalera — *stairs*
el garaje — *garage*
la habitación — *bedroom*
la lavandería — *laundry room*
el pasillo — *corridor, hall*
la piscina — *swimming pool*
el piso — *floor; apartment*
la planta baja — *first floor, ground floor*
la sala — *living room*
la terraza — *terrace*

Los muebles y accesorios — *Furniture and accessories*

la alfombra — *carpet, rug*
la butaca — *armchair*
la cama — *bed*
la cómoda — *dresser*
la cortina — *curtain*
el cuadro — *picture, painting*
el espejo — *mirror*
la lámpara — *lamp*
el sofá — *sofa*

Los electrodomésticos — *Appliances*

la aspiradora — *vacuum cleaner*
la lavadora — *washer*
el lavaplatos — *dishwasher*
el (horno) microondas — *microwave (oven)*
el/la radio — *radio*
el refrigerador — *refrigerator*
la secadora — *dryer*
el ventilador — *fan*

Para la cama — *For the bed*

la almohada — *pillow*
la manta — *blanket*
la sábana — *sheet*

En el baño — *In the bathroom*

la bañera — *bathtub*
la ducha — *shower*
el inodoro — *toilet*
el jabón — *soap*

el lavabo — *bathroom sink*
la toalla — *towel*

En la cocina — *In the kitchen*

la estufa — *stove*
el fregadero — *kitchen sink*
el plato — *dish, plate*

En el jardín — *In the garden*

la barbacoa — *barbecue pit; barbecue (event)*
el césped — *lawn*
la hoja — *leaf*

Los lugares — *Places*

las afueras — *outskirts*
el barrio — *neighborhood*
la calle — *street*
el centro — *downtown, center*
cerca (de) — *near, close (to)*
lejos (de) — *far (from)*
el pueblo — *village*
la zona — *area*

Las descripciones — *Descriptions*

limpio/a — *clean*
ordenado/a — *tidy*
seco/a — *dry*
sucio/a — *dirty*

Verbos — *Verbs*

ayudar — *to help*
barrer — *to sweep*
cocinar — *to cook*
cortar — *to cut; to mow (lawn)*
creer — *to believe*
doblar — *to fold*
limpiar — *to clean*
ordenar — *to tidy up*
pasar la aspiradora — *to vacuum*
planchar — *to iron*
preparar — *to prepare*
recoger (j) — *to pick up*
regar (ie) — *to water*
sacar — *to take out*
tender (ie) — *to hang (clothes)*

Palabras útiles — *Useful words*

la desventaja — *disadvantage*
el trabajo — *work*
la ventaja — *advantage*
la vista — *view*

See page 157 for ordinal numbers.
See *Lengua* box on page 160 for more electronic items.
See page 167 for expressions with **tener**.
See page 171 for direct object pronouns.
See pages 175–176 for demonstrative adjectives and pronouns.

Expansión gramatical

This grammatical supplement includes structures often considered optional for the introductory level, because the functions and forms presented here are far beyond the performance level of most first-year students. Many instructors choose to present them for recognition only, if at all. The *vosotros* command forms are included in this section for the instructors who use them to address their students.

The explanation and activities in this section use the same format as the grammatical material throughout *Mosaicos* in order to facilitate their incorporation into the core lessons of the program or their addition as another chapter in the book.

Funciones y formas

1. Giving informal orders or commands to two or more people (in Spain): *Vosotros* commands
2. Expressing an indirect wish that a third party do something: Indirect commands
3. Suggesting that someone and the speaker do something: The Spanish equivalents of English *let's*
4. Reacting to a past occurrence or event: The present perfect subjunctive
5. Hypothesizing about an occurrence or event in the past: The conditional perfect and the pluperfect subjunctive
6. Expressing contrary-to-fact conditions in the past: *If*-clauses (using the perfect tense)
7. Emphasizing a fact resulting from an action by someone or something: The passive voice

1. Giving informal orders or commands to two or more people (in Spain): *Vosotros* commands

	AFFIRMATIVE	NEGATIVE
hablar	habla**d**	no **habléis**
comer	come**d**	no **comáis**
escribir	escribi**d**	no **escribáis**

■ To use the affirmative **vosotros** command, change the final **-r** of the infinitive to **-d**.

■ Use the **vosotros** form of the present subjunctive for the **vosotros** negative command.

■ For the affirmative **vosotros** command of reflexive verbs, drop the final **-d** and add the pronoun **os: levantad + os = levantaos.** The verb **irse** is an exception: **idos.**

EG-1 Buenos consejos. Usted quiere que sus mejores amigos cambien sus hábitos y vivan una vida más sana. Dígales qué deben hacer.

MODELO: caminar dos kilómetros todos los días
            Caminad dos kilómetros todos los días.

1. comer muchas frutas y vegetales
2. empezar un programa de ejercicios
3. no respirar por la boca
4. no cansarse mucho los primeros días
5. relajarse para evitar el estrés
6. dormir no menos de ocho horas

EG-2 Órdenes en grupo. Cada uno/a de ustedes va a hacer el papel de profesor/a de educación física y le va a dar una orden a los otros estudiantes del grupo. Los estudiantes deben hacer lo que el/la profesor/a les indica.

MODELO: *Levantad los brazos y las piernas.*

SITUACIONES

You and your partner have rented a cabin in the mountains for a month. Some of your friends are going to use the cabin part of the time and you would like to give them some rules to make sure they leave everything in order. Write the rules and then compare them with those of another couple.

2. Expressing an indirect wish that a third party do something: Indirect commands

You have used commands directly to tell others to do something: **Salga/Salgan ahora.** Now you are going to use indirect commands to say what someone else should do: **Que salga Berta.** Note that this indirect command is equivalent to saying **Quiero que Berta salga,** but without expressing the main verb **quiero.**

■ The word **que** introduces the indirect command. The subject, if stated, normally follows the verb.

Que cocine Roberto.	*Let Roberto cook.*
Que descanse María.	*Let María rest.*

■ Reflexive and object pronouns always precede the verb.

Que **se siente** a la mesa.	*Let him sit at the table.*
Que **le sirvan** la cena.	*Let them serve him dinner.*
Que **se la sirvan** ahora.	*Let them serve it to him now.*

 EG-3 Una clase de cocina. Un chef muy conocido ha accedido a dar una clase de cocina con el fin de recaudar (*raise*) dinero para una obra social. Usted y su compañero/a forman parte del comité que organiza la clase. Su compañero/a tiene la lista de las personas que desean ayudar y usted tiene la lista de las tareas pendientes. Háganse preguntas y contéstense con la información que cada uno/a tiene.

MODELO: *Eduardo, Alicia y Pedro preparar los anuncios, comprar los refrescos*
   E1:   *¿Quién va a preparar los anuncios?*
   E2:   *Que los preparen Alicia y Pedro. ¿Y qué va a hacer Eduardo?*
   E1:   *Que compre los refrescos.*

Personas

Beatriz
Alberto y Rubén
Miguel
Elena y Amanda
Ana María
Emilio
Un camarero

Tareas

traer los platos
tener los ingredientes listos
buscar las sillas
copiar las recetas
servir el vino
recibir a las personas
ayudar al chef

EG-4 Una fiesta hispana. PRIMERA FASE. Para celebrar el final de curso ustedes han decidido organizar una fiesta en el departamento de español. Hagan una lista de todo lo que necesitan y otra lista de todas las personas que van a invitar, además de sus compañeros/as de clase.

SEGUNDA FASE. Decidan qué otras personas de la clase pueden encargarse de cada sección y por qué. Su compañero/a, que está de acuerdo con usted, le dará algunas ideas.

MODELO: E1:   *Que se encargue Juan de comprar las invitaciones porque tiene que ir al supermercado esta tarde.*
                E2:   *Sí, pero que las escriban María y Pedro que escriben mejor.*

SITUACIONES

Role A. You are a new manager for the Student Union who wants to improve the food and the service at the cafeteria. In a meeting with the cafeteria manager, say a) that it is important that students receive a better service, b) inform the manager of the type of food you would like to find in the cafeteria and of the ways in which the service could be improved, and c) say that you hope the prices will not increase (**subir**) this semester.

Role B. You are the cafeteria manager. Agree with the Student Union manager and tell him/her a) that you have a good team and you want everyone to do a good job, b) that you will be happy to meet with a student committee and have students suggest (**sugerir**) menus, and c) that you will do your best (**hacer lo posible**) to convince your team to incorporate your suggestions.

3. Suggesting that someone and the speaker do something: The Spanish equivalents of English *let's*

In Spanish, you may suggest that two or more people, including yourself, do something together in the following ways.

- **Vamos + a** + *infinitive* is commonly used in Spanish to express English *let's* + *verb*.

Vamos a llamar al doctor.	*Let's call the doctor.*

- Use **vamos** by itself to mean *let's go*. The negative *let's not go* is **no vayamos**.

Vamos al hospital.	*Let's go to the hospital.*
No vayamos al hospital.	*Let's not go to the hospital.*

- Another equivalent for *let's* + *verb* is the **nosotros** form of the present subjunctive.

Hablemos con el médico.	*Let's talk to the doctor.*
No hablemos con la enfermera.	*Let's not talk to the nurse.*

- The final **-s** of reflexive affirmative commands is dropped when the pronoun **nos** is attached. Note the additional written accent.

Levantemos + nos	→	**Levantémonos.**
Sirvamos + nos	→	**Sirvámonos.**

- Placement of object and reflexive pronouns is the same as with **usted(es)** commands.

Comprémosla.	*Let's buy it.*
No la compremos.	*Let's not buy it.*

 EG-5 ¿Qué debemos hacer? Usted y un/a compañero/a están estudiando y cuidando a su hermanito al mismo tiempo. El niño les dice que se siente mal. Cada uno/a de ustedes debe escoger tres de las siguientes opciones y decirle a su compañero/a lo que deben o no deben hacer.

MODELO: llevarlo a su cuarto   llamar a tus padres
E1: *Llevémoslo a su cuarto.*   E2: *Llamemos a tus padres.*

1. darle agua
2. llevarlo al parque
3. comprarle juguetes
4. ponerle el termómetro
5. llamar al médico
6. preguntarle qué le duele
7. prepararle una hamburguesa
8. explicarle los síntomas al doctor
9. ponerle la televisión
10. acostarlo

EG-6 Resoluciones. Usted y su compañero/a deciden llevar una vida más sana. Túrnense para decir lo que piensan hacer. Su compañero/a va a decirle si está de acuerdo o no con su sugerencia.

MODELO: comer más verduras
   E1: *Vamos a comer más verduras.*
   E2: *Sí, comamos más verduras./No, (no comamos más verduras,)*
      comamos más frutas.

1. tomar vitaminas y minerales
2. caminar tres kilómetros diariamente
3. beber ocho vasos de agua todos los días
4. acostarse más temprano
5. dormir ocho horas todas las noches
6. ...

 EG-7 Los preparativos para un beneficio. En pequeños grupos, decidan qué actividades van a hacer para recaudar (*collect*) fondos a beneficio de un hospital. Deben mencionar cinco actividades.

MODELO: *Organicemos un partido del equipo de basquetbol.*

SITUACIONES

You and your partner are planning to visit a classmate who is in the hospital. Decide a) when you will visit him/her, b) what you are going to take him/her, and c) what you can do for your classmate after he/she leaves the hospital. Then, exchange this information with another pair of students.

4. Reacting to a past occurrence or event: The present perfect subjunctive

Use the present perfect subjunctive to react to a past occurrence, event or condition. The present perfect subjunctive is formed with the present subjunctive of the verb **haber** + *past participle*.

PRESENT SUBJUNCTIVE OF *HABER* + *PAST PARTICIPLE*		
yo	haya	
yú	hayas	
Ud., él/ella	haya	hablado
nosotros/as	hayamos	comido
vosotros/as	hayáis	vivido
Uds., ellos/as	hayan	

Note that the dependent clause using the present perfect subjunctive describes what has happened before the time expressed or implied in the main clause, which is the present. Its English equivalent is normally *has/have* + *past participle*, but it may vary according to the context.

Your friend tells you:

Mis hijos volvieron de sus vacaciones. →

Your reaction to this past event:

Me alegro de que **hayan llegado**.
I'm glad they arrived early.

Your secretary informs you:

El gerente de ventas no vino a trabajar ayer. →

Your reaction to this past news:

Es posible que **haya estado** enfermo.
It's possible that he may have been sick.

 EG-8 ¿Qué espera usted? Escoja la oración que complete lógicamente las siguientes situaciones. Compare sus respuestas con las de su compañero/a.

1. Su computadora no estaba funcionando bien y usted se la dio a un técnico para que la reparara. Usted espera que...
   a. la haya vendido.
   b. haya destruido sus programas.
   c. haya encontrado el problema.
2. Su amigo acaba de regresar de Puerto Rico, donde fue a pasar sus vacaciones. Usted le dice: "Espero que...
   a. hayas visitado el Viejo San Juan".
   b. te hayas aburrido mucho".
   c. hayas perdido todo tu dinero".
3. Uno de sus compañeros ha estado muy grave en el hospital, pero ya está en la casa. Usted le habla y le dice: "Siento mucho que...
   a. hayas vendido la casa".
   b. hayas estado tan mal".
   c. hayas salido del hospital".

4. Usted llama por teléfono a un amigo para invitarlo a cenar, pero nadie contesta el teléfono. Es probable que su amigo…

   a. haya cenado ya.

   b. haya salido de su casa.

   c. haya cambiado su teléfono.

5. Uno de sus parientes dijo una mentira (*lie*). Como es natural, a usted le molesta mucho que no…

   a. haya dicho la verdad.

   b. haya dicho nada.

   c. haya hablado con sus parientes.

EG-9 Un viaje. Uno de sus amigos pasó un semestre en Los Ángeles. Túrnese con su compañero/a para decirle lo que esperan que haya hecho en su visita.

MODELO: ir a Beverly Hills / visitar la Biblioteca Huntington

     E1:   *Espero que hayas ido a Beverly Hills.*

     E2:   *Y yo espero que hayas visitado la Biblioteca Huntington.*

1. ver las Torres de Watts

2. ir a los Estudios Universal

3. caminar por la calle Olvera

4. comer comida mexicana

5. manejar hasta el observatorio del Monte Wilson

6. asistir al Desfile de las Rosas

EG-10 Los adelantos científicos. Usted y su compañero/a trabajan con otros científicos en un laboratorio de ingeniería genética. Háganse preguntas para saber qué han logrado o no en sus investigaciones.

MODELO: aislar el nuevo virus / es posible que

     E1:   *¿Han aislado el nuevo virus?*

     E2:   *Es posible que lo hayamos / hayan aislado.*

1. cambiar la estructura de la célula / dudar

2. no hacer implantes nuevos / es una lástima

3. duplicar órganos / no creer que

4. regular el ritmo del corazón / esperar

5. reactivar los músculos atrofiados / es probable que

6. modificar los genes / es importante que

En directo

To express that you remember or recognize someone in a photo:

Mira, mira, este/esta es…
Look, this is . . .

Te equivocas
You are wrong.

Pero, ¿no ves que es…/ Tiene/lleva…
But, don't you see it is . . .
(a person's name)

¿Has visto a…?

SITUACIONES

You and your classmate graduated years ago and are remembering the times when you were at the university. You have found a group photo of your Spanish class. Talk about each of your classmates saying a) what you know they have done in their lives, b) what you hope they have done, and c) what you doubt they have done. Use your imagination and the expressions in the box to sound more natural.

5. Hypothesizing about an occurrence or event in the past: The conditional perfect and the pluperfect subjunctive

In this section you will study two new verb tenses: the conditional perfect and the pluperfect subjunctive. Use this tense to hypothesize about an occurrence or event in the past.

■ Use the conditional of **haber** + *past participle* to form the conditional perfect.

CONDITIONAL PERFECT		
yo	habría	
tú	habrías	
Ud., él, ella	habría	hablado
nosotros/as	habríamos	comido
vosotros/as	habríais	vivido
Uds., ellos/as	habrían	

■ The conditional perfect usually corresponds to English *would have + past participle.*

Sé que le **habría gustado** esta casa.	*I know you/he/she would have liked this house.*

■ Use the past subjunctive of **haber** + *past participle* to form the pluperfect subjunctive.

PLUPERFECT SUBJUNCTIVE		
yo	hubiera	
tú	hubieras	
Ud., él, ella	hubiera	hablado
nosotros/as	hubiéramos	comido
vosotros/as	hubierais	vivido
Uds., ellos/as	hubieran	

■ The pluperfect subjunctive corresponds to English *might have, would have,* or *had + past participle.* It is used in constructions where the subjunctive is normally required.

Dudaba que **hubiera venido** temprano.	*I doubted that he had/would have come early.*
Esperaba que **hubieran comido** en casa.	*I was hoping that they would have eaten at home.*
Ojalá que **hubieran visto** ese letrero.	*I wish they had seen that sign.*

EG-11 ¿Qué habría hecho en estas situaciones? PRIMERA FASE. Digan qué habría hecho cada uno/a de ustedes en las siguientes situaciones. Después escojan la respuesta que les parezca mejor para cada situación.

MODELO: Usted recibió una invitación para una recepción en la Casa Blanca.
      E1:   *Se lo habría dicho a todos mis compañeros.*
      E2:   *Habría leído la invitación varias veces porque habría pensado que era una broma.*

1. En el aeropuerto le dijeron que podía viajar en primera clase todo el año sin pagar.
2. Le pidieron sugerencias para mejorar la situación de los vuelos y los aeropuertos.
3. La NASA lo/la llamó para ver si le interesaba vivir tres meses en una estación espacial.
4. Le dijeron que organizara la fiesta de fin de curso de su clase.
5. Le pidieron que revisara los programas en su universidad y sugiriera los cambios necesarios.

SEGUNDA FASE. Comparen las respuestas que escogieron con las de otra pareja y decidan cuál es la mejor. Después compartan sus respuestas con el resto de la clase.

 EG-12 Nuestras esperanzas. Usted y su compañero/a esperaban que el nuevo gobierno hiciera muchas cosas en beneficio de la sociedad. Se lograron algunas cosas, pero otras no. Túrnense para decir qué esperaban que el nuevo gobierno y su gabinete hubieran hecho y si lo han hecho o no.

MODELO: subir el sueldo mínimo / mejorar el sistema de educación
      E1:   *Esperaba que hubieran subido el sueldo mínimo y (no) lo han hecho.*
      E2:   *Y yo esperaba que hubieran mejorado el sistema de educación y (no) lo han hecho.*

1. bajar los impuestos (*taxes*)
2. mejorar el transporte público
3. terminar con la corrupción
4. construir viviendas (*housing*) para familias pobres
5. ofrecer mejores planes de salud
6. proteger el medio ambiente
7. ...

SITUACIONES

Role A. You had an argument (**pelea**) with your significant other. Explain to your best friend what happened and ask him/her what he/she would have done in your place. Then tell him/her what you intend to do.

Role B. Your best friend explains to you that he/she had an argument (**pelea**) with his/her significant other. Ask questions to obtain some details. Then a) tell him/her what you would have done in the same situation, b) ask him/her what he/she intends to do and c) give him/her your advice.

6. Expressing contrary-to-fact conditions in the past: *If*-clauses (using the perfect tenses)

The conditional perfect and pluperfect subjunctive are used in contrary-to-fact if-statements which refer to actions, events, experiences related to the past.

Si **hubieras venido**, te **habría**
  gustado la conferencia.

If you had come (which you did not),
  you would have liked the lecture.

 EG-13 La vida sería diferente. Con su compañero/a, diga cuáles habrían sido las consecuencias si...

MODELO: no se hubieran inventado los aviones
      E1: *Habríamos viajado en barco, en tren o en autobús.*
      E2: *Habríamos contaminado menos la atmósfera.*

1. no se hubiera inventado la bomba atómica
2. no se hubieran deforestado los bosques
3. los ingleses hubieran descubierto América
4. las mujeres hubieran tenido siempre las mismas oportunidades que los hombres
5. no se hubieran creado las vacunas (*vaccination*)
6. los jóvenes hubieran gobernado el mundo

 EG-14 Unas excusas. ¿Qué excusas darían ustedes en las siguientes situaciones?

MODELO: Un amigo le pidió que participara en un experimento.
      E1: *Si mis padres me lo hubieran permitido, habría participado.*
      E2: *Si hubiera tenido tiempo, habría participado.*

1. Una organización quería que usted donara botellas y papeles para reciclar.
2. Le pidieron su coche para llevar unas ratas al laboratorio.
3. Lo/La necesitaban de voluntario/a para probar una vacuna contra el catarro.
4. Un/a compañero/a quería venderle su computadora portátil.
5. Una compañía necesitaba probar unos paracaídas (*parachutes*) y buscaba personas interesadas en las pruebas.
6. Alquilaban un robot para que hiciera las tareas domésticas.

 EG-15 Volver a vivir. Piense en una experiencia negativa que usted haya tenido. Cuéntele a su compañero/a qué le pasó y dígale qué habría hecho si hubiera sabido en ese momento lo que sabe hoy. Después, su compañero/a debe hacer lo mismo.

SITUACIONES

Role A. You attended a conference/lecture about the city of the future. Tell your classmate a) where and when the conference/lecture took place, b) that he/she would have found it very interesting, and c) the things that he/she would have learned if he/she had attended.

Role B. Your classmate has attended a conference/lecture about the city of the future. Ask him/her questions to find out more about the things he/she learned.

7. Emphasizing a fact resulting from an action by someone or something: The passive voice

The passive voice emphasizes a fact resulting from the action by someone or something.

■ The passive voice in Spanish is formed with the verb **ser** + *past participle*; the passive voice is most commonly used in the preterit, though at times you may see it used in other tenses.

La planta nuclear **fue construida** en 1980.	*The nuclear plant was built in 1980.*

■ Use the preposition **por** when indicating who or what performs the action.

El bosque **fue destruido**. (Who or what did it is not expressed.)	*The forest was destroyed.*
El bosque **fue destruido por** el fuego. (The fire did it.)	*The forest was destroyed by the fire.*

■ The past participle functions as an adjective and therefore agrees in gender and number with the subject.

Los árboles fueron **destruidos** por la lluvia ácida.	*The trees were destroyed by acid rain.*
La cura fue **descubierta** el año pasado.	*The cure was discovered last year.*

■ You'll most often find the passive voice in written Spanish, especially in newspapers and formal writing. However, in conversation, Spanish speakers normally use two different constructions that you have already studied—a third person plural verb or a **se** construction.

Vendieron el laboratorio.	*They sold the laboratory.*
Se vendió el edificio.	*The building was sold.*

EG-16 La comunicación oral. Túrnense para decir lo que pasó en una reunión del presidente y los ministros. ¿Cómo lo dirían los periódicos? ¿Cómo lo dirían ustedes en una conversación?

MODELO: ministros / recibir / el presidente
      E1: *Los ministros fueron recibidos por el presidente.*
      E2: *El presidente recibió a los ministros.*

1. la agenda / preparar / el secretario
2. la agenda / aprobar / todos
3. el proyecto para disminuir la contaminación / escribir / el Sr. Sosa
4. el proyecto / presentar / la Ministra de Salud
5. unos comentarios / leer / el presidente
6. las preguntas / contestar / el ministro

EG-17 Dos reporteros. Túrnense para decir cómo escribirían las siguientes noticias para un periódico.

MODELO: la lluvia ácida dañó las cosechas
Las cosechas fueron dañadas por la lluvia ácida.

1. La zona del Amazonas se conoce como el "pulmón" del planeta.
2. Los campesinos deforestaron la selva.
3. Los campesinos cultivaron la tierra.
4. Estos grupos cortaron muchos árboles.
5. La invasión de los seres humanos exterminó muchas especies de animales.
6. El gobierno plantará mil árboles para mejorar la situación.

SITUACIONES

You and your classmate are TV newscasters. You must write and give a piece of news to your viewers on a great discovery. Inform them that a) some very secret plans have been discovered by the CIA, b) that important security measures have been taken, c) that politicians are now deliberating on how to respond to a possible threat (**peligro**) to the population, d) that public transport has been interrupted in major cities, e) that the situation is under control and f) that nobody should be afraid.

Appendix 1

Stress and Written Accents in Spanish

Rules for Written Accents

The following rules are based on pronunciation.

1. If a word ends in *n*, *s*, or a vowel, the penultimate (second-to-last) syllable is usually stressed.

    Examples: cami**nan**
                muchos
                silla

2. If a word ends in a consonant other than *n* or *s*, the last syllable is stressed.

    Example: fa**tal**

3. Words that are exceptions to the preceding rules have an accent mark on the stressed vowel.

    Examples: sar**tén**
                lápices
                ma**má**
                fácil

4. **Separation of diphthongs.** When *i* or *u* are combined with another vowel, they are pronounced as one sound (a diphthong). When each vowel sound is pronounced separately, a written accent mark is placed over the stressed vowel (either the *i* or the *u*).

    Example: gracias   día

Because the written accents in the following examples are not determined by pronunciation, the accent mark must be memorized as part of the spelling of the words as they are learned.

5. **Homonyms.** When two words are spelled the same, but have different meanings, a written accent is used to distinguish and differentiate meaning.

    Examples:

de	*of*	**dé**	*give* (formal command)
el	*the*	**él**	*he*
mas	*but*	**más**	*more*
mi	*my*	**mí**	me
se	*him/herself,* *(to) him/her/them*	**sé**	*I know, be* (formal command)
si	*if*	**sí**	*yes*
te	*(to) you*	**té**	*tea*
tu	*your*	**tú**	*you*

6. **Interrogatives and exclamations.** In questions (direct and indirect) and exclamations, a written accent is placed over the following words: **dónde, cómo, cuándo, cuál(es), quién(es), cuánto(s)/cuánta(s),** and **qué.**

Word Formation in Spanish

Recognizing certain patterns in Spanish word formation can be a big help in deciphering meaning. Use the following information about word formation to help you as you read.

■ **Prefixes.** Spanish and English share a number of prefixes that shade the meaning of the word to which they are attached: **inter-** (between, among); **intro/a-** (within); **ex-** (former, toward the outside); **en-/em-** (the state of becoming); **in-/a-** (not, without), among others.

inter-	interdisciplinario, interacción
intro/a-	introvertido, introspección
ex-	exponer (*expose*)
en-/em-	enrojecer (*to turn red*), empobrecer (*to become poor*)
in-/a-	inmoral, incompleto, amoral, asexual

■ **Suffixes.** Suffixes and, in general, word endings will help you identify various aspects of words such as part of speech, gender, meaning, degree, etc. Common Spanish suffixes are **-ría, -za, -miento, -dad/tad, -ura, -oso/a, -izo/a, -(c)ito/a,** and **-mente**.

-ría	place where something is made and/or bought: **panadería, zapatería** (*shoe store*), **librería**.
-za	feminine, abstract noun: **pobreza** (*poverty*), **riqueza** (*wealth, richness*).
-miento	masculine, abstract noun: **empobrecimiento** (*impoverishment*), **entrenamiento** (*training*).
-dad/tad	feminine noun: **ciudad** (*city*), **libertad** (*liberty, freedom*)
-ura	feminine noun: **verdura, locura** (*craziness*).
-oso/a	adjective meaning having the characteristics of the noun to which it's attached: **montañoso, lluvioso** (*rainy*).
-izo/a	adjective meaning having the characteristics of the noun to which it's attached: **rojizo** (*reddish*), **enfermizo** (*sickly*).
-(c)ito/a	diminutive form of noun or adjective: **Juanito, mesita** (*little table*), **Carmencita**.
-mente	attached to the feminine form of adjective to form an adverb: **rápidamente, felizmente** (*happily*).

■ **Compounds.** Compounds are made up of two words (e.g., *mailman*), each of which has meaning in and of itself: **altavoz** (*loudspeaker*) from **alto/a** and **voz**; **sacacorchos** (*corkscrew*) from **sacar** and **corcho**. Your knowledge of the root words will help you recognize the compound; and likewise, learning compounds can help you to learn the root words. What do you think **sacar** means?

■ **Spanish-English associations.** Learning to associate aspects of word formation in Spanish with aspects of word formation in English can be very helpful. Look at the associations below.

SPANISH	ENGLISH
es/ex + consonant	*s* + consonant
esclerosis, extraño	*sclerosis, strange*
gu-	*w-*
guerra, Guillermo	*war, William*
-tad/dad	*-ty*
libertad, calidad	*liberty, quality*
-sión/-ción	*-sion/-tion*
tensión, emoción	*tension, emotion*

Appendix 2

Verb Charts

Regular Verbs: Simple Tenses

Infinitive Present Participle Past Participle	Indicative					Subjunctive		Imperative
	Present	Imperfect	Preterit	Future	Conditional	Present	Imperfect	Commands
hablar hablando hablado	hablo hablas habla hablamos habláis hablan	hablaba hablabas hablaba hablábamos hablabais hablaban	hablé hablaste habló hablamos hablasteis hablaron	hablaré hablarás hablará hablaremos hablaréis hablarán	hablaría hablarías hablaría hablaríamos hablaríais hablarían	hable hables hable hablemos habléis hablen	hablara hablaras hablara habláramos hablarais hablaran	habla (tú), no hables hable (usted) hablemos hablad (vosotros), no habléis hablen (Uds.)
comer comiendo comido	como comes come comemos coméis comen	comía comías comía comíamos comíais comían	comí comiste comió comimos comisteis comieron	comeré comerás comerá comeremos comeréis comerán	comería comerías comería comeríamos comeríais comerían	coma comas coma comamos comáis coman	comiera comieras comiera comiéramos comierais comieran	come (tú), no comas coma (usted) comamos comed (vosotros), no comáis coman (Uds.)
vivir viviendo vivido	vivo vives vive vivimos vivís viven	vivía vivías vivía vivíamos vivíais vivían	viví viviste vivió vivimos vivisteis vivieron	viviré vivirás vivirá viviremos viviréis vivirán	viviría vivirías viviría viviríamos viviríais vivirían	viva vivas viva vivamos viváis vivan	viviera vivieras viviera viviéramos vivierais vivieran	vive (tú), no vivas viva (usted) vivamos vivid (vosotros), no viváis vivan (Uds.)

Regular Verbs: Perfect Tenses

Indicative											Subjunctive			
Present Perfect		Past Perfect		Preterit Perfect		Future Perfect		Conditional Perfect			Present Perfect		Past Perfect	
he	hablado	había	hablado	hube	hablado	habré	hablado	habría	hablado		haya	hablado	hubiera	hablado
has	comido	habías	comido	hubiste	comido	habrás	comido	habrías	comido		hayas	comido	hubieras	comido
ha	vivido	había	vivido	hubo	vivido	habrá	vivido	habría	vivido		haya	vivido	hubiera	vivido
hemos		habíamos		hubimos		habremos		habríamos			hayamos		hubiéramos	
habéis		habíais		hubisteis		habréis		habríais			hayáis		hubierais	
han		habían		hubieron		habrán		habrían			hayan		hubieran	

Irregular Verbs

Infinitive / Present Participle / Past Participle	Indicative					Subjunctive		Imperative
	Present	Imperfect	Preterit	Future	Conditional	Present	Imperfect	Commands
andar andando andado	ando andas anda andamos andáis andan	andaba andabas andaba andábamos andabais andaban	anduve anduviste anduvo anduvimos anduvisteis anduvieron	andaré andarás andará andaremos andaréis andarán	andaría andarías andaría andaríamos andaríais andarían	ande andes ande andemos andéis anden	anduviera anduvieras anduviera anduviéramos anduvierais anduvieran	anda (tú), no andes ande (usted) andemos andad (vosotros), no andéis anden (Uds.)
caer cayendo caído	caigo caes cae caemos caéis caen	caía caías caía caíamos caíais caían	caí caíste cayó caímos caísteis cayeron	caeré caerás caerá caeremos caeréis caerán	caería caerías caería caeríamos caeríais caerían	caiga caigas caiga caigamos caigáis caigan	cayera cayeras cayera cayéramos cayerais cayeran	cae (tú), no caigas caiga (usted) caigamos caed (vosotros), no caigáis caigan (Uds.)
dar dando dado	doy das da damos dais dan	daba dabas daba dábamos dabais daban	di diste dio dimos disteis dieron	daré darás dará daremos daréis darán	daría darías daría daríamos daríais darían	dé des dé demos deis den	diera dieras diera diéramos dierais dieran	da (tú), no des dé (usted) demos dad (vosotros), no deis den (Uds.)
decir diciendo dicho	digo dices dice decimos decís dicen	decía decías decía decíamos decíais decían	dije dijiste dijo dijimos dijisteis dijeron	diré dirás dirá diremos diréis dirán	diría dirías diría diríamos diríais dirían	diga digas diga digamos digáis digan	dijera dijeras dijera dijéramos dijerais dijeran	di (tú), no digas diga (usted) digamos decid (vosotros), no digáis digan (Uds.)

Irregular Verbs (continued)

Infinitive / Present Participle / Past Participle	Indicative						Subjunctive		Imperative
	Present	Imperfect	Preterit	Future	Conditional		Present	Imperfect	Commands
estar estando estado	estoy estás está estamos estáis están	estaba estabas estaba estábamos estabais estaban	estuve estuviste estuvo estuvimos estuvisteis estuvieron	estaré estarás estará estaremos estaréis estarán	estaría estarías estaría estaríamos estaríais estarían		esté estés esté estemos estéis estén	estuviera estuvieras estuviera estuviéramos estuvierais estuvieran	está (tú), no estés esté (usted) estemos estad (vosotros), no estéis estén (Uds.)
haber habiendo habido	he has ha hemos habéis han	había habías había habíamos habíais habían	hube hubiste hubo hubimos hubisteis hubieron	habré habrás habrá habremos habréis habrán	habría habrías habría habríamos habríais habrían		haya hayas haya hayamos hayáis hayan	hubiera hubieras hubiera hubiéramos hubierais hubieran	
hacer haciendo hecho	hago haces hace hacemos hacéis hacen	hacía hacías hacía hacíamos hacíais hacían	hice hiciste hizo hicimos hicisteis hicieron	haré harás hará haremos haréis harán	haría harías haría haríamos haríais harían		haga hagas haga hagamos hagáis hagan	hiciera hicieras hiciera hiciéramos hicierais hicieran	haz (tú), no hagas haga (usted) hagamos haced (vosotros), no hagáis hagan (Uds.)
ir yendo ido	voy vas va vamos vais van	iba ibas iba íbamos ibais iban	fui fuiste fue fuimos fuisteis fueron	iré irás irá iremos iréis irán	iría irías iría iríamos iríais irían		vaya vayas vaya vayamos vayáis vayan	fuera fueras fuera fuéramos fuerais fueran	ve (tú), no vayas vaya (usted) vamos, no vayamos id (vosotros), no vayáis vayan (Uds.)
oír oyendo oído	oigo oyes oye oímos oís oyen	oía oías oía oíamos oíais oían	oí oíste oyó oímos oísteis oyeron	oiré oirás oirá oiremos oiréis oirán	oiría oirías oiría oiríamos oiríais oirían		oiga oigas oiga oigamos oigáis oigan	oyera oyeras oyera oyéramos oyerais oyeran	oye (tú), no oigas oiga (usted) oigamos oíd (vosotros), no oigáis oigan (Uds.)

Irregular Verbs (continued)

Infinitive / Present Participle / Past Participle	Indicative					Subjunctive		Imperative
	Present	Imperfect	Preterit	Future	Conditional	Present	Imperfect	Commands
poder / pudiendo / podido	puedo / puedes / puede / podemos / podéis / pueden	podía / podías / podía / podíamos / podíais / podían	pude / pudiste / pudo / pudimos / pudisteis / pudieron	podré / podrás / podrá / podremos / podréis / podrán	podría / podrías / podría / podríamos / podríais / podrían	pueda / puedas / pueda / podamos / podáis / puedan	pudiera / pudieras / pudiera / pudiéramos / pudierais / pudieran	
poner / poniendo / puesto	pongo / pones / pone / ponemos / ponéis / ponen	ponía / ponías / ponía / poníamos / poníais / ponían	puse / pusiste / puso / pusimos / pusisteis / pusieron	pondré / pondrás / pondrá / pondremos / pondréis / pondrán	pondría / pondrías / pondría / pondríamos / pondríais / pondrían	ponga / pongas / ponga / pongamos / pongáis / pongan	pusiera / pusieras / pusiera / pusiéramos / pusierais / pusieran	pon (tú), no pongas / ponga (usted) / pongamos / poned (vosotros), no pongáis / pongan (Uds.)
querer / queriendo / querido	quiero / quieres / quiere / queremos / queréis / quieren	quería / querías / quería / queríamos / queríais / querían	quise / quisiste / quiso / quisimos / quisisteis / quisieron	querré / querrás / querrá / querremos / querréis / querrán	querría / querrías / querría / querríamos / querríais / querrían	quiera / quieras / quiera / queramos / queráis / quieran	quisiera / quisieras / quisiera / quisiéramos / quisierais / quisieran	quiere (tú), no quieras / quiera (usted) / queramos / quered (vosotros), no queráis / quieran (Uds.)
saber / sabiendo / sabido	sé / sabes / sabe / sabemos / sabéis / saben	sabía / sabías / sabía / sabíamos / sabíais / sabían	supe / supiste / supo / supimos / supisteis / supieron	sabré / sabrás / sabrá / sabremos / sabréis / sabrán	sabría / sabrías / sabría / sabríamos / sabríais / sabrían	sepa / sepas / sepa / sepamos / sepáis / sepan	supiera / supieras / supiera / supiéramos / supierais / supieran	sabe (tú), no sepas / sepa (usted) / sepamos / sabed (vosotros), no sepáis / sepan (Uds.)
salir / saliendo / salido	salgo / sales / sale / salimos / salís / salen	salía / salías / salía / salíamos / salíais / salían	salí / saliste / salió / salimos / salisteis / salieron	saldré / saldrás / saldrá / saldremos / saldréis / saldrán	saldría / saldrías / saldría / saldríamos / saldríais / saldrían	salga / salgas / salga / salgamos / salgáis / salgan	saliera / salieras / saliera / saliéramos / salierais / salieran	sal (tú), no salgas / salga (usted) / salgamos / salid (vosotros), no salgáis / salgan (Uds.)

Irregular Verbs (continued)

ser / siendo / sido

Indicative Present	Imperfect	Preterit	Future	Conditional	Subj. Present	Subj. Imperfect	Commands
soy	era	fui	seré	sería	sea	fuera	sé (tú),
eres	eras	fuiste	serás	serías	seas	fueras	no seas
es	era	fue	será	sería	sea	fuera	sea (usted)
somos	éramos	fuimos	seremos	seríamos	seamos	fuéramos	seamos
sois	erais	fuisteis	seréis	seríais	seáis	fuerais	sed (vosotros),
son	eran	fueron	serán	serían	sean	fueran	no seáis / sean (Uds.)

tener / teniendo / tenido

Indicative Present	Imperfect	Preterit	Future	Conditional	Subj. Present	Subj. Imperfect	Commands
tengo	tenía	tuve	tendré	tendría	tenga	tuviera	ten (tú),
tienes	tenías	tuviste	tendrás	tendrías	tengas	tuvieras	no tengas
tiene	tenía	tuvo	tendrá	tendría	tenga	tuviera	tenga (usted)
tenemos	teníamos	tuvimos	tendremos	tendríamos	tengamos	tuviéramos	tengamos
tenéis	teníais	tuvisteis	tendréis	tendríais	tengáis	tuvierais	tened (vosotros),
tienen	tenían	tuvieron	tendrán	tendrían	tengan	tuvieran	no tengáis / tengan (Uds.)

traer / trayendo / traído

Indicative Present	Imperfect	Preterit	Future	Conditional	Subj. Present	Subj. Imperfect	Commands
traigo	traía	traje	traeré	traería	traiga	trajera	trae (tú),
traes	traías	trajiste	traerás	traerías	traigas	trajeras	no traigas
trae	traía	trajo	traerá	traería	traiga	trajera	traiga (usted)
traemos	traíamos	trajimos	traeremos	traeríamos	traigamos	trajéramos	traigamos
traéis	traíais	trajisteis	traeréis	traeríais	traigáis	trajerais	traed (vosotros),
traen	traían	trajeron	traerán	traerían	traigan	trajeran	no traigáis / traigan (Uds.)

venir / viniendo / venido

Indicative Present	Imperfect	Preterit	Future	Conditional	Subj. Present	Subj. Imperfect	Commands
vengo	venía	vine	vendré	vendría	venga	viniera	ven (tú),
vienes	venías	viniste	vendrás	vendrías	vengas	vinieras	no vengas
viene	venía	vino	vendrá	vendría	venga	viniera	venga (usted)
venimos	veníamos	vinimos	vendremos	vendríamos	vengamos	viniéramos	vengamos
venís	veníais	vinisteis	vendréis	vendríais	vengáis	vinierais	venid (vosotros),
vienen	venían	vinieron	vendrán	vendrían	vengan	vinieran	no vengáis / vengan (Uds.)

ver / viendo / visto

Indicative Present	Imperfect	Preterit	Future	Conditional	Subj. Present	Subj. Imperfect	Commands
veo	veía	vi	veré	vería	vea	viera	ve (tú),
ves	veías	viste	verás	verías	veas	vieras	no veas
ve	veía	vio	verá	vería	vea	viera	vea (usted)
vemos	veíamos	vimos	veremos	veríamos	veamos	viéramos	veamos
veis	veíais	visteis	veréis	veríais	veáis	vierais	ved (vosotros),
ven	veían	vieron	verán	verían	vean	vieran	no veáis / vean (Uds.)

Stem-Changing and Orthographic-Changing Verbs

Infinitive / Present Participle / Past Participle	Indicative					Subjunctive		Imperative
	Present	Imperfect	Preterit	Future	Conditional	Present	Imperfect	Commands
almorzar (z, c) almorzando almorzado	almuerzo almuerzas almuerza almorzamos almorzáis almuerzan	almorzaba almorzabas almorzaba almorzábamos almorzabais almorzaban	almorcé almorzaste almorzó almorzamos almorzasteis almorzaron	almorzaré almorzarás almorzará almorzaremos almorzaréis almorzarán	almorzaría almorzarías almorzaría almorzaríamos almorzaríais almorzarían	almuerce almuerces almuerce almorcemos almorcéis almuercen	almorzara almorzaras almorzaras almorzáramos almorzarais almorzaran	almuerza (tú) no almuerces almuerce (usted) almorcemos almorzad (vosotros) no almorcéis almuercen (Uds.)
buscar (c, qu) buscando buscado	busco buscas busca buscamos buscáis buscan	buscaba buscabas buscaba buscábamos buscabais buscaban	busqué buscaste buscó buscamos buscasteis buscaron	buscaré buscarás buscará buscaremos buscaréis buscarán	buscaría buscarías buscaría buscaríamos buscaríais buscarían	busque busques busque busquemos busquéis busquen	buscara buscaras buscara buscáramos buscarais buscaran	busca (tú) no busques busque (usted) busquemos buscad (vosotros) no busquéis busquen (Uds.)
corregir (g, j) corrigiendo corregido	corrijo corriges corrige corregimos corregís corrigen	corregía corregías corregía corregíamos corregíais corregían	corregí corregiste corrigió corregimos corregisteis corrigieron	corregiré corregirás corregirá corregiremos corregiréis corregirán	corregiría corregirías corregiría corregiríamos corregiríais corregirían	corrija corrijas corrija corrijamos corrijáis corrijan	corrigiera corrigieras corrigiera corrigiéramos corrigierais corrigieran	corrige (tú) no corrijas corrija (usted) corrijamos corregid (vosotros) no corrijáis corrijan (Uds.)
dormir (ue, u) durmiendo dormido	duermo duermes duerme dormimos dormís duermen	dormía dormías dormía dormíamos dormíais dormían	dormí dormiste durmió dormimos dormisteis durmieron	dormiré dormirás dormirá dormiremos dormiréis dormirán	dormiría dormirías dormiría dormiríamos dormiríais dormirían	duerma duermas duerma durmamos durmáis duerman	durmiera durmieras durmiera durmiéramos durmierais durmieran	duerme (tú), no duermas duerma (usted) durmamos dormid (vosotros), no durmáis duerman (Uds.)
incluir (y) incluyendo incluido	incluyo incluyes incluye incluimos incluís incluyen	incluía incluías incluía incluíamos incluíais incluían	incluí incluiste incluyó incluimos incluisteis incluyeron	incluiré incluirás incluirá incluiremos incluiréis incluirán	incluiría incluirías incluiría incluiríamos incluiríais incluirían	incluya incluyas incluya incluyamos incluyáis incluyan	incluyera incluyeras incluyera incluyéramos incluyerais incluyeran	incluye (tú), no incluyas incluya (usted) incluyamos incluid (vosotros), no incluyáis incluyan (Uds.)

Stem-Changing and Orthographic-Changing Verbs (continued)

Infinitive / Present Participle / Past Participle	Indicative Present	Imperfect	Preterit	Future	Conditional	Subjunctive Present	Imperfect	Imperative Commands
llegar (g, gu) / llegando / llegado	llego / llegas / llega / llegamos / llegáis / llegan	llegaba / llegabas / llegaba / llegábamos / llegabais / llegaban	llegué / llegaste / llegó / llegamos / llegasteis / llegaron	llegaré / llegarás / llegará / llegaremos / llegaréis / llegarán	llegaría / llegarías / llegaría / llegaríamos / llegaríais / llegarían	llegue / llegues / llegue / lleguemos / lleguéis / lleguen	llegara / llegaras / llegara / llegáramos / llegarais / llegaran	llega (tú), no llegues, llegue (usted), lleguemos, llegad (vosotros), no lleguéis, lleguen (Uds.)
pedir (i, i) / pidiendo / pedido	pido / pides / pide / pedimos / pedís / piden	pedía / pedías / pedía / pedíamos / pedíais / pedían	pedí / pediste / pidió / pedimos / pedisteis / pidieron	pediré / pedirás / pedirá / pediremos / pediréis / pedirán	pediría / pedirías / pediría / pediríamos / pediríais / pedirían	pida / pidas / pida / pidamos / pidáis / pidan	pidiera / pidieras / pidiera / pidiéramos / pidierais / pidieran	pide (tú), no pidas, pida (usted), pidamos, pedid (vosotros), no pidáis, pidan (Uds.)
pensar (ie) / pensando / pensado	pienso / piensas / piensa / pensamos / pensáis / piensan	pensaba / pensabas / pensaba / pensábamos / pensabais / pensaban	pensé / pensaste / pensó / pensamos / pensasteis / pensaron	pensaré / pensarás / pensará / pensaremos / pensaréis / pensarán	pensaría / pensarías / pensaría / pensaríamos / pensaríais / pensarían	piense / pienses / piense / pensemos / penséis / piensen	pensara / pensaras / pensara / pensáramos / pensarais / pensaran	piensa (tú), no pienses, piense (usted), pensemos, pensad (vosotros), no penséis, piensen (Uds.)
producir (zc) / produciendo / producido	produzco / produces / produce / producimos / producís / producen	producía / producías / producía / producíamos / producíais / producían	produje / produjiste / produjo / produjimos / produjisteis / produjeron	produciré / producirás / producirá / produciremos / produciréis / producirán	produciría / producirías / produciría / produciríamos / produciríais / producirían	produzca / produzcas / produzca / produzcamos / produzcáis / produzcan	produjera / produjeras / produjera / produjéramos / produjerais / produjeran	produce (tú), no produzcas, produzca (usted), produzcamos, pruducid (vosotros), no produzcáis, produzcan (Uds.)
reír (i, i) / riendo / reído	río / ríes / ríe / reímos / reís / ríen	reía / reías / reía / reíamos / reíais / reían	reí / reíste / rio / reímos / reísteis / rieron	reiré / reirás / reirá / reiremos / reiréis / reirán	reiría / reirías / reiría / reiríamos / reiríais / reirían	ría / rías / ría / riamos / riáis / rían	riera / rieras / riera / riéramos / rierais / rieran	ríe (tú), no rías, ría (usted), riamos, reíd (vosotros), no riáis, rían (Uds.)

Stem-Changing and Orthographic-Changing Verbs (continued)

Infinitive / Present Participle / Past Participle	Indicative					Subjunctive		Imperative
	Present	Imperfect	Preterit	Future	Conditional	Present	Imperfect	Commands
seguir (i, i) (ga) siguiendo seguido	sigo sigues sigue seguimos seguís siguen	seguía seguías seguía seguíamos seguíais seguían	seguí seguiste siguió seguimos seguisteis siguieron	seguiré seguirás seguirá seguiremos seguiréis seguirán	seguiría seguirías seguiría seguiríamos seguiríais seguirían	siga sigas siga sigamos sigáis sigan	siguiera siguieras siguiera siguiéramos siguierais siguieran	sigue (tú), no sigas siga (usted) sigamos seguid (vosotros), no sigáis sigan (Uds.)
sentir (ie, i) sintiendo sentido	siento sientes siente sentimos sentís sienten	sentía sentías sentía sentíamos sentíais sentían	sentí sentiste sintió sentimos sentisteis sintieron	sentiré sentirás sentirá sentiremos sentiréis sentirán	sentiría sentirías sentiría sentiríamos sentiríais sentirían	sienta sientas sienta sintamos sintáis sientan	sintiera sintieras sintiera sintiéramos sintierais sintieran	siente (tú), no sientas sienta (usted) sintamos sentid (vosotros), no sintáis sientan (Uds.)
volver (ue) volviendo vuelto	vuelvo vuelves vuelve volvemos volvéis vuelven	volvía volvías volvía volvíamos volvíais volvían	volví volviste volvió volvimos volvisteis volvieron	volveré volverás volverá volveremos volveréis volverán	volvería volverías volvería volveríamos volveríais volverían	vuelva vuelvas vuelva volvamos volváis vuelvan	volviera volvieras volviera volviéramos volvierais volvieran	vuelve (tú), no vuelvas vuelva (usted) volvamos volved (vosotros), no volváis vuelvan (Uds.)

Appendix 3

Spanish to English Glossary

This vocabulary includes all words presented in the text, except for proper nouns spelled the same in English and Spanish, diminutives with a literal meaning, typical expressions of the Hispanic countries presented in the *Enfoque cultural,* and cardinal numbers (found on page 14). Other cognates and words easily recognized because of the context are not included either.

The number following each entry corresponds to the **capítulo** in which the word was first introduced. Numbers followed by "r" signal that the item was presented for recognition rather than as active vocabulary.

A

a *at, to* P
abajo *below, under* 4r
el/la abogado/a *lawyer* 9
abordar *to board* 12r
abrazar(se) (c) *to embrace* 13
el abrazo *hug* 4r
el abrigo *coat robe* 6
abril *April* Pr
abrir *to open* 12r
la abuela *grandmother* 4
el abuelo *grandfather* 4
abundar *to abound* 13
aburrido/a *bored* 6r; *boring* 1
acabar(se) *to complete, to finish; to run out of* 9r
el acceso *access* 15
el accesorio *accessory* 5
el aceite *oil* 10
la aceituna *olive* 3r
el achiote *paprika* 10r
acompañar *to accompany* 8
aconsejable *advisable* 11r
aconsejar *to advise* 5r
el acontecimiento *event* 13r
acostar(se) (ue) *to put to bed; to go to bed* 4
la actividad *activity* 1r
activo/a *active* Pr
el actor/la actriz *actor/actress* 9
actual *present, current* 14
actualmente *at the present time* 9
actuar *to act* 13
la adaptación *adjustment, adaptation* 14
adaptar *to adapt* 11r

Adelante. *Come in.* 5r
el adelanto *advance* 15, 15r
adelgazar *to lose weight* 10r
el ademán *gesture* 15r
además *besides* 11r
el aderezo *salad dressing* 10
adinerado/a *well-off* 8r
adiós *good-bye* Pr
adivinar *to guess* 6r
¿adónde? *where (to)?* 3
adornado/a *decorated* 8
la aduana *customs* 12
la aerolínea/línea aérea el asiento *airline seat* 12
el/la aeromozo *flight attendant* 12r
el aeropuerto *airport* 12
afeitar(se) *to shave; to shave (oneself)* 4
el afiche *poster* 4r
afirmar *to affirm* 7r
afortunadamente *fortunately* 4r
afuera *outside* 4r
las afueras *outskirts* 5
la agencia de viajes *travel agency* 12
el/la agente de viajes *travel agent* 12
agosto *August* Pr
agradable *agreeable* 11r; *nice* 2
agregar *to add* 10
el/la agricultor/a *farmer* 9
agrio/a *sour* 10
el aguacate *avocado* 10, 10r
agudo/a *sharp, acute* 11r
el águila *eagle* 14r
el/la ahijado/a *godchild* 4
ahora *now* 1
ahorrar *to save* 6r
los ahorros *savings* 9r

el aire acondicionado *air conditioning* 5
el ají *chile pepper* 10r
el ajo *garlic* 10, 10r
al *to the (contraction of a+el)* 3
la alacridad *alacrity* 13r
al aire libre *outdoors* 3
la alberca *swimming pool* 5r
el albergue juvenil *youth hostel* 13r
el alcalde *mayor* 14r
la alcoba *bedroom* 5r
al lado (de) *next to* P
alegrarse (de) *to be glad (about)* 11; *to be happy* 4r
alegre *happy, glad* 2
alegremente *happily* 4r
la alegría *joy* 8
alemán/alemana *German* 2
alérgico/a *allergic* 11r
el alfiler *pin* 15r
la alfombra *carpet, rug* 5
al fondo *at the back, in the rear* 13
la álgebra *algebra* 11r
algo *anything* 13r; *something* 1
alguien *everyone* 13r; *someone* 13r
algún/alguno(s)/alguna(s) *any* 13r; *any, some* Pr; *several* 13r
algunas veces *sometimes* 13r
alguna vez *ever* 13r; *sometime* 13r
aliviar *to relieve* 12r
el alivio *relief* 15r
allí *there* 4r
el alma *soul* 15r
el almacén *department store; warehouse* 6
la almeja *clam* 10r

la almohada *pillow* 5
almorzar (ue) *to have lunch* 4
el almuerzo *lunch* 3, Pr
¿Aló? *Hello? (on the telephone)* 3r
el alojamiento *lodging* 11r, 12
el alquiler *rent* 5
alquilar *to rent* 3
alternativo/a *alternative* 1r
alto *loudly* Pr
alto/a *tall* 2
el/la alumno/a *student* 1
el ama/o de casa *housewife, homemaker* 9
amarillo/a *yellow* 2
ambicioso/a *ambitious* Pr
a menos que *unless* 14r
el/la amigo/a *friend* P
la amistad *friendship* 13, 13r
el amor *love* 13
amplio/a *ample* 14
añadir *to add* 10
el analfabetismo *illiteracy* 14
analfabeto/a *illiterate* 14
anaranjado/a *orange* 2
la anatomía *anatomy* 1r
ancho/a *wide* 6
andar *to go* 14r
el anillo *ring* 6
animado/a *lively* 8
el año *year* P
anoche *last night* 6r
el Año Nuevo *New Year's Day* 8r
el año pasado *last year* 6r
la ansiedad *anxiety* 12r
ante(a)noche *night before last* 6r
anteayer *day before yesterday* 6r
el antepasado *ancestor* 8
antes *before* 6r, 8
antes (de) que *before* 14r
el antibiótico *antibiotic* 11
antiguo/a *old* 1
antipático/a *unpleasant* 2
la antropología *anthropology* 1
el anuncio *ad, advertisement* 9
apagar *to extinguish, to turn off* 9
el apagón *blackout* 8r
el apartamento *apartment* 5
a petición *on demand* 5r
el apio *celery* 10r
la aplicación *application* 15r
apoyar *to support* 7r
aprender *to learn* 1
apropiado/a *appropriate* 6r
aprovechar *to take advantage* 7
el apunte *note* 1

aquel/aquella *that (over there)* 5r
el árbitro *umpire, referee* 7
el árbol *tree* 7
el arete *earring* 6
argentino/a *Argentinian* 2
el armario *cabinet* 5r; *closet, armoire* 5
el aro *earring* 6r
el arpa *harp* 13r
el/la arquitecto/a *architect* 9, 9r
la arquitectura *architecture* 1, 5
arrepentirse (ie) *to regret* 7r
arrogante *arrogant* Pr
el arroz *rice* 3
el arte *art* 1r
la artesanía *handicrafts* 6
el/la artesano/a *craftsman/woman* 9; *craftsperson* 9
los artes plásticas *plastic arts* 1r
el artículo de belleza *beauty item* 11
el/la artista *artist* 9r
asar *to roast* 10r
asegurar *to assure* 7r
el aserrín *sawdust* 8
el asiento *seat* 12
el asiento de pasillo *aisle seat* 12
el asiento de ventanilla *window seat* 12
asistir *to attend* 1
la aspiradora *vacuum cleaner* 5
el astronomía *astronomy* 1r
asumir *to assume* 12r
asustado/a *scared* 12r
atar *to bind* 13r
aterrizar (c) *to land* 15
el ático *attic* 5r
atlético/a *athletic* Pr
la atmósfera *atmosphere* 7
atractivo/a *attractive* Pr
atrás *back, behind, backwards* 6r
a través de *through* 13
atreverse *to dare* 7r
aun *event* 14r
aunque *although* 14r; *even if* 14r; *even though* 14r
el auto *car* 2
el autobús/bus *bus* 12
la autopista *freeway* 12
el autorretrato *self-portrait* 13
el/la auxiliar de vuelo *flight attendant* 12, 12r
avanzar *to advance* 15r
a veces *sometimes* 1r; *at times* 13r
la avenida *avenue* Pr

a la venta *for sale* 6r
averiguar *to find out* 5r
las aves *poultry, fowl* 10
el avión *plane* 12
ayer *yesterday* 6r
ayudar *to help* 5, 5r
la azafata *flight attendant* 12r
el azar *chance* 13r
el/la azúcar *sugar* 10
azul *blue* 2

B

el bailarín/la bailarina *dancer* 13
bailar *to dance* 1
la bajada *slope* 7r
bajar *to download* 15
bajo/a *short (in stature)* 2
el balón *ball* 7r
el baloncesto/el básquetbol *basketball* 7
la bañadera *bathtub* 5r
la banana *banana, plantain* 10
el banano *banana, plantain* 10r
bañar(se) *to bathe; to take a bath* 4
el banco *bank* 9
el banco de peces *shoal; school of fish* 15
la banda ancha *broadband* 5r
la bandeja *tray* 10
la bañera *bathtub* 5, 5r
el baño *bathroom* 5
barato/a *inexpensive, cheap* 6
la barbacoa *barbecue pit; barbecue (event)* 5
el barco *ship/boat* 12
barrer *to sweep* 5
el barrio *neighborhood* 5
basar *to base* 13r
básicamente *basically* 4r
el básquetbol *basketball* 7
bastante *enough* Pr; *rather* P
la basura *garbage, trash* 5
la bata *robe* 6
el bate *bat* 7
el batido *milkshake, smoothie* 10r
batir *to beat* 10, 10r
el baúl *trunk* 12
el bautizo *baptism, christening* 4
beber *to drink* 1
la bebida *drink* 3
el béisbol *baseball* 7
las bellas artes *fine arts* 1r
beneficiar *to benefit* 6r
besar *to kiss* 11r

el **beso** *kiss* 4r

la **biblioteca** *library* 1; *library cafe, coffee shop cafeteria* 1

el/la **bibliotecario/a** *librarian* 9, 9r

la **biblioteca virtual** *virtual library* 15

la **bicicleta** *bicycle* 3r

bien *well* P

bienes raíces *real estate* 5r

bien parecido *good-looking* 2r

bilingüe *bilingual* 2

el **billete** *ticket (Spain)* 12r

la **billetera** *wallet* 6

la **bioquímica** *biochemistry* 1r

el **bisonte** *bison* 13r

el **bistec** *steak* 3

blando/a *soft* 13

la **blusa** *blouse* 6

blanco/a *white* 2

la **boca** *mouth* 11

la **boda** *wedding* 3

la **bodega** *wine cellar* 5

la **bola** *bowling ball* 7r

el **boleto** *ticket* 12r

el **boliche** *bowling* 7r

el **bolígrafo** *ballpoint pen* P

boliviano/a *Bolivian* 2

el **bolo** *bowling ball* 7r

la **bolsa/el bolso** *purse* 6

el/la **bombero/a** *firefighter* 9

bonito/a *pretty* 2

el **laboratorio** *laboratory* 1, Pr

el **borrador** *eraser* P

el **bosque** *forest* 15

el **bosque tropical** *rain forest* 15

la **bota** *boot* 6

la **botella** *bottle* 10

el **bowling** *bowling* 7r

el **brazo** *arm* 6r, 11

la **broma** *joke* 10r

brujo/a *broke* 2r

el **buceo** *snorkeling* 12r

buenas noches *good evening* P

buenas tardes *good afternoon* P

¡Buena suerte! *Good luck!* 1

buen mozo *good-looking guy* 2r

¡Bueno! *Hello? (on the telephone)* 3r

bueno/a *good* 1; *well (health); physically attractive* 6r

buenos días *good morning* P

la **bufanda** *scarf* 6, 6r

el **burgués** *middle class* 13r

el **bus** *bus (Puerto Rico, Cuba)* 12r

el **buscador** *search engine* 15

buscar *to look for* 1

la **butaca** *armchair* 5, 7r

C

el **cabello** *hair* 11

la **cabeza** *head* 6r, 11

la **cabuya** *ammunition* 2r

cada *each* 7

cada... horas *every . . . hours* 11

la **cadera** *hip* 11

caer *to drop* 8r

caer bien *to like* 6r

caer mal *to dislike* 6r

caer(se) *to fall* 11

café *brown* 2r

el **café** *cafe, coffee shop* 1; *coffee* 3

la **cafetería** *cafeteria* 1

caigue *lazy (Bolivia)* 13r

la **caja** *box* 6r

la **caja fuerte** *safe* 12

el/la **cajero/a** *cashier* 9

el/la **cajero/a** *cashier* 9r

el **cajero automático** *ATM* 12

el **calcetín** *sock* 6

el **calcio** *calcium* 10r

la **calculadora** *calculator* P

el **cálculo** *calculus* 1r

callado/a *quiet* 2

la **calefacción** *heating* 5

el **calendario** *calendar* Pr

el **calentamiento** *warming* 15

la **calidad** *quality* 6r, 13

caliente *hot* 3

callarse *to keep quiet* 14r

la **calle** *street* 5, Pr

calmar *to calm, alleviate* 11r

el **calor** *heat* 5r

el **calzado** *footwear* 6r

calzar *to wear a shoe size* 6r

el **calzoncillo** *boxer shorts* 6

la **cama** *bed* 5

la **cámara** *camera* 9r

el **camarero/la camarera** *server, waiter/waitress* 3

el **camarón** *shrimp* 10

cambiar *to change, to exchange* 6

el **cambio** *change* 4r, 14

el **cambur** *banana, plantain* 10r

caminar *to walk* 1; *walk* 3r

el **camino** *road; way* 8

el **camión** *bus (Mexico)* 12r

la **camioneta** *bus (Guatemala)* 9r

la **camisa** *shirt* 6

la **camisa de manga corta** *short-sleeved shirt* 6r

la **camiseta** *T-shirt* 6

el **camisón** *nightgown* 6

la **campaña de publicidad** *publicity campaign* 15r

el **campeonato** *championship* 7; *tournament* 7r

el **campeón/la campeona** *champion* 7

el/la **campesino/a** *peasant* 10

el **campo** *countryside* 9

canadiense *Canadian* 2

el **canal** *channel* 7r

cancelar *to cancel* 12

el **cáncer** *cancer* 11

la **canción** *song* 3

la **canela** *cinnamon* 10r

el **cangrejo** *crab* 10r

cansado/a *tired* 2

cantar *to sing* 3

la **cantidad** *quantity* 9r

la **capa de ozono** *ozone layer* 15

el **capítan** *captain* 3r

la **capitanía general** *administrative unit of the Spanish Empire* 3r

el **capó** *hood* 12

la **cápsula** *capsule* 15

la **cara** *face* 4r, 11; *expression* 15r

el **cargador de celular (del móvil)** *cell phone charger* 5r

cariños *love (closing)* 3r

caritativo/a *charitable* 13r

carmelita *brown* 2r

el **carnaval** *carnival* 8

la **carne** *meat* 10

la **carne de res** *beef/steak* 10

la **carne molida/picada** *ground meat* 10

el **carnet de conducir** *driver's license* 15r

caro/a *expensive* 6, 6r

el/la **carpintero/a** *carpenter* 9

la **carrera** *major* 1r; *race* 7

la **carreta** *cart, wagon* 8

la **carretera** *highway* 12

el **carro** *car* 2

la **carroza** *float (in a parade)* 8

el **cartero/la cartera** *mail carrier* 12

la **casa** *house, home* 1

casado/a *married* 2

la **casa editorial** *editorial house* 13r

casar(se) *to get married* 4

castaño/a *brown* 2r

el **catarro** *cold* 11

la **cebolla** *onion* 10

la ceja *eyebrow* 11
la celebración *celebration* 3
celebrar *to celebrate* 3
el cementerio *cemetery* 8
la cena *dinner, supper* 3
cenar *to have dinner* 3
el centro *downtown, center* 5
el centro comercial *shopping center* 6
el centro de entrenamiento *training resort* 7r
el centro de salud *hospital* 11
el/la ceramista *potter* 9
cerca *near* 3r
cerca de *close to, near* 3
el cerdo *pork* 10
el cereal *cereal* 3
el cerebro *brain* 11
la cereza *cherry* 10
cerrar (ie) *to close* 4r
la certeza *certainty* 13r
la cerveza *beer* 1r, 3
el césped *lawn* 5
el cesto *wastebasket* P
el cesto/la cesta *basket, hoop* 7
el ceviche *dish of marinated raw fish* 3
las chanclas *flip-flops* 9r
la chancona *nerd (Peru)* 3r
chao *good-bye* Pr
la chaqueta *jacket* 6
chau *good-bye* Pr
el/la chef *chef* 9
el cheque *check* 9r
el/la chico/a *boy/girl* P
el chile *chile pepper* 10r
chileno/a *Chilean* 2
la chimenea *fireplace* 5
la chivita *bus* 1r; *bus (Colombia)* 12r
el choclo *corn* 10r
el/la chofer (chófer) *driver; chauffeur* 9
la chuleta *chop* 10
el chunche *thing (Costa Rica)* 12r
los churros *fried dough* 10
el ciclismo *cycling* 7
el/la ciclista *cyclist* 7, 7r
la ciencia *science* 1
las ciencias políticas *political science* 1
cien/ciento *hundred* 3r
el/la científico/a *scientist* 9, 9r
cierto/a *true* Pr
el cilantro *cilantro* 10r
el cine *cinema* 13r; *movies* 1r, 3

el/la cineasta *filmmaker* 13r
la cintura *waist* 11
el cinturón *belt* 6
el/la cirujano/a *surgeon* 11r
la cita *date* 6r
citar *to quote* 14r
la cita textual *quotation* 7r
la ciudad *city* 3
el ciudadano *citizen* 14r
clarear el día *dawn* 13r
¡claro! *of course!* 3
la clase turista *coach class* 12r; *tourist class* 12
el/la cliente/clienta *client* 6r, 9
climatizado/a *air-conditioned* 15
la clínica, el centro *clinic* 11
la clonación *cloning* 15
el clóset *closet* 5r
la cobija *blanket* 5r
el coche *car* 2
cocido/a *cooked* 3r
la cocina *kitchen* 5; *stove* 5r
la cocina fusión *fusion cuisine* 10r
cocinar *to cook* 5
el/la cocinero/a *cook* 5r
codiciado/a *sought after* 13r
el código *code* 15r
el codo *elbow* 11
el cognado *cognate* Pr
colapsar *to collapse* 9r
el colectivo *bus (Argentina)* 12r
el colesterol *cholesterol* 10r
colocar *to place* 5r
colombiano/a *Colombian* 2
los colores *colors* 2
el collar *necklace* 6
el comedor *dining room* 5, 5r
comenzar (ie) *to begin* 8
comer *to eat* 1
cómico/a *comic* Pr
la comida *food; meal; dinner, supper* 3
la comida chatarra *junk food* 10r
el comienzo *beginning* 7r, 8
el comino *cumin* 10r
¿cómo? *how/what?* 1r
la cómoda *dresser* 5
cómodo/a *comfortable* 9r
¿Cómo es? *What is he/she/it like?* P
¿Cómo está? *How are you (formal)?* P
¿Cómo estás? *How are you (informal)?* P

¡Cómo no! *Of course!* 9
¿Cómo se dice... ? *How do you say . . . ?* Pr
¿Cómo se escribe... ? *How do you spell . . . ?* Pr
¿Cómo se llama usted? *What's your name? (formal)* P
¿Cómo te llamas? *What's your name? (familiar)* P
¿Cómo te va? *How is it going?* 1
el/la compañero/a *partner, classmate* 1
la compañía de danza *dance company* 13
la compañía de teatro *theater company* 13
la compañía/empresa *company* 9
la comparsa *group dressed in similar costumes* 8
cómplice *complicit* 14r
el comportamiento *behavior* 9r
comprar *to buy* 1
comprender *to understand* 1
el compromiso *engagement* 8r
la computación *computer science* 1r
la computadora *computer* P
la computadora portátil *laptop* P
la comunicación *communication* 1r
comunicar *to communicate* 14r
comunicarse *to reach out to* 14r
con *with* 1
con cariño *affectionately* 4r
el concejo municipal *city council* 14r
la concha *shell* 8r
la conclusión *conclusion* 14r
la concordancia *agreement* 6r
el concurso *contest* 5r
el condimento *seasoning* 10
conducir *to drive* 15r
conectar *to connect* 15r
conectarse *to connect* 15
la conexión *connection* 12r
la confianza *trust* 14
el conflicto *conflict* 1r
congelar(se) *to freeze* 7
conmigo *with me* 7
conocer (zc) *to know* 3; *to meet* 13r
el conocimiento *knowledge* 15
con permiso *pardon me, excuse me* Pr
el/la consejero/a vocacional *career counselor* 9r
el consenso *consensus* 13r

la **conservación** *preservation* 15

construir (y) *to build* 15; *to construct* 12r

el **consultorio** *office (of doctor, dentist, etc.)* 9

consumir *to consume* 10r

la **contabilidad** *accounting* 1r

el/la **contable** *accountant* 9r

el/la **contador/a** *accountant* 9r

con tal (de) que *provided that* 14r

contaminado/a *polluted, contaminated* 7

contar *to count* 6r; *to tell* 7r

contemporáneo/a *contemporary* 1r

contento/a *happy, glad* 2

contestar *to answer* Pr

contigo *with you (familiar)* 7

continuar *to continue* 15r

contraer *to contract* 11r

contrario/a *opposing* 7, 7r

el **contraste** *contrast* 4r

el/la **contratista** *contractor* 9

contribuir (y) *to contribute* 15

conversador/a *talkative* 2

conversar *to talk, to converse* 1

la **copa** *(stemmed) glass* 10

la **Copa Mundial** *World Cup* 7r

el **corazón** *heart* 11, 11r

la **corbata** *tie* 6

el **cordero** *lamb* 10

el **coroto** *thing (Venezuela)* 6r

el **correo** *mail* 12

correr *to run* 1

la **correspondencia** *correspondence* 9r

la **corrida (de toros)** *bullfight* 8

cortar *to cut; to mow (lawn)* 5

la **cortina** *curtain* 5

corto/a *short (in length)* 2

la **cosa** *thing* 6

cosechar *to harvest* 9

costarricense *Costa Rican* 2

costar (ue) *to cost* 4

la **costilla** *rib* 10

la **costumbre** *custom* 8

creativo/a *creative* Pr

creer *to believe* 5

la **crema** *cream* 10

claro *of course* 4r

el **crucero** *cruise* 12

la **clase** *class* Pr

el **cuaderno** *notebook* P

la **cuadra** *city block* 12

el **cuadro** *picture, painting* 5

¿cuál(es)? *which?* 1r

¿Cuál es la fecha? *What is the date?* Pr

cuando *when* 14r

¿cuándo? *when?* 1r

¿cuánto/a? *how much?* 1r

¿Cuánto cuesta? *How much is it?* 1

¿cuántos/as? *how many?* 1r

el **cuarto** *bedroom* 5r; *room; bedroom* 5

el/la **cuate** *friend (Mexico)* 8r

cubano/a *Cuban* 2

cubista *cubist* 13

la **cuchara** *spoon* 10

la **cucharada** *spoonful* 10r

la **cucharita** *teaspoon* 10

el **cuello** *neck* 11

la **cuenca** *river basin* 15

la **cuenta corriente** *checking account* 9r

el **cuento** *story* 13

el **cuero** *leather* 6r

el **cuerpo** *body* 6r

el **cuidado** *care* 5r

cuidadosamente *carefully* 4r

cuidar(se) (de) *to take care of* 11

el **culantro** *cilantro* 10r

el **cumpleaños** *birthday* 3

cumplir *to fulfill* 7r

curar *to cure* 11

la **curiosidad** *curiosity* 12r

el **currículum** *résumé* 9

D

dañino/a *harmful* 10r

la **danza** *dance* 13r

dar *to give, to hand* 6

dar de comer *to feed* 9r

dar un paseo *to take a walk* 8

los **datos** *data* 14

de *of, from* 2

debajo (de) *under* P

deber *should* 1

debido a *due to* 15

débil *weak* 2

decepcionado/a *disappointed* 6r

decir (g, i) *to say, to tell* 4

la **decisión** *decision* 13r

el **dedo** *finger* 11

de estatura mediana *average, medium (height)* 2

la **deforestación** *deforestation* 15

de ida y vuelta *round trip* 12

dejar *to leave* 9

del *of the (contraction of de + el)* 2

delgado/a *thin* 2

la **democracia** *democracy* 14

de moda *stylish* 6r

de nada *you're welcome* Pr

denunciar *to denounce* 13

el **departamento** *apartment* 5r

el **dependiente/la dependienta** *salesperson* 1

el **deporte** *sport* 7

el/la **deportista** *athlete* 7r

la **depresión** *depression* 1r

deprimido/a *depressed* 11

¿de quién? *whose?* 2

la **derecha** *right* 4

el **derecho** *right* 14

derecho *straight* 12r

derretir *to melt* 10r

desamparado/a *homeless* 14r

la **desaparición** *disappearence* 15

desarmar *to disassemble* 9r

desarrollar(se) *to develop* 8r

el **desarrollo** *development* 13

desayunar *to have breakfast* 4

el **desayuno** *breakfast* 3

descansar *to rest* 3

descomponer(se) *to break* 9r

describir *to describe* 6r

la **descripción** *description* 1

el **descubrimiento** *discovery* 15

descuidado/a *careless* 9r

desde *since* 13

desear *to desire* 5r; *to wish, to want* 2

desechable *disposable* 15r

el **desempleo** *unemployment* 14

el **desfile** *parade* 8

el **deshielo** *thaw, thawing* 15

despacio *slowly* Pr

la **despedida** *closing* 4r

despedir (i) *to fire* 9r

despedir(se) (i) *to say goodbye* 7r

despegar (u) *to take off (airplane)* 15

despertar(se) (ie) *to wake (someone up)* 4

la **despidida** *farewell* Pr

el **desplazamiento** *movement, displacement* 14

después *after, later* 3

después (de) que *after* 14r

destacado/a *outstanding* 13

destacarse *to stand out* 14

el **destino** *destination* 12r

la **desventaja** *disadvantage* 5

el **detalle** *detail* 12r
detener *to stop* 9r
detrás (de) *behind* P
devolver *to return* 6r, 15r
el **día** *day* P
diabético/a *diabetic* 11r
el **Día del Amor y la Amistad** *Valentine's Day* 8r
el **Día de Acción de Gracias** *Thanksgiving* 8r
el **Día de la Independencia** *Independence Day* 8r
el **Día de la Independencia de México** *Mexican Independence Day* 8r
el **Día de las Brujas** *Halloween* 8r
el **Día de los Enamorados** *Valentine's Day* 8r
el **Día de los Muertos** *Day of the Dead* 8r
el **Día de la Madre** *Mother's Day* 8r
el **Día del Padre** *Father's Day* 8r
el **día feriado** *legal holiday* 8
el **día festivo** *holiday* 8
dialogar *to talk* 14r
el **diccionario** *dictionary* 1
diciembre *December* Pr
dictatorial *dictatorial* 14
el **diente** *tooth* 10r, 11
el **diente de ajo** *clove of garlic* 10r
la **dieta** *diet* 3r
difícil *difficult* 1
difícilmente *difficultly* 4r
difundir *to spread, to disseminate* 15
difunto/a *dead* 8
¿Diga?, ¿Dígame? *Hello? (on the telephone)* 3r
digitalmente *digitally* 13r
dinámico/a *dynamic* Pr
el **dinero en efectivo** *money in cash* 6
dirigir (j) *to direct* 13
dirigirse (j) *to address* 4r
la **discoteca** *dance club* 1
disculparse *to apologize* 7r
discutir *to argue* 7
la **diseminación** *dispersal, dissemination* 15
el **diseñador** *designer* 5r
el **diseño** *design* 1r
el **diseño gráfico** *graphic design* 1r
disfrazarse *to wear a costume* 8
disfrutar *to enjoy* 10
disponible *available* 5r
el **dispositivo** *device* 5r
distinguir *to distinguish* 13
la **distribución** *layout* 5r

la **diversificación** *diversification* 14
las **diversiones** *leisure activities* 3
divertido/a *fun, funny* 1r; *funny, amusing* 2
divertirse (ie, i) *to have a good time* 8
divorciado/a *divorced* 4
el **lado** *side* 4r
doblar *to turn* 12
doblar *to fold* 5, 5r
el **documento adjunto** *attached document* 15; *attachment* 15
el **dólar** *dollar* 3r
doler (ue) *to hurt, ache* 11
el **dolor** *pain* 11
doméstico/a *domestic* 5r
el **domingo** *Sunday* Pr
dominicano/a *Dominican* 2
dónde *where?* Pr
¿Dónde está... ? *Where is . . . ?* P
dorar *to brown* 10r
dormir(se) (ue) *to sleep; to fall asleep* 4
dormir (ue) la siesta *to take a nap* 4
el **dormitorio** *bedroom* 5r
el **drama** *drama* 1r
la **droga** *drug* 1r
la **ducha** *shower* 5
duchar(se) *to give a shower to; (to take a shower)* 4
la **duda** *doubt* 13r
dudoso/a *doubtful* 13r
el **dulce** *candy/sweets* 10
duplicar *to double* 10r
durante *during* 3; *for (time)* 3r
durar *to last* 7
el **durazno** *peach* 10r
el **DVD** *DVD; DVD player* P

E

la **economía** *economics* 1
económicamente *economically* 5r
ecuatoriano/a *Ecuadorian* 2
el **edificio** *building* 5
eficaz *efficient* 12r
la **eficiencia** *efficiency* 14
eficiente *efficient* Pr
el/la **ejecutivo/a** *executive* 9
el **ejercicio aeróbico** *aerobic exercise* 11r
él *he* P
elaborar *to produce* 9
la **elección** *election* 14r
el/la **electricista** *electrician* 9r
el **electrodoméstico** *appliance* 5

elegante *elegant* Pr
elegir (i, i) *to choose, to elect* 14
ellos/ellas *they* 1
el **elote** *corn* 10r
el/la **tenista** *tennis player* 7
el **embarque** *departure* 12r
la **emergencia** *emergency* 9r
la **emigración** *emigration* 14
el/la **emigrante** *emigrant* 14
emigrar *to emigrate* 9
empezar (ie) *to begin, to start* 4
el/la **empleado/a** *employee* 9
en *in* P
en la actualidad *at the present time* 13
en busca de *in search of* 15
el **encaje** *lace* 13r
en cambio *on the other hand* 4r
encantado/a *pleased/nice to meet you* P
encantar *to delight, to love* 6
encargar *to order* 9r
encauzar *to channel* 7
encender (ie) *to turn on* 15
encerrar (ie) *to lock up* 8
encontrar (ue) *to find* 6
en contraste *in contraste* 4r
en cuanto *as soon as* 14r
la **encuesta** *Surveys/Polls* 14
la **encuesta de opinión** *opinion poll* 14r
la **energía solar** *solar energy* 15
enérgico/a *energetic* 14
enero *January* Pr
enfadarse *to get angry* 7
enfermarse *to become sick* 11
la **enfermedad** *illness* 11
el/la **enfermero/a** *nurse* 9
enfermo/a *sick* 11
enfocarse (qu) *to focus* 15
enfrente (de) *in front of* P
el **enlace** *link* 15
enojado/a *angry* 2
enojar(se) *to get angry* 7r
¿En qué puedo servirle(s)? *How may I help you?* 6
en realidad *in fact, really* 9
la **ensalada** *salad* 3
enseguida *immediately* 6
entender (ie) *to understand* 4
enterar *to find out* 7r
enterrar *to bury* 8r
entonces *then* 8

entrar (en) *to go in, to enter* 6
entre *between, among* P
entregar *to deliver* 5r
el entrenador/la entrenadora *coach* 7
el entrenamiento *training* 7r
entretenerse *to have fun* 5r
la entrevista *interview* 9
entrevistar *to interview* 7r
en vez de *instead of* 14
enviar *to send* 9
el equipaje *luggage* 12
el equipo *team; equipment* 7
el equipo deportivo *sports equipment* 7
eres *you are (familiar)* P
la ermita *hermitage* 8r
es *you are (formal), he/she is* P
la escala *stopover* 12
la escalera *stairs* 5
el escaparate *store window* 6
la escena *scene* 13
la escena retrospectiva *flashback* 13r
escribir *to write* 1, 6r, Pr
el escritorio *desk* P
el escritor/la escritora *writer* 13
escuchar *to listen (to)* 1
la escuela *school* 6r
el escultor/la escultora *sculptor* 13
ese/a *that (adjective)* P
el eslogan *motto* 12r
eso *that* 5r
los espaguetis *spaghetti* 3
la espalda *back* 11
el español *Spanish* Pr
español/a *Spanish* 2
la especialidad *specialty* 9
el/la especialista *specialist* 11r
las especias *spices* 10
el espejo *mirror* 5
el espejo retrovisor *rearview mirror* 12
la esperanza de vida *life expectancy* 14
esperar *to wait for* 9
las espinacas *spinach* 10
el espíritu *spirit* 8r
la esposa *wife* 4
el esposo *husband* 4
el esquí *skiing, ski* 7
esquiar *to ski* 7
la esquina *corner* 12, 12r
está *he/she is, you are (formal)* P
está despejado *it's clear* 7
el estadio *stadium* 7r
la estadística *statistics* 1

el estado de ánimo *mood* 5r
Estados Unidos *United States* 2r
estadounidense *U.S. citizen* 2
esta noche *tonight* 3r
está nublado *it's cloudy* 7
estar *to be* 1, Pr
estar de acuerdo *to agree* 11r
estar de moda *to be fashionable* 6
estar en forma *to keep in shape* 7r
estás *you are (familiar)* P
este/a *this* 1
el estilo *style* 5, 5r
Estimado/a *Dear* 3r
esto *this* 5r
el estómago *stomach* 11
estornudar *to sneeze* 11
estrecho/a *narrow, tight* 6
la estrella *star* 13
la estructura *structure* 1r
el/la estudiante *student* P
estudiar *to study* 1
el estudio *to show* 7r
estudioso/a *studious* 1
la estufa *stove* 5
estupendo/a *fabulous* 3; *stupendous, marvelous* 10r
el evento *event* 7
evidente *evident* 12r
evitar *to avoid* 10r
el examen *test* 1
examinar *to examine* 11
excelente *excellent* 1
la excentricidad *eccentricity* 15r
exigir *to demand, exact, require* 14r
el éxito *success* 10r, 13, Pr
la experiencia *experience* 9
el experto *expert* 7r
explicar *to explain* 6r, 15r
exponer (g) *to exhibit* 13
la exportación *export* 14
la exposición *exhibit* 12r
expresion *expression* P
la extinción *extinction* 15
extinguido/a *extinct* 15r; *extinguished* 15
extrovertido/a *extroverted* Pr

F

fabuloso/a *fabulous, great* 3
fácil *easy* 1
fácilmente *easily* 4r
facturar *to check in (luggage)* 12

la facultad *school, department* 1
la falda *skirt* 6
falso/a *false* Pr
la falta *lack* 4r
la familia *The family* 4
famoso/a *famous* 10r
el/la farmacéutico/a *pharmacist* 11
la farmacia *pharmacy* 1r, 11
fascinar *to fascinate, to be pleasing to* 6
favorito/a *favorite* 1
febrero *February* Pr
la fecha *date* Pr
felicidades *congratulations* 3
las felicitaciones *congratulations* 11r
felicitar *to congratulate* 11r
feo/a *ugly* 2
el festival *festival* 8
la festividad *festivity; holiday* 8
la fibra *fiber* 10r
la ficha *note card* 7r
la fiebre *fever* 11
la fiesta *celebration* 8; *party* 3, 7r
la figura de autoridad *authority figure* 6r
fijarse *to check out* 3r; *to take note* 14r
¡Fíjate qué noticia! *How about that!* 3r
la filología *philology* 1r
la filosofía *philosophy* 1r
finalmente *finally, at last* 6r
el Fin de Año *New Year's Eve* 8r
el fin de semana *weekend* 1
firmar *to sign* 9r
la física *physics* Pr
la fisiología *physiology* 1r
la flor *flower* 2
fluir *to flow* 10r
fomentar *to encourage* 13r
el fondo *background* 8r
el/la fontanero/a *plumber* 9
la forma *shape, form* 13
la foto(grafía) *photo(graph)* 4
el fracaso *failure* 13
fracturar(se) *to fracture, to break* 11
francés/francesa *French* 2
la frazada *blanket* 5r
frecuentemente *frequently* 4r
el fregadero *kitchen sink* 5
freír (i) *to fry* 10, 10r

la frente *forehead* 11
la fresa *strawberry* 10
el frijol *bean* 3
el frío *cold* 5r
frío/a *cold* 3
frito/a *fried* 3, 3r
la fruta *fruit* 3, 10
el fruto de pasión *passion fruit* 10r
la fuente *bowl* 10r; *source* 15
fuerte *strong* 2
fumar *to smoke* 11
la fundación *founding* 13
el fútbol *soccer* 7
el fútbol americano *football* 7r

G

las gafas *glasses* 13r
las gafas de sol *sunglasses* 6r
la galleta *cookie* 10
la gamba *shrimp* 10
el ganado *cattle* 10r
el ganador *winner* 5r
ganar *to win* 5r, 7
la ganga *bargain* 6r
el garaje *garage* 5
la garganta *throat* 11
gastar *to spend* 6
gemelo/a *twin* 4, 4r
generalmente *generally* 4r
generoso/a *generous* Pr
genéticamente *genetically* 15, 15r
la gente *people* 8
la geografía *geography* 1
el/la gerente (de ventas) *(sales) manager* 9
el gimnasio *gymnasium* 1
globalizar *to globalize* 11r
la gobernación *administrative unit of the Spanish Empire* 3r
el gobernador *governor* 3r
gobernar (ie) *to govern* 14
el gobierno *government* 11
el gol *goal* 7
el golf *golf* 7
golpear *to knock* 7r
gordo/a *fat* 2
la gorra *cap* 6, 6r
grabar *to record* 13r
gracias *thanks, thank you* Pr
gracioso/a *funny* 15r
gradualmente *gradually* 15r

graduarse *to graduate* 14r
gráfico/a *graphic* 15r
grande *big* 1
la grasa *fat* 10r
grave *serious* 11; *seriously ill* 6r
la gripe *flu* 11
gris *gray* 2
el grupo *group* 14r
la guagua *bus (Puerto Rico, Cuba)* 12r
el guajolote *turkey* 10r
el guante *glove* 6
la guantera *glove compartment* 12
la guía *guide* 6r
la guitarra *guitar* 3, 8r
el/la guitarrista *guitar player* 13
gustar (le) *to be pleasing to, to like* 6; *to like* 2r

H

la habitación *bedroom, room* 5
la habitación doble/sencilla *double/single room* 12
el/la habitante *inhabitant* 14
hablar *to speak* 1
hace *ago* 4r; *since* 6r
hace fresco *it's cool* 7
hacer *to do, to make* 3r
hacer cola *to stand in line* 12, 12r
hacer la cama *to make the bed* 3
hacerse *to become* 14r
Hace sol. *It's sunny.* Pr
el hacha *hachet* 13r
la hambre *hunger* 5r
la hamburguesa *hamburger* 3
la harina *flour* 10
hasta *including; until* 13
Hasta luego. *See you later.* Pr
Hasta mañana. *See you tomorrow.* Pr
Hasta pronto. *See you soon.* Pr
hasta que *until* 14r
hay *there is, there are* P
el hecho *fact* 6r
la heladería *ice creamery* 6r
el helado *ice cream* 3, 6r
heredar *to inherit* 14r
el/la herencia *inheritance* 14r

la herida *wound* 11r
el/la herido/a *injured person* 9r
herido/a *wounded, injured* 9r
la hermana *sister* 4
la hermanastra *stepsister* 4
el hermanastro *stepbrother* 4
el hermano *brother* 4
el herrero *blacksmith; ironworker* 9
hervir (ie, i) *to boil* 10
el hielo *ice* 7
la hierba *herb* 10
el higo *fig* 10r
la hija *daughter* 4
el hijo *son* 4
el hijo único/ la hija única *only child* 4
hinchar *to swell* 11r
la hinchazón *swelling* 11r
la hipótesis *hypothesis* 13r
hispano/a *Hispanic* 2
la historia *history* 1
hola *hi, hello* P
el hogar *home* 4r
la hoja *leaf* 5
el hombre *man* 3
el hombre/la mujer de negocios *businessman/woman* 9
el hombro *shoulder* 11
hondureño/a *Honduran* 2
la honestidad *honesty* 14
la hora *time; hour* Pr
el horario *schedule* Pr
hornear *to bake, to microwave* 10r
el (horno) microondas *microwave (oven)* 5
horrible *horrible* 15r
el hospital *hospital* 11
el hotel *hotel* 12
hoy *today* P
hoy en día *nowadays* 8
Hoy es... *Today is . . .* Pr
el hueso *bone* 11
el huevo *egg* 3
las humanidades *humanities* 1
humano/a *human* 11

I

la idea *idea* 10r
idealista *idealistic* Pr

la iglesia *church* 8
la igualdad *equality* 14
igualmente *likewise* P
imaginar *imagine* 3r
el imperfecto *imperfect* 6r
el impermeable *raincoat* 6
implementar *to implement* 14r
importante *important* Pr
imposible *impossible* 6r
la impresora *printer* 5r
impulsivo/a *impulsive* Pr
inapropiado/a *inappropriate* 6r
el incendio *fire* 9
increíble *incredible* 4r
independiente *independent* Pr
indicar *to indicate* 7r
la infancia *childhood* 6r
infantil *children's* 14
la infección *infection* 11
influir *to influence* 13r
la información *information* 7r
la informática *computer science* 1
la infraestructura *infrastructure* 15
el/la ingeniero/a *engineer* 9
el iniciado *apprentice* 13r
la inmigración *immigration* 14
el inodoro *toilet* 5
inolvidable *unforgettable* 13
el inspector *inspector* 12r
la instrucción *instruction* 14r
el instrumento *instrument* 3
inteligente *intelligent* Pr
el intercambio *exchange* 15
interesante *interesting* 1, Pr
interesar *to interest* 6
internacional *international* 7r
el/la intérprete *interpreter* 9; *performer, artist* 13
la intimidad *intimacy* 4r
introvertido/a *introverted* Pr
la inundación *flood* 15
la investigación *research* 7r
investigar *to study, research* 11r
el invierno *winter* 6r
la invitación *invitation* 3r, 8
invitar *to invite* 8
la inyección *injection* 11
el ipod *iPod* 5r
ir *to go* 3r, Pr
ir de compras *to go shopping* 6
ir de tapas *to go out for tapas* 1r

ir(se) *to go away, to leave* 7
la izquierda *left* 4

J

el jabón *soap* 5
jamás *never* 13r; *(not) ever* 13r
el jamón *ham* 3
japonés/japonesa *Japanese* 2
el jardín *garden* 5
los jeans *jeans* 6
el jefe/la jefa *boss* 9
joven *young* 2, 8r
el/la joven *young man/woman* 3
la joya *piece of jewelry* 6
el/la joyero/a *jeweller* 9
jubilarse *to retire* 14r
el juego/partido *game* 7
el jueves *Thursday* Pr
el/la juez *judge* 9
el jugador/la jugadora *player* 7
jugar (ue) *to play (a game, sport)* 4
jugar (ue) a los bolos *to bowl* 7
el jugo *juice* 3
el juguete *toy* 5r, 6
julio *July* Pr
junio *June* Pr
la junta directiva *board of directors* 14r
juntos/as *together* 4
el juramento *oath* 13r

L

ella *she* P
el labio *lip* 11
laboral *labor-related* 13r
la consola *game station* 5r
lácteo/a *dairy (product)* 10
el lago *lake* 7
lamentar *to be sorry* 11r
la lana *wool* 6r
la langosta *lobster* 10
lanzar *to throw* 7r
el lápiz *pencil* P
el lavabo *bathroom sink* 5
la lavadora *washer* 5
la lavandería *dry cleaner* 6r
lavar en seco *dry clean* 6r
la lección *lesson* 1r
la leche *milk* 3
la leche de coco *coconut milk* 10
la lechuga *lettuce* 3

la lectura *reading* Pr
leer *to read* 1, 7r, Pr
leer por encima *to skim* 15r
las legumbres *legumes* 10
lejano/a *distant* 14r
lejos (de) *far; (far from)* 3r, 5
la lengua *language* 1r; *tongue* 15r
lentamente *slowly* 4r
las lentejas *lentils* 10
los lentes de contacto *contact lenses* 2
levantar *to raise* Pr
levantar la mano *to raise one's hand* Pr
levantar(se) *to raise; to get up* 4
la librería *bookstore* 1
el libro *book* 1r, 6r, P
la licuadora *blender* 10r
ligero/a *lightweight* 15r
el limón *lemon* 10
el limpiaparabrisas *windshield wiper* 12
limpiar *to clean; to tidy up* 5
lindo/a *pretty, attractive* 2r
el lío *mess* 3r
la lista *list* 10r
listo/a *clever* 6r; *smart; ready* 2
la literatura *literature* 1, 13r
el living *living room* 5r
llamar *to call* 7r
la llanta *tire* 12
la llave *key* 12
la llegada *arrival* 12r
llegar *to arrive* 1
llenar *to fill (out)* 9
lleno/a *full* 12
llevar *to wear, to take* 6
llevarse bien *to get along well* 13r
llover (ue) *to rain* 7
la lluvia *rain* 7
la lluvia de ideas *brainstorming* 7r
loco/a *crazy* 11r
el/la locutor/a *radio announcer* 9
lógicamente *logically* 4r
lograr *to achieve* 4r
el logro *achievement* 4r
lo importante *the important thing* 9
Lo siento. *I'm sorry (to hear that).* Pr
lo siguiente *the following* 13r

los recursos *resources* 15
Lo vamos a pasar muy bien. *We are going to have a good time.* 3r
la lucha *fight* 14
luchar *to fight* 14r
el lucro *non-profit* 14r
luego *later* 3; *then* 4r
el lugar *place* 1
el lujo *luxury* 12r
el lunes *Monday* Pr

M

machacar *to crush* 10r
la madera *wood* 9
la madrastra *stepmother* 4
la madre *mother* 4
la madrina *godmother* 4
magnífico/a *great* 6
el maíz *corn* 10
mal *bad* P
la maleta *suitcase* 12, 12r
el maletero *trunk* 12
el maletín *briefcase* 12r
malo/a *bad* 1; *ill* 6r
la mamá *mom* 4
la mañana *morning* P, Pr
mañana *tomorrow* P
mandar *to send* 9
mandar saludos *to say hello* 5r
el mandato *command* 9r
manejar *to drive* 12
la mano *hand* 6r, 11, Pr
la manta *blanket* 5, 5r
la manteca/la mantequilla *butter* 10
el mantel *tablecloth* 10
mantener (g, ie) *to maintain* 8
mantenerse en contacto *to stay in touch* 5r
la manzana *apple* 10
la manzanilla *chamomile* 11r
el mapa *map* P
maquillar(se) *to put makeup on (someone);* 4
el mar *sea* 3
el maracuyá *passion fruit* 10
la maravilla *marvel* 3r
maravilloso/a *marvelous* 8
la marca *brand* 7r
el marcador *highlighter* 5r; *marker* P
la margarina *margarine* 10
los mariscos *shellfish* 10
marrón *brown* 2, 2r
marroquí *Moroccan* 2

el martes *Tuesday* Pr
marzo *March* Pr
más *more* Pr
más o menos *more or less* P
más tarde *later* 3r; *much later* 4r
las matemáticas *mathematics* Pr
el material *material* 6r
mayo *May* Pr
la mayonesa *mayonnaise* 10
mayor *old* 2
la mayoría *majority* 14
el/la mecánico/a *mechanic* 9r
el médano *dune* 7r
el/la mediador *mediator* 13r
la media hermana *half-sister* 4
las medias *stockings* 6r
la medicina *medicine* 1, 11
el/la médico/a *medical doctor* 9
la medida *measure* 12r
el medio ambiente *environment* 15
el medio hermano *half-brother* 4
los medios de transporte *means of transportation* 12
me gusta(n) *I like* 2
Me gustaría... *I would like . . .* 6
la mejilla *cheek* 11
mejor *better* 11r
mejorar *to improve* 14
el melocotón *peach* 10r
la melodía *melody* 8, 13
el melón *melon* 10
los menonitas *Mennonites* 13r
el/la menor *the youngest* 4
menos *minus* Pr
el mensaje *message* 14r, 15
mentir *to lie* 11r
la mentira *lie* 7r
el menú *menu* 3r
el mercado *market* 6
el mes *month* P
la mesa *table* 10, P
metal *metal* 2r
meter *to insert* 15
meter un gol *to score a goal* 7
el metro *subway* 12
el metro cuadrado *square meter* 5r
mexicano/a *Mexican* 2
mi amor *my love (term of endearment)* 3r
mi cielo *term of endearment* 3r
el micro *bus (Chile)* 12r
el miedo *fear* 5r
mientras *while* 3, 8

el miércoles *Wednesday* Pr
la migración *migration* 14
migrar *to migrate* 11r
mil *thousand* 3r
mil gracias *many thanks* 7r
el/la millonario/a *millionaire* 15r
millón *million* 3r
mirar *to look (at)* 1
mi(s) *my* P
mi vida *my life (term of endearment)* 3r
la mochila *backpack* P
moderno/a *modern* 1r, Pr
módico/a *moderate* 12r
molestar(le) *to bother* 11
molido/a *ground* 10
montar (en bicicleta) *to ride (a bicycle)* 1
morado/a *purple* 2
moreno/a *brunette* 2
morir *to die* 6r
la mortalidad *mortality* 14
la mostaza *mustard* 10
el mostrador *counter* 12, 12r
mostrar (ue) *to show* 6
el motor *motor* 12
mover (ue) *to move* 11r
muchas veces *often* 1r
mucho *much, a lot (adv.)* 2
mucho/a *many (adj.)* 2
mucho gusto *pleased/nice to meet you* P
mudarse *to move* 5r
los muebles *furniture* 5
muerto/a *dead* 8; *dead (atmosphere); deceased* 6r
la mujer *woman* 3
la mujer de negocios *businesswoman* 9
la multa *fine/ticket* 15r
mundial *world, worldwide* 7
la muñeca *wrist* 11
el mural *mural* 13
el/la muralista *muralist* 1r, 13
el músculo *muscle* 11
el museo *museum* 12r
la música *music* 1r, 3; *Music* 8
muy *very* P

N

el nacimiento *birth* 7r
nacional *national* 7r
las nacionalidades *Nationalities* 2

nada *nothing* 13r

nadar *to swim* 3

nadie *nobody, no one* 13r

la naranja *orange* 3

naranja *orange (color)* 2r

la nariz *nose* 11

natal *native* 10r

la naturaleza *nature* 15

la nave *ship* 15r

la Navidad *Christmas* 8r

necesario/a *necessary* 11r

el negocio *business* 1r

negrita *bold* 4r

negro/a *black* 2

el nervio *nerve* 11

nervioso/a *nervous* 2, Pr

nevar (ie) *to snow* 7

la nevera *refrigerator* 5r

ni... ni *neither . . . nor* 13r

nicaragüense *Nicaraguan* 2

la nieta *granddaughter* 4

el nieto *grandson* 4

la nieve *snow* 6r, 7

nigeriano/a *Nigerian* 2

ningún/ninguno/ninguna *no; no one; not any* 13r

el niño/a *child* 4

el nivel *level* 14

no *no* Pr

la noche *night* Pr

la Nochebuena *Christmas Eve* 8r

la Nochevieja *New Year's Eve* 8r

No comprendo. *I don't understand* Pr

¡No me digas! *Really!* 4r

nominar *to nominate* 13

no obstante *however* 11r

normalmente *normally* 4r

norteamericano/a *North American* 1

No sé. *I don't know* Pr

nosotros/nosotras *we* 1

nostálgico *nostalgic* 14r

la nota *note* 1

la noticia *news* 3r, 4

la novela *novel* 13

el/la novelista *novelist* 13, 15r

la novia *fiancée, girlfriend* 4

noviembre *November* Pr

el novio *fiancé, boyfriend* 4

nuevo/a *new* 2

el número *size* 6r

nunca *never* 1r; *(not) ever* 13r

O

o *or* 13r

o... o *either . . . or* 13r

el objeto *object* 6r

la obra *work* 13

el/la obrero/a *worker, laborer* 9r

obtener *to obtain* 10r

obvio/a *obvious* 13r

el ocio *free time* 11r

octubre *October* Pr

la ocupación *occupation* 9r

ocupado/a *busy* 4

ocurrir *to occur* 10r

odiar *to hate* 8r

la oficina *office* 1, Pr

ofrecer (zc) *to offer* 9

el oído *(inner) ear* 11

Oiga, por favor. *Listen, please.* 1r

¡Oigo! *Hello? (on the telephone)* 3r

oír *to hear* 3r; *to listen* 1r

oír hablar *to hear about* 7r

ojalá que... *I/we hope that . . .* 11r

el ojo *eye* 2

las Olimpiadas *Olympics* 7r

olvidar *to forget* 10r

el ómnibus *bus (Peru)* 12r

la operación *surgery* 11r

la opinión *opinion* 14r

optimista *optimistic* Pr

el ordenador *computer* 1r

ordenar *to clean* 5

la oreja *ear* 6r; *(outer) ear* 11

la organización *organization* 14r

organizar *to organize* 7r

oro *gold* 2r

la orquesta *orchestra* 8

la oscuridad *dark* 15r

oscuro/a *dark* 2

el otoño *fall, autumn* 6r

otra cosa *something else* 6r

otra vez *again* Pr

otro/a *other* 4r; *other, another* 3

la oveja *sheep* 10

el OVNI *UFO* 15r

¡Oye! *Listen!* 1r

P

palabra *word* P

el/la paciente *patient* 11

paciente *patient (adj.)* Pr

el padrastro *stepfather* 4

el padre *father* 4

los padres *parents* 4

el padrino *godfather* 4

pagar *to pay (for)* 6

la página *page* Pr

el país *country, nation* 3

el paisaje *landscape* 13

la palabra *word* 6r

la palabra clave *key word* 6r

el paladar *palate* 13r

el palo *golf club* 7

las palomitas de maíz *popcorn* 10r

la palta *avocado* 10r

el pan *bread* 3

la panadería *bakery* 6r

panameño/a *Panamanian* 2

el pan dulce *bun, small cake* 10

la pantalla *screen* P

los pantalones *pants* 6

los pantalones cortos *shorts* 6

las pantimedias *pantyhose* 6

el pan tostado *toast* 3

el pañuelo *handkerchief* 6

el papá *dad* 4

la papa *potato* 3

las papas fritas *French Fries* 3

el penalti *penalty* 7r

el pendiente *earring* 6r

la pendiente *slope* 7r

pensar de *to think of/about (opinion)* 4r

pensar en *to think of/about* 4r

pensar (ie) *to plan to* 4; *to think* 4

el pepino *cucumber* 10

pequeño/a *small* 1

la pera *pear* 10

perder (ie) *to lose* 7

perderse (ie) *to get lost* 12

la pérdida *loss* 15

perdón *pardon me, excuse me* Pr

el perejil *parsley* 10r

perezoso/a *lazy* 2

perfeccionista *perfectionistic* Pr

perfectamente *perfectly* 4r

perfecto/a *perfect* 10r

el **periódico** *newspaper* 3; *periodical, newspaper* 1r

el/la **periodista** *journalist* 9, 9r

el **permiso de conducir** *driver's license* 15r

pero *but* 1

el **perro** *dog* 4, 11r

la **persona** *person* P

el **personaje principal** *main character* 13

la **perspectiva** *perspective* 11r

las **pertenencias** *belongings* 12r

peruano/a *Peruvian* 2

la **pesa** *weight* 10r

la **pesadilla** *nightmare* 12r

el **pescado** *fish* 3, 10

pesimista *pessimistic* Pr

la **pestaña** *eyelash* 11

el **petróleo** *petroleum* 15r

picado/a *chopped* 10r; *ground* 10

picar *to chop* 10r

picar(se) *to itch* 11r

el **pie** *foot* 2r, 5r, 11

la **piel** *skin* 10r

la **piel de gallina** *goosebumps* 15r

la **pierna** *leg* 2r, 6r, 11

el/la **piyama** *pajamas* 6

la **pileta** *swimming pool* 5r

el **pimentón** *paprika* 10r

la **pimienta** *pepper* 10

la **pimienta roja** *red pepper* 10r

el **pimiento (verde)** *(green) pepper* 10

la **piña** *pineapple* 10

el **pintor/la pintora** *painter* 13

la **pintura** *painting* 13

la **piscina** *swimming pool* 5, 5r

el **piso** *floor; apartment* 5

pitar *to whistle* 7

la **pizarra** *chalkboard* P

la **placa** *license plate* 12

el **placer** *pleasure* 7r

el **plan** *plan* 7r

el **planeta** *planet* 15

plástico *plastic* 2r

el **plátano** *banana, plantain* 10

el **plato** *plate, dish* 10

la **plaza** *city square* 13r

el/la **plomero/a** *plumber* 9

planchar *to iron* 5

la **planta baja** *first floor, ground floor* 5

la **población** *population* 14

pobre *poor* 2

la **pobreza** *poverty* 14

poco *few, little* 4r; *a little* 4r

polaco/a *Polish* 2

poco a poco *little by little* 4r

poco después *a little later* 4r

poder (ue) *to be able to, can* 4

el **poema** *poem* 13; *poema* 1r

la **poesía** *poetry* 13

el/la **poeta** *poet* 13

el/la **policía** *policeman/woman* 9

políglota *polyglot, multilingual* 14

el **pollo** *chicken* 3

el **pomelo** *grapefruit* 10

poner *to put* 3r

poner la mesa *to set the table* 3

ponerse en marcha *to go into effect* 15r

ponerse (g) *to become* 14r; *to put on (clothes)* 6r

popular *popular* Pr

la **popularidad** *popularity* 7r

popularizar (c) *to popularize* 13

por *by; for; along; through; in (time)* 3r

el **porcentaje** *percentage* 14

por ciento *percent* 3r

por cierto *by the way* 9

por ejemplo *for example* 3r

por eso *that is why* 3r

por favor *please* Pr

por fin *finally, at last* 3r, 15r

por lo menos *at least* 3r

por la mañana *in the morning* 3r

por la noche *in the evening* 3r

el **poroto** *bean* 10r

por otro lado *on the other hand* 4r

porque *because* 1r

¿por qué? *why?* 1r

por supuesto *of course* 3r

por la tarde *in the afternoon* 3r

por teléfono *by telephone* 3r

portugués/portuguesa *Portuguese* 2

por último *finally, at last* 4r

por un lado *on the one hand* 4r

posible *possible* 13r

la **posición** *position* P

potente *powerful* 15r

practicar *to practice* 1

preceder *to precede* 14

el **precio** *price* 6, 6r

precioso/a *beautiful* 6

preferir (ie) *to prefer* 4

la **pregunta** *question* Pr

premiar *to reward* 9r

el **premio** *award, prize* 13

preocupar(se) *to concern; to be concerned, worried* 11r

preparar *to prepare* 5

el **preparativo** *preparation* 8

la **presentación** *introduction* P

presente *here (present)* Pr

presidencial *presidential* 14r

el **presidente/la presidenta** *president* 14

prestar *to lend* 6r

el **pretérito** *preterit* 6r

prever *to foresee, to predict* 13r

la **primavera** *spring* 6r

la **primera clase** *first class* 12, 12r

primero/a *first* 4r

el **primo/a** *cousin* 4

la **prisa** *speed, haste* 5r

probable *probable* 13r

probar *to try* 10r

probarse (ue) *to try on* 6

el **problema** *problem* 1r, 13r

la **procesión** *procession* 8

producir *to produce* 15r

el **producto** *product* 10

el **profesor/la profesora** *professor, teacher* P

el **programa** *program* 1r

el **progreso** *progress* 14r

prohibir *to prohibit* 11r

el **promedio** *average* 8r, 14

prometedor/a *promising* 13

promocionar *to advertise* 6r

el **pronóstico del tiempo** *weather forecast* 7r

propio/a *own* 9

la **propuesta** *proposal* 7r

la **proteína** *protein* 10r

el **proveedor de comida** *caterer* 9r

el **proveedor de salud** *health care provider* 11

la **proximidad** *proximity* 14

próximo/a *next* 3r

la **(p)sicología** *psychology* 1, Pr

el/la **(p)sicólogo/a** *psychologist* 9

el/la **(p)siquiatra** *psychiatrist* 11r

el **plato** *dish, plate* 5

la **publicidad** *publicity* 6r

el **pueblo** *village* 5

la **puerta** *door* P

la **puerta (de salida)** *gate* 12

puertorriqueño/a *Puerto Rican* 2

el **puesto** *position* 9

el pulmón *lung* 11
la pulsera *bracelet* 6
el punto culminante *climax* 13r
el punto de vista *point of view* 11r
el pupitre *student desk* P
la playa *beach* 1
la plaza *plaza, square* 1

Q

¿qué? *what?* 1r
¡Qué bárbaro! *Great!* 7r
¡Qué bien/bueno! *That's great!* 4r
¡Qué casualidad! *What a suprise/coincidence!* 1r
quedar *to arrange to meet* 8; *to fit; to be left over* 6
¿Qué día es hoy? *What day is it?* Pr
¿Qué fecha es hoy? *What is the date?* Pr
¿Qué hay? *Hello? (on the telephone)* 3r
¿Qué hora es? *What time is it?* Pr
¡Qué increíble! *How incredible!* 1r
la queja *complaint* 13r
quejarse *to complain* 7r
¡Qué lástima! *What a pity!* 1
querer (ie) *to want* 4
querido/a *dear* 3r
Querido/a *Dear* 3r
el queso *cheese* 3
el queso crema *cream cheese* 10
¿Qué tal? *What's up, What's new? (informal)* P
¿Qué te/le(s) pasa? *What's wrong (with you/them)?* 11
¿Qué te parece? *What do you think?* 3
¿Qué tiempo hace? *What is the weather like?* Pr
¿Quién es... ? *Who is . . . ?* P
¿quién(es)? *who?* 1r
la quijada *jawbone* 13r
Quisiera... *I would like . . .* 6
quitar(se) *to take away; to take off* 4

R

el radiador *radiator* 12
el/la radio *radio* 5
el/la radiólogo/a *radiologist* 11r
rallar *to grate* 10r

rápidamente *quickly* 4r
rápido/a *fast* 3
la raqueta *racquet* 7
el rasgo *feature, trait* 12r
la razón *reason* 5r
la realidad *reality* 13r
realizar (c) *to carry out* 14
realmente *of course* 9; *in fact, really* 9; *really* 4r
reaparecer *to reappear* 11r
la rebaja *sale* 6
rebajado/a *marked down* 6
la recámara *bedroom* 5r
la recepción *front desk* 12
la receta *prescription* 11; *receipt* 10r; *recipe* 10
recetar *to prescribe* 11
recibir *to receive* 14r
reciclado/a *recycled* 15
reclamar *to claim* 12r
recoger (j) *to pick up* 5
la recomendación *recommendation* 15r
recomendar (ie) *to recommend* 10
recopilar *to compile* 14r
recordar(se) (ue) *to remember* 4r, 8
recorrer *to cover, to travel* 12; *to travel, to cover (distance)* 7
el recuerdo *memory* 13; *souvenir* 6r
la red *net* 7; *network* 5r
reducir *to reduce* 11r
reflejar *to reflect* 5r, 13
el refrán *proverb* 12r
el refresco *soda; soft drink* 3
el refrigerador *refrigerator* 5, 5r
regalar *to give (a present)* 6
el regalo *gift* 3r; *present* 6
regar (ie) *to water* 5
regatear *to haggle* 6r
el régimen *regime* 14
la región *region* 15r
regular *fair* Pr
regularmente *regularly* 4r
reír (i) *to laugh* 7r
religioso/a *religious* Pr
el relleno *filling* 10r
relleno/a *filled* 3r
el reloj *clock* P
el remedio *remedy, medicine* 11
el renacimiento *rebirth* 8r
el rendimiento *performance* 9r
repetir (i) *to repeat* 4r
repoblar *to reforest* 15; *to repopulate* 15r
el reproductor de CDs *CD player* 5r

el reproductor de DVDs *DVD player* 5r
la reputación *reputation* 7r
la reseña *review* 13r
la reserva natural *nature preserve* 15
reservar *to make a reservation* 12
respetar *to respect* 13r
respirar *to breathe* 11
responder *to respond* 15r
responsable *responsible* Pr
el restaurante *restaurant* 1r
el resultado *the result* 7r
resumir *to summarize* 4r
relativamente *relatively* 4r
el reto *challenge* 15
retornar *to return* 11r
retratar *to portray* 13
la reunión *meeting, gathering* 3
reunirse *to get together, to meet* 8
revisar *to inspect* 12
la revista *magazine* 3
la revista de corazón *gossip magazine* 13
el rey/la reina *king/queen* 8
largo/a *long* 2
el riachuelo *creek* 4r
rico/a *delicious (food)* 6r; *rich, wealthy* 2, 6r
el riel *rail* 15, 15r
la risa *laughter* 12r
el robo *robbery* 10r
el robot *robot* 15
rociar *to spray* 8r
el rocoto *pepper* 3r
rodear *to surround* 13
la rodilla *knee* 11
rojo/a *red* 2
romántico/a *romantic* Pr
romper *to break* 15r; *to tear* 15r
la ropa *clothes* 6
la ropa de estar en casa *loungewear* 6r
la ropa deportiva *sportswear* 6r
la ropa formal *formalwear* 6r
la ropa informal *casualwear* 6r
la ropa interior *underwear* 6, 6r
rosa *pink* 2
rosado/a *pink* 2
el rotulador *marker* P
rubio/a *blond* 2
la ruda *rue (herb)* 11r
la rueda *wheel* 12
el ruido *noise* 5r, 8

las ruinas *ruins* 5
la rutina *routine* 3r

S

la sala *living room* 5, 5r
el sábado *Saturday* Pr
la sábana *sheet* 5
saber *to know* 3r, Pr
sacar *to take out* 5
sacar buenas/malas notas *to get good/bad grades* 1
el saco *blazer, jacket* 6
la sala de espera *waiting area* 12r
la sal *salt* 10
la salida *departure* 12r
la salida de emergencia *emergency exit* 12
la salida del sol *sunrise* 13r
salir *to go out* 3r
el salón *living room* 5r
el salón de clase *classroom* P
la salsa con queso *nacho cheese sauce* 10r
la salsa de tomate *tomato sauce* 10
saltear *to sauté* 10r
la salud *Health* 11
saludable *healthy* 10r
el saludo *greeting* 1
salvadoreño/a *Salvadorian* 2
la sandalia *sandal* 6
el sándwich *sandwich* 1r, 3
el sanatorio *hospital* 11r
las compras *shopping* 6
la secadora *dryer* 5
secar(se) *to dry (oneself)* 4
la sed *thirst* 5r
sedentario/a *sedentary* 11r
seguir (i) *to follow, to go on* 4
seguir (i) derecho *to go straight* 12
según *as* 14r; *according to* 14r
seguramente *surely, certainly* 4r
la seguridad *security* 13r
seguro/a *certain* 13r
la semana *week* P, Pr
la semilla *seed* 8
el seminario *seminar* 1r
la señal *signal* 9
el senderista *hiker* 4r
la señora (Sra.) *Ms., Mrs.* P
la señorita (Srta.) *Ms, Miss* P
el señor (Sr.) *Mr.* P

sentarse (ie) *to sit down* 4
sentimental *sentimental* Pr
sentir(se) (ie, i) *to be sorry* 11r; *to feel* 4, 11
septiembre *September* Pr
ser *to be* 2, Pr
serio/a *serious* 11, Pr
la servilleta *napkin* 10
servir (i) *to serve* 4
si *if* 3
sí *yes* P
siempre *always* 1r
sigilosamente *discreetly* 13r
el significado *meaning* 4r
siguiente *following* 14r
la silla *chair* P
el silencio *silence* 14r
silvestre *wild* 10r
el símbolo *symbol* 13
simpático/a *friendly* 14r; *nice, charming* 2
simplemente *simply* 4r
sin *without* 7r
sincero/a *sincere* Pr
sin embargo *nevertheless* 9, 9r
sin que *without* 14r
el síntoma *symptom* 11
las medias *stockings, socks* 6
sobre *on, above* P
sobrevivir *to survive* 9
la sobrina *niece* 4
el sobrino *nephew* 4
sobrio/a *sober* 14r
social *social* 1r
la sociedad *Society* 14
la sociología *sociology* 1
el sofá *sofa* 5
sofreír *to fry lightly* 10r
el sol *sun* Pr
solicitar *to apply (for)* 9
la solicitud *application* 9
sólo *only (adv.)* 1
soltero/a *single* 2
el sombrero *hat* 6, 6r
son *equals* Pr
sonar *to sound* 7r
la sopa *soup* 3
la sorpresa *surprise* 7r
sorprender *to surprise* 12r
el sostén *bra* 6
el sótano *basement* 5r
soy *I am* P
suave *soft* 8
subir *to get into* 15r; *to go up* 10r

subrayar *to underline* 4r
subvencionar *subsidize* 13r
la sucursal *branch (business)* 14
la sudadera *sweatshirt; jogging suit* 6
el sueldo *salary* 9
el sueño *dream* 5r; *sleep* 5r
la suerte *luck* 3r, 5r
el suéter *sweater* 6
sugerir *to suggest* 14r
el supermercado *supermarket* 6, 10r
surgir (j) *to emerge* 13
surrealista *surrealist* 13
su(s) *his/her/their* P
sustentar *to support* 12r
el susto *fear* 12r

T

la talla *size (clothes)* 6
el taller *workshop* 9
el tamale *tamale* 3r
el tamaño *size* 6r
también *also, too* 1
tampoco *neither; not* 13r
tan pronto (como) *as soon as* 14r
tanto/a... como *as much ... as* 8r
tapar *to cover* 10r
las tapas *tapas* 1r
la tarde *afternoon* Pr
tarde *late* 4
la tarea *chore, task* 5r; *homework* 1, Pr
la tarjeta de crédito *credit card* 6
la tarjeta de embarque *boarding pass* 12, 12r
la tarjeta magnética *key card* 12
la tarta *pie* 10r
la tasa *rate* 14
la tasa de cambio *exchange rate* 8r
la taza *cup* 10, 10r
la tela *fabric* 2r
el té *tea* 3
el teatro *theater* 8, 13r
el/la técnico/a *technician* 9
la tecnología *technology* 15
te gusta(n) *you (familiar) like* 2
el tejado *roof* 9r
el teléfono *telephone* 3
el teléfono celular/móvil *cell phone* 15r

la telenovela *soap opera* 11r
el televisor *television set* P
el tema *theme* 13
temer *to fear* 11
temprano *early* 4
tender (ie) *to hang (clothes)* 5
el tenedor *fork* 10
tener (g, ie) *to have* 4
tener... años *to be . . . old* 5r
tener calor *to be hot* 5r
tener cuidado *to be careful* 5r
tener dolor de... *to have a(n) . . . ache* 11
tener éxito *to be successful* 10r, 13
tener frío *to be cold* 5r
tener hambre *to be hungry* 5r
tener mala cara *to look terrible* 11
tener miedo *to be afraid* 5r
tener prisa *to be in a hurry, rush* 5r
tener que *to have to* 4r
tener razón *to be right, correct* 5r
tener sed *to be thirsty* 5r
tener sueño *to be sleepy* 5r
tener suerte *to be lucky* 5r
Tengo... años. *I am . . . years old.* 2
tengo/tienes *I have/you have* 1
el tenis *tennis* Pr
el/la tenista *tennis player* 7r
la tensión (arterial) *(blood) pressure* 11
la terapia *therapy* 13r
tercero/a *third* 5r
terminar *to finish* 14r
el termómetro *thermometer* 11
la terraza *deck* 9r; *terrace* 5
el terrorismo *terrorism* 14r
el testamento *will* 14r
la tía *aunt* 4
el tiempo *time; weather* Pr; *weather* 7
el tiempo libre *free time* 3
la tienda *store* 6
tiene *he/she has; you (formal) have* 2
la tierra *land, soil* 15
tímido/a *timid* Pr
la tina *bathtub* 5r
la tintorería *dry cleaner* 14r
el tío *uncle* 4
típico/a *typical* 3
titular(se) *to be called* 13
el título *motto* 12r; *title* 4r
la tiza *chalk* P
la toalla *towel* 5

el tobillo *ankle* 11
tocar (un instrumento) *to play (an instrument)* 3
todas las semanas *every week* 1r
todavía *still, yet* 10
todo *everything* 13r
todo/a *every* 1r
todos/as *all* 13r; *everybody* 2, 13r
todos los días *every day* 1r
todos los meses *every month* 1r
tomar *to take; to drink* 1
tomar apuntes/notas *to take notes* 1
tomar asiento *to take a seat* 9r
tomar el sol *sunbathe* 1r; *to sunbathe* 3
el tomate *tomato* 3
el tono *tone* 14r
tonto/a *silly, foolish* 2
torcer(se) (ue) *to twist* 11
el torneo *tournament* 7r
el toro *bull* 8
la toronja *grapefruit* 10
torpe *clumsy* 6r
la tos *cough* 11
toser *to cough* 11
tostar *to toast* 10r
la tostada *toast*
tóxico/a *toxic* 1r
trabajador/a *hardworking* 2
trabajar *to work* 1
el trabajo *work* 5, 9
el trabajo de campo *fieldwork* 13r
la tradición *tradition* 8
tradicional *traditional* Pr
tradicionalmente *traditionally* 4r
traducir (zc) *to translate* 7
traer *to bring* 3r
el tráfico *traffic* 15r
el tráfico de drogas *drug trafficking* 14
el traje *suit* 6
el traje de baño *bathing suit* 6
el traje de chaqueta *suit* 6
el traje pantalón *pantsuit* 6
tranquilo/a *tranquil* Pr
tranquilamente *tranquilly* 4r
transitar *to cross; to move back and forth* 12
el tratamiento médico *medical treatment* 11
tratar *to treat* 11; *to be about* 13; *to try* 5r
el trayecto *route* 12
el tren *train* 12

triste *sad* 2, 14r
tropezarse *to stumble* 15r
tú *you (familiar)* P
tu(s) *your (familiar)* P
último/a *last* 8

U

la uña de gata *cat's claw (herb)* 11r
una semana atrás *a week ago* 6r
una vez *once* 12, 13r
unificar (qu) *to unify* 15
la universidad *university* 1
un poco *a little* 4
un/una *a, an* P
urgente *urgent* 11r
uruguayo/a *Uruguayan* 2
usar *to use* 2
usted *you (formal)* P
ustedes *you (plural)* 1
útil *useful* P
la uva *grape* 10

V

las vacaciones *vacation* 3
la vacante *opening* 9
vacío/a *empty* 12
la vainilla *vanilla* 10
valer *to be worth* 6
los vaqueros/jeans *jeans* 6
el vaso *glass* 10
Vaya. *Go.* Pr
la vecina *neighbor* 5r
el/la vecino/a *neighbor* 5r
el vegetal/la verdura *vegetable* 3
vegetariano/a *vegetarian* 12r
la velocidad *speed* 12
la vena *vein* 11
¡Ven/Anda, anímate! *Come on, cheer up!* 3r
el/la vendedor/a *salesperson,* 9; *seller* 6r
vender *to sell* 6, 6r
venezolano/a *Venezuelan* 2
venir (g, ie) *to come* 4
la venta *sale* 9r
la ventaja *advantage* 5
la ventana *window* 1r, P
la ventanilla *window* 12r
el ventilador *fan* 5
ver *to see* 1
el verano *summer* 6r
verbos *verbs* P

¿**verdad?** *right?* 1
verdad *true* 13r
la verdad *truth* 7r
verde *green; not ripe* 2
la verdura *vegetable* 10
ver(se) *to look, appear* 11r
el vestido *dress* 6
el vestido de verano *summer dress* 6r
vestir(se) (i) *to dress; to get
    dressed* 4
el/la veterinario/a *veterinarian* 9r
viajar *to travel* 12
el viaje *trips* 12
el videojuego *video game* 15, 15r
el vidrio *glass* 2r
viejo/a *old* 2, 8r
el viento *wind* 7
el viernes *Friday* Pr
el vinagre *vinegar* 10
el vino *wine* 3

el virreinato *administrative unit of
    the Spanish Empire* 3r
virtualmente *virtually* 15
la viruela *smallpox* 11r
visitar *to visit* 4
la vista *view* 5
la vitamina *vitamin* 11r
la vivienda *dwelling; apartment* 5r;
    housing 5
vivir *to live* 1
vivo/a *alive* 6r; *lively
    (personality)* 6r
volador/a *flying* 15, 15r
el volante *steering wheel* 12
volar (ue) *to fly* 12
el vóleibol *volleyball* 7
el volibol *volleyball* 7r
volver (ue) *to return* 4
la voz *voice* 13
el vuelo *flight* 12

Y

y *and* P; *plus* Pr
ya *already* 10
yo *I* P
el yogur *yogurt* 10
la yuca *yucca* 3r

Z

la zanahoria *carrot* 10
las zapatillas de deporte *tennis
    shoes* 6
las zapatillas *slippers* 6
los zapatos *shoes* 6
los zapatos de tacón *high-heeled
    shoe* 6
el zarcillo *earring* 6r
la zona *area* 5
la zona peatonal *pedestrian area* 10r

Appendix 4

English to Spanish Glossary

A

a un/una
a little later poco después
a lot (of) mucho/a (adj.); mucho (adv.)
to abound abundar
above sobre
access el acceso
accessory el accesorio
to accompany acompañar
according to según
accountant el/la contador/a (contable)
accounting la contabilidad
to ache doler (ue)
to achieve lograr
achievement el logro
to act actuar
active activo/a
activity la actividad
actor el actor
actress la actriz
ad, advertisement el anuncio
to adapt adaptar
adaptation la adaptación
to add agregar; añadir
to address dirigirse
adjustment la adaptación
advance el adelanto
to advance avanzar
advantage la ventaja
to advertise promocionar
advisable aconsejable
to advise aconsejar
aerobic exercise el ejercicio aeróbico
affectionately con cariño
to affirm afirmar
after después; después (de) que
afternoon la tarde
again otra vez
ago hace
to agree estar de acuerdo
agreeable agradable
agreement la concordancia
air-conditioned climatizado/a
air conditioning el aire acondicionado

airline la aerolínea/línea aérea
airport el aeropuerto
aisle seat el asiento de pasillo
alacrity la alacridad
algebra la álgebra
alive vivo/a
all todos/as
allergic alérgico/a
to alleviate calmar
along por
already ya
also también
alternative alternativo/a
although aunque
always siempre
ambitious ambicioso/a
ammunition la cabuya
ample amplio/a
amusing divertido/a
anatomy la anatomía
ancestor el antepasado
and y
angry enojado/a
ankle el tobillo
to answer contestar
Antarctica la Antártida
antes before
antes (de) que before
anthropology la antropología
antibiotic el antibiótico
anxiety la ansiedad
any, some algún/alguno/alguna
anything algo
apartment el apartamento; el departamento; el piso; la vivienda
to apologize disculparse
apple la manzana
appliance el electrodoméstico
application la aplicación; la solicitud
to apply (for) solicitar
apprentice el iniciado
appropriate apropiado/a
April abril
architect el/la arquitecto/a
architecture la arquitectura
area la zona
Argentinian argentino/a
to argue discutir

arm el brazo
armchair la butaca
arrival la llegada
to arrive llegar
arrogant arrogante
art el arte
artist el/la artista; el/la intérprete
as según
as much . . . as tanto … como
as soon as as en cuanto
to ask for pedir (i)
to assist ayudar
to assume asumir
to assure asegurar
astronomy el astronomía
at a
at times a veces
athlete el/la deportista
athletic atlético/a
ATM el cajero automático
atmosphere la atmósfera
attached document el documento adjunto
to attend asistir
attic el ático
attractive atractivo/a; bonito/a; bueno/a; guapo/a; lindo/a
August agosto
aunt la tía
authority figure la figura de autoridad
available disponible
avenue la avenida
average el promedio
avocado el aguacate; la palta
to avoid evitar
award, prize el premio

B

back al fondo, atrás; la espalda
background el fondo
backpack la mochila
backwards atrás
bad mal; malo/a
bakery la panadería
ball el balón/la pelota
ballpoint pen el bolígrafo

banana el banano; el cambur; el plátano; la banana

bank el banco

baptism, christening el bautizo

barbecue pit; barbecue (event) la barbacoa

bargain la ganga

to base basar

baseball el béisbol

basement el sótano

basically básicamente

basket (hoop) el/la cesto/a

basketball el baloncesto/el básquetbol

bat el bate

to bathe; to take a bath bañar(se)

bathing suit el traje de baño

bathroom el baño

bathroom sink el lavabo

bathtub la bañera; la tina; la bañadera; la bañera

to be estar; ser

to be able to, can poder (ue)

to be afraid tener miedo

to be called titular(se)

to be careful tener cuidado

to be cold tener frío

to be crazy (Cuba) estar trocá

to be fashionable estar de moda

to be glad (about) alegrarse (de)

to be happy alegrarse

to be hot tener calor

to be hungry tener hambre

to be in a hurry (Colombia) estar de afán

to be in a hurry, rush tener prisa

to be lucky tener suerte

to be . . . old tener ... años

to be pleasing to, to like gustar

to be right, correct tener razón

to be sleepy tener sueño

to be sorry lamentar; sentir(se) (ie, i)

to be successful tener éxito

to be thirsty tener sed

to be worth valer

beach la playa

bead la cuenta

bean el frijol; el poroto

to beat batir

beautiful precioso/a

beauty item el artículo de belleza

beauty salon, barbershop la peluquería

because porque

to become hacerse; poner(se)

to become sick enfermarse

bed la cama

bedroom el cuarto; el dormitorio; la habitación; la alcoba; la recámara

beef/steak la carne de res

beer la cerveza

to begin comenzar (ie)

to begin, to start empezar (ie)

beginning el comienzo

behavior el comportamiento

behind atrás; detrás (de)

to believe creer

belongings las pertenencias

below abajo

belt el cinturón

to benefit beneficiar

besides además

better mejor

between, among entre

bicycle la bicicleta

big grande

bilingual bilingüe

to bind atar

biochemistry la bioquímica

birth el nacimiento

birthday el cumpleaños

bison el bisonte

black negro/a

blackout el apagón

blacksmith; ironworker el herrero

blanket la manta; la cobija; la frazada

blazer, jacket el saco

blender la licuadora

blond rubio/a

(blood) pressure la tensión (arterial)

blouse la blusa

blue azul

to board abordar

board of directors la junta directiva

boarding pass la tarjeta de embarque;

boat el barco

body el cuerpo

to boil hervir (ie, i)

bold negrita

Bolivian boliviano/a

bone el hueso

book el libro

bookstore la librería

boot la bota

bored aburrido/a

boring aburrido/a

boss el jefe/la jefa

to bother molestar(le)

bottle la botella

to bowl jugar (ue) a los bolos

bowl la fuente

bowling el boliche; el bowling

bowling ball el bolo; la bola

box la caja

boxer shorts el calzoncillo

boy el chico

boyfriend el novio

bra el sostén

bracelet la pulsera

brain el cerebro

brainstorming la lluvia de ideas

branch (business) la sucursal

brand la marca

bread el pan

to break descomponer(se); fracturar(se); romper

breakfast el desayuno

to breathe respirar

briefcase el maletín

to bring traer

broadband la banda ancha

broke brujo/a

brother el hermano

to brown dorar

brown marrón

brunette moreno/a

to build construir (y)

building el edificio

bull el toro

bullfight la corrida (de toros)

bumper el parachoques

bun, small cake el pan dulce

to bury enterrar

bus el autobús, el bus

business el negocio

businessman/woman el hombre/la mujer de negocios

busy ocupado/a

but pero

butter la manteca/la mantequilla

to buy comprar

by por

by telephone por teléfono

by the way por cierto

C

cabinet el armario

cafe, coffee shop el café

cafeteria la cafetería

calcium el calcio

calculator la calculadora

calculus el cálculo

calendar el calendario

to call llamar

to calm, alleviate calmar

camera la cámara

Canadian canadiense

to cancel cancelar

cancer   el cáncer
candy/sweets   el dulce
cap   la gorra
capsule   la cápsula
captain   el capitán
car   el auto; el carro; el coche
care   el cuidado
career counselor   el/la consejero/a
   vocacional
carefully   cuidadosamente
careless   descuidado/a
carnival   el carnaval
carpenter   el/la carpintero/a
carpet, rug   la alfombra
carrot   la zanahoria
to carry out   realizar (c)
cart, wagon   la carreta
cashier   el/la cajero/a
casualwear   la ropa informal
caterer   el/la proveedor/a de comida
cattle   el ganado
CD player   el reproductor de CDs
to celebrate   celebrar
celebration   la celebración; la fiesta
celery   el apio
cell phone   el teléfono celular; el
   teléfono móvil
cell phone charger   el cargador de
   celular; el cargador del móvil
cemetery   el cementerio
cereal   el cereal
certain   seguro/a
certainly   seguramente
certainty   la certeza
chair   la silla
chalk   la tiza
chalkboard   la pizarra
challenge   el reto
chamomile   la manzanilla
champion   el campeón/la campeona
championship   el campeonato
chance   el azar
to change   cambiar
change   el cambio
channel   el canal
charitable   caritativo/a
charming   simpático/a
chauffeur   el/la chofer (chófer)
cheap   barato/a
check   el cheque
to check in (luggage)   facturar
to check out   fijarse
checking account   la cuenta corriente
cheek   la mejilla
cheese   el queso
chef   el/la chef
cherry   la cereza

chest   el pecho
chicken   el pollo
chicken breast   la pechuga de pollo
child   el niño/ la niña
childhood   la infancia
children's   infantil
Chile   Chile
chile pepper   el ají; el chile
Chilean   chileno/a
cholesterol   el colesterol
to choose   elegir (i, i)
chop   la chuleta
to chop   picar
chopped   picado/a
chore   la tarea
Christmas   la Navidad
Christmas Eve   la Nochebuena
church   la iglesia
cilantro   el cilantro; el culantro
cinema   el cine
cinnamon   la canela
citizen   el ciudadano
city   la ciudad
city block   la cuadra
city council   el concejo municipal
city square   la plaza
to claim   reclamar
clam   la almeja
class   la clase
classmate   el/la compañero/a
classroom   el salón de clase
to clean   limpiar; ordenar
clever   listo/a
client   el/la cliente/clienta
climax   el punto culminante
clinic   la clínica, el centro
clock   el reloj
clone   la clonación
cloning   la clonación
to close   cerrar (ie)
close to, near   cerca de
closet   el armario; el clóset
closing   la despedida
clothes   la ropa
clove of garlic   el diente de ajo
clumsy   torpe
coach   el/la entrenador/a
coach class   la clase turista
coat   el abrigo
coconut milk   la leche de coco
code   el código
coffee   el café
cognate   el cognado
cold   el catarro; el frío; frío/a
to collapse   colapsar
Colombian   colombiano/a
colors   los colores

to comb (someone's hair)   peinar(se)
to come   venir (g, ie)
Come in.   Adelante.; Pase(n).
Come on, cheer up!   ¡Ven/Anda,
   anímate!
comfortable   cómodo/a
comic   cómico/a
command   el mandato
to communicate   comunicar
communication   la comunicación
company   la compañía/empresa
to compile   recopilar
to complain   quejarse
complaint   la queja
to complete, to finish; to run out of
   acabar(se)
complicit   cómplice
computer   la computadora; el
   ordenador
computer science   la informática; la
   computación
conclusion   la conclusión
conflict   el conflicto
to congratulate   felicitar
congratulations   las felicidades; las
   felicitaciones
to connect   conectar(se)
connection   la conexión
consensus   el consenso
to construct   construir
to consume   consumir
contact lenses   los lentes de
   contacto
contaminated   contaminado/a
contemporary   contemporáneo/a
contest   el concurso
to continue   continuar
to contract   contraer
contractor   el/la contratista
contrast   el contraste
to contribute   contribuir (y)
convenience store   la tienda de
   conveniencia
to converse   conversar
to cook   cocinar
cook   el/la cocinero/a
cooked   cocido/a
cookie   la galleta
corn   el choclo; el elote; el maíz
corner   la esquina
correspondence   la correspondencia
corridor, hall   el pasillo
to cost   costar (ue)
Costa Rican   costarricense
cough   la tos
to cough   toser
council   el concejo

to count   contar
counter   el mostrador
country, nation   el país
countryside   el campo
cousin   el primo/la prima
to cover   recorrer; tapar
crab   el cangrejo
craftsperson   el/la artesano/a
crazy   loco/a
cream   la crema
cream cheese   el queso crema
creative   creativo/a
credit card   la tarjeta de crédito
creek   el riachuelo
to cross   cruzar; transitar
cruise   el crucero
to crush   machacar
Cuban   cubano/a
cubist   cubista
cucumber   el pepino
cumin   el comino
cup   la taza
to cure   curar
curiosity   la curiosidad
current   actual
curtain   la cortina
custom   la costumbre
customs   la aduana
to cut   cortar
cycling   el ciclismo
cyclist   el/la ciclista

D

dad   el papá
dairy (product)   lácteo/a
to dance   bailar
dance   la danza
dance club   la discoteca
dance company   la compañía de
   danza
dancer   el bailarín/la bailarina
dangerous   peligroso/a
to dare   atreverse
dark   la oscuridad; oscuro/a
data   los datos
date   la fecha; la cita
daughter   la hija
dawn   clarear el día
day   el día
day after tomorrow   pasado mañana
day before yesterday   anteayer
Day of the Dead   el Día de los
   Muertos
dead   difunto/a; muerto/a
Dear   Estimado/a; Querido/a
dear   querido/a

December   diciembre
decision   la decisión
deck   la terraza
decorated   adornado/a
deforestation   la deforestación
delicious   rico/a
to delight   encantar
to deliver   entregar
to demand   exigir
democracy   la democracia
to denounce   denunciar
department, school   la facultad
department store   el almacén
departure   la salida
depressed   deprimido/a
depression   la depresión
to describe   describir
description   a descripción
design   el diseño
designer   el diseñador
to desire   desear
desk   el escritorio
destination   el destino
detail   el detalle
to develop   desarrollar(se)
development   el desarrollo
device   el dispositivo
diabetic   diabético/a
dictatorial   dictatorial
dictionary   el diccionario
to die   morir
diet   la dieta
difficult   difícil
difficultly   difícilmente
digitally   digitalmente
dining room   el comedor
dinner   la comida
dinner, supper   la cena
to direct   dirigir (j)
disadvantage   la desventaja
disappearence   la desaparición
disappointed   decepcionado/a
to disassemble   desarmar
discovery   el descubrimiento
discreetly   sigilosamente
dish, plate   el plato
dishwasher   el lavaplatos
to dislike   caer mal
dispersal, dissemination   la
   diseminación
displacement   el desplazamiento
disposable   desechable
distant   lejano/a
to distinguish   distinguir
diversification   la diversificación
divorced   divorciado/a
to do   hacer

dog   el perro
dollar   el dólar
domestic   doméstico/a
Dominican   dominicano/a
door   la puerta
to double   duplicar
double/single room   la habitación
   doble/sencilla
doubt   la duda
doubtful   dudoso/a
to download   bajar
downtown, center   el centro
drama   el drama
dream   el sueño
dress   el vestido
to dress; to get dressed   vestir(se) (i)
dresser   la cómoda
to drink   beber
drink   la bebida
to drink   tomar
to drive   conducir; manejar
driver   el/la chofer (chófer)
driver's license   el carnet de conducir;
   el permiso de conducir
to drop   caer
drug   la droga
drug trafficking   el tráfico de drogas
dry clean   lavar en seco
dry cleaner   la lavandería; la
   tintorería
to dry (oneself)   secar(se)
dryer   la secadora
due to   debido a
dune   el médano
during   durante
DVD   el DVD
DVD player   el reproductor de DVDs
dwelling   la vivienda
dynamic   dinámico/a

E

each   cada
eagle   el águila
ear   el oído; la oreja; la oreja
early   temprano
earring   el arete
easily   fácilmente
Easter   la Pascua
easy   fácil
to eat   comer
eccentricity   la excentricidad
economically   económicamente
economics   la economía
Ecuadorian   ecuatoriano/a
editorial house   la casa editorial
efficiency   la eficiencia

efficient   eficaz; eficiente
egg   el huevo
either . . . or   o . . . o
elbow   el codo
to elect   elegir (i, j)
election   la elección
electrician   el/la electricista
elegant   elegante
to embrace   abrazar(se) (c)
to emerge   surgir (j)
emergency   la emergencia
emergency exit   la salida de
   emergencia
emigrant   el/la emigrante
to emigrate   emigrar
emigration   la emigración
employee   el/la empleado/a
empty   vacío/a
to encourage   fomentar
energetic   enérgico/a
engagement   el compromiso
engineer   el/la ingeniero/a
to enjoy   disfrutar
enough   bastante
to enter   entrar (en)
entertainment   la diversión
environment   el medio ambiente
equality   la igualdad
equals   son
equipment   el equipo
eraser   el borrador
even if   aunque
even though   aunque
evening   por la noche
event   el acontecimiento; aun; el
   evento
ever   alguna vez
every   todo/a
every day   todos los días
every . . . hours   cada ... horas
every month   todos los meses
every week   todas las semanas
everybody   todos/as
everyone   alguien
everything   todo
evident   evidente
to exact   exigir
to examine   examinar
excellent   excelente
to exchange   cambiar
exchange   el intercambio
exchange rate   la tasa de cambio
excuse me   con permiso, perdón
executive   el/la ejecutivo/a
to exert effort   fajar(se)
to exhibit   exponer (g)
exhibit   la exposición

expensive   caro/a
experience   la experiencia
expert   el experto
to explain   explicar
export   la exportación
expression   la cara; expresion
extinct   extinguido/a
extinction   la extinción
to extinguish, to turn off   apagar
extinguished   extinguido/a
extroverted   extrovertido/a
eye   el ojo
eyebrow   la ceja
eyelash   la pestaña

F

fabric   la tela
fabulous   fabuloso/a
face   la cara
fact   el hecho
failure   el fracaso
fair   regular
to fall   caer(se)
fall   el otoño
false   falso/a
family   la familia
famous   famoso/a
fan   el ventilador
far (from)   lejos (de)
farewell   la despedida
farmer   el/la agricultor/a
to fascinate   fascinar
fast   rápido/a
fat   gordo/a; la grasa
father   el padre
Father's Day   el Día del Padre
favorite   favorito/a
fear   el miedo; el susto
to fear   temer
feature, trait   el rasgo
February   febrero
to feed   dar de comer
to feel   sentir (se) (ie)
festival   el festival
festivity; holiday   la festividad
fever   la fiebre
few   poco
fiancé(e)   el/la novio/a
fiber   la fibra
fieldwork   el trabajo de campo
fig   el higo
fight   la lucha
to fight   luchar
to fill (out)   llenar
filled   relleno/a
filling   el relleno

film   la película
filmmaker   el/la cineasta
finally, at last   finalmente; por fin;
   por último
to find   encontrar (ue)
to find out   averiguar; enterar(se)
fine arts   las bellas artes
fine/ticket   la multa
finger   el dedo
to finish   terminar
to fire   despedir (i)
fire   el incendio
firefighter   el/la bombero/a
fireplace   la chimenea
first   primero/a
first class   la primera clase
first floor   la planta baja
fish   el pescado
flashback   la escena retrospectiva
flight   el vuelo
flight attendant   el/la auxiliar de
   vuelo; el/la aeromozo/a; la
   azafata
flip-flops   las chanclas
float (in a parade)   la carroza
flood   la inundación
floor   el piso; la planta
flour   la harina
to flow   fluir
flower   la flor
flu   la gripe
to fly   volar (ue)
flying   volador/a
to focus   enfocarse (qu)
to fold   doblar
to follow   seguir (i)
following   siguiente
food   la comida
foot   el pie
football   el fútbol americano
footwear   el calzado
for   durante (time); para; por
for example   por ejemplo
for sale   a la venta
forehead   la frente
to foresee   prever
forest   el bosque
to forget   olvidar
fork   el tenedor
form   la forma
formalwear   la ropa formal
fortunately   afortunadamente
to fracture   fracturar(se)
free time   el ocio; el tiempo libre
freeway   la autopista
to freeze   congelar(se)
French   francés/francesa

French fries   las papas fritas
frequently   frecuentemente
Friday   el viernes
fried   frito/a
fried dough   los churros
friend   el/la amigo/a
friendly   simpático/a
friendship   la amistad
from   de
front desk   la recepción
fruit   la fruta
to fry   freír (i)
to fry lightly   sofreír
to fulfill   cumplir
full   lleno/a
fun   divertido/a
funny   divertido/a; gracioso/a
furniture   los muebles
furrier   el/la peletero/a
fusion cuisine   la cocina fusión

G

game   el juego; el partido
game station   la consola
garage   el garaje
garbage   la basura
garden   el jardín
garlic   el ajo
gas station   la tienda de gasolina
gate   la puerta (de salida)
generally   generalmente
generous   generoso/a
genetically   genéticamente
geography   la geografía
German   alemán/alemana
gesture   el ademán
to get along well   llevarse bien
to get angry   enfadarse; enojar(se)
to get good/bad grades   sacar buenas/malas notas
to get into   subir
to get lost   perderse (ie)
to get married   casar(se)
to get together   reunirse
to get up   levantar
gift   el regalo
girl   la chica; la chica
girlfriend   la novia
to give   dar
to give (a present)   regalar
glad   alegre; contento/a
glass   la copa; el vaso; el vidrio
glasses   las gafas
to globalize   globalizar
glove   el guante
glove compartment   la guantera
to go   andar; ir

Go.   Vaya.
to go away   ir(se)
to go in   entrar (en)
to go into effect   ponerse en marcha
to go out   salir
to go shopping   ir de compras
to go straight   seguir (i) derecho
to go to bed   acostarse
to go up   subir
goal   el gol
godchild   el/la ahijado/a
godfather   el padrino
godmother   la madrina
gold   oro
golf   el golf
golf club   el palo
good   bueno/a
good afternoon   buenas tardes
good-bye   adiós; chao; chau
good evening   buenas noches
good-looking   bien parecido
good-looking   guapo/a
Good luck!   ¡Buena suerte!
good morning   buenos días
goosebumps   la piel de gallina
gossip magazine   la revista de corazón
to govern   gobernar (ie)
government   el gobierno
governor   el gobernador
gradually   gradualmente
to graduate   graduarse
granddaughter   la nieta
grandfather   el abuelo
grandmother   la abuela
grandson   el nieto
grape   la uva
grapefruit   el pomelo; la toronja
graphic   gráfico/a
graphic design   el diseño gráfico
to grate   rallar
gray   gris
Great!   ¡Estupendo!
great   fabuloso/a; magnífico/a
green   verde
green pepper   el pimiento verde
greeting   el saludo
grill   la parrilla
ground   molido/a; picado/a
ground floor   la planta baja
ground meat   la carne molida/picada
group   el grupo
Guatemalan   guatemalteco/a
to guess   adivinar
guide   la guía
guitar   la guitarra
guitar player   el/la guitarrista
gymnasium   el gimnasio

H

hachet   el hacha
to haggle   regatear
hair   el cabello; el pelo
hairdresser   el/la peluquero/a
half-brother   el medio hermano
half-sister   la media hermana
Halloween   el Día de las Brujas
hallway   el pasillo
ham   el jamón
hamburger   la hamburguesa
to hand   dar
hand   la mano; la mano; la mano
handicrafts   la artesanía
handkerchief   el pañuelo
handsome   guapo/a
to hang (clothes)   tender (ie)
to happen   pasar
happily   alegremente
happy   alegre; contento/a
hardworking   trabajador/a
harmful   dañino/a
harp   el arpa
to harvest   cosechar
hat   el sombrero
to hate   odiar
to have   tener (g, ie)
to have a good time   divertirse (ie, i); pasar bien
to have a(n) . . . ache   tener dolor de...
to have breakfast   desayunar
to have dinner   cenar
to have fun   divertirse (ie); entretenerse
to have lunch   almorzar (ue)
to have to   tener que
he   él
he/she is   es
head   la cabeza
health   la salud
health care provider   el proveedor de salud
health center   el centro de salud
healthy   saludable
to hear   oír
to hear about   oír hablar
heart   el corazón
heat   el calor
heating   la calefacción
height   la estatura
hello   hola
Hello? (on the telephone)   ¿Aló?; ¡Bueno!; ¿Diga?; ¿Dígame?; ¡Oigo!; ¿Qué hay?
to help   ayudar
her   su(s)
herb   la hierba

here (present) presente
hi hola
high-heeled shoe el zapato
  de tacón
highlighter el marcador
highway la carretera
hiker el senderista
hip la cadera
his/her/their su(s)
Hispanic hispano/a
history la historia
holiday el día festivo
home el hogar
homeless desamparado/a
homemaker el ama/o de casa
homework la tarea
Honduran hondureño/a
honesty la honestidad
hood el capó
horrible horrible
hospital el hospital; el sanitorio
hot caliente
hotel el hotel
hour la hora
house, home la casa
housewife el ama/o de casa
housing la vivienda
How about that! ¡Fíjate qué noticia!
How are you (formal)? ¿Cómo está?
How are you (informal)? ¿Cómo estás?
How do you say . . . ? ¿Cómo se
  dice … ?
How do you spell . . . ? ¿Cómo se
  escribe … ?
How incredible! ¡Qué increíble!
How is it going? ¿Cómo te va?
how many? ¿cuántos/as?
How may I help you? ¿En qué puedo
  servirle(s)?
how much? ¿cuánto/a?
How much is it? ¿Cuánto cuesta?
how/what? ¿cómo?
however no obstante
hug el abrazo
human humano/a
humanities las humanidades
hundred cien/ciento
hunger la hambre
to hurt doler (ue)
husband el esposo
hypothesis la hipótesis

I

I yo
I am soy
I am . . . years old. Tengo … años.
I don't know No sé.

I don't understand No comprendo.
I have/you have tengo/tienes
I like me gusta(n)
I/we hope that . . . ojalá que …
I would like . . . Me gustaría …
I would like . . . Quisiera …
ice el hielo
ice cream el helado
ice creamery la heladería
idea la idea
idealistic idealista
if si
ill malo/a
ill person el/la enfermo/a
illiteracy al analfabetismo
illiterate analfabeto/a
illness la enfermedad
I'm sorry (to hear that) lo siento
imagine imaginar
immediately enseguida
immigration la inmigración
imperfect el imperfecto
to implement implementar
important importante
impossible imposible
to improve mejorar
impulsive impulsivo/a
in boldface en negrita
in contrast en contraste
in fact en realidad/realmente
in front of enfrente (de)
in search of en busca de
in (time) por
inappropriate inapropiado/a
including hasta
incredible increíble
Independence Day el Día de la
  Independencia
independent independiente
to indicate indicar
inexpensive barato/a
infection la infección
to influence influir
information la información
infrastructure la infraestructura
inhabitant el/la habitante
to inherit heredar
inheritance el/la herencia
injection la inyección
injured herido/a
injured person el/la herido/a
to insert meter
to inspect revisar
inspector el inspector
instead of en vez de
instruction la instrucción
intelligent inteligente
interesante en

to interest interesar
interesting interesante
international internacional
interpreter el/la intérprete
interview la entrevista
to interview entrevistar
intimacy la intimidad
introduction la presentación
introverted introvertido/a
invitation la invitación
to invite invitar
iPod el ipod
to iron to planchar
to itch picar(se)
it's clear está despejado
it's cloudy está nublado
it's cool hace fresco
It's sunny. Hace sol.
it's sunny hace sol

J

jacket la chaqueta
January enero
Japanese japonés/japonesa
jawbone la quijada
jeans los jeans; los vaqueros/
  jeans
jeweller el/la joyero/a
jewelry, piece of la joya
job el trabajo
jogging suit la sudadera
joke la broma
journalist el/la periodista
joy la alegría
judge el/la juez
juice el jugo
July julio
June junio
junk food la comida chatarra

K

to keep in shape estar en forma
to keep quiet callarse
to keep silent guardar silencio
key la llave
key card la tarjeta magnética
key word la palabra clave
king el rey
to kiss besar
kiss el beso
kitchen la cocina
kitchen sink el fregadero
knee la rodilla
to knock golpear
to know conocer; saber
knowledge el conocimiento

L

labor-related   laboral
laboratory   el laboratorio
laborer   el/la obrero/a
lace   el encaje
lack   la falta
lake   el lago
lamb   el cordero
to land   aterrizar (c)
land   la tierra
landscape   el paisaje
language   la lengua
laptop   la computadora portátil
to last   durar
last   último/a
last night   anoche
last year   el año pasado
late   tarde
later   después; luego; más tarde
to laugh   reír (i)
laughter   la risa
laundry room   la lavandería
lawn   el césped
lawyer   el/la abogado/a
layout   ladistribución
lazy   perezoso/a
leaf   la hoja
to learn   aprender
least   at por lo menos
leather   el cuero
to leave   dejar; ir(se)
left   la izquierda
leg   la pierna
leg (animal)   la pata
legal holiday   el día feriado
legumes   las legumbres
leisure activities   las diversiones
lemon   el limón
to lend   prestar
lentils   las lentejas
lesson   la lección
lettuce   la lechuga
level   el nivel
librarian   el/la bibliotecario/a
library   la biblioteca
license plate   la placa
to lie   mentir
lie   la mentira
life expectancy   la esperanza de vida
lightweight   ligero/a
to like   caer bien; gustar
likewise   igualmente
link   el enlace
lip   el labio
list   la lista
to listen   oír

Listen!   ¡Oye!
Listen, please.   Oiga, por favor.
to listen (to)   escuchar
literature   la literatura
little   a poco; poco; a un poco
little by little   poco a poco
to live   vivir
lively   animado/a; vivo/a
living room   el living; la sala; el salón
lobster   la langosta
to lock up   encerrar (ie)
lodging   el alojamiento
logically   lógicamente
long   largo/a
to look, appear   ver(se)
to look (at)   mirar
to look for   buscar
to look terrible   to tener mala cara
to lose   perder (ie)
to lose weight   adelgazar
loss   la pérdida
loudly   alto
loungewear   la ropa de estar en casa
love   el amor
Love (closing)   Cariños
luck   lasuerte
luggage   el equipaje
lunch   el almuerzo
lung   el pulmón
luxury   el lujo

M

magazine   la revista
mail   el correo
mail carrier   el/la cartero/a
main character   el personaje principal
to maintain   mantener (g, ie)
major   la carrera
majority   la mayoría
to make   hacer
to make a reservation   reservar
to make the bed   to hacer la cama
man   el hombre
manager   el/la gerente
many   mucho/a (adj.)
many . . . as   as tanto(s)/a(s) … como
map   el mapa
March   marzo
margarine   la margarina
marked down   rebajado/a
marker   el marcador; el rotulador
market   el mercado
married   casado/a
marvel   la maravilla
marvelous   estupendo/a;
   maravilloso/a

material   el material
mathematics   las matemáticas
May   mayo
mayonnaise   la mayonesa
mayor   el alcalde
meal   la comida
meaning   el significado
means of transportation   los medios de
   transporte
measure   la medida
meat   la carne
mechanic   el/la mecánico/a
mediator   el/la mediador
medical doctor   el/la médico/a
medical treatment   el tratamiento
   médico
medicine   la medicina
to meet   conocerse; reunir(se)
meeting, gathering   la reunión
melody   la melodía
melon   el melón
to melt   derretir
memory   el recuerdo
Mennonites   los menonitas
menu   el menú
mess   el lío; el majarete
message   el mensaje
metal   metal
mexican   mexicano/a
Mexican   mexicano/a
Mexican Independence Day   el Día de
   la Independencia de México
to microwave   hornear
microwave (oven)   el (horno)
   microondas
middle class   el burgués
to migrate   migrar
migration   la migración
milk   la leche
milkshake, smoothie   el batido
million   millón
millionaire   el/la millonario/a
minus   menos
mirror   el espejo
moderate   módico/a
modern   moderno/a
mom   la mamá
Monday   el lunes
money in cash   el dinero en efectivo
month   el mes
mood   el estado de ánimo
more   más
more or less   más o menos
morning   la mañana
Moroccan   marroquí
mortality   la mortalidad
mother   la madre

Mother's Day   el Día de la Madre
motor   el motor
motto   el eslogan; el título
mouth   la boca
to move   mover; mudarse
movement   el desplazamiento
movies   el cine
to mow (lawn)   cortar
Mr.   el señor (Sr.)
Ms, Miss   la señorita (Srta.)
Ms., Mrs.   la señora (Sra.)
much   mucho/a (adj.); mucho (adv.)
much later   más tarde
multilingual   políglota
mural   el mural
muralist   el/la muralista
muscle   el músculo
museum   el museo
music   la música
must   tener que
mustard   la mostaza
my   mi(s)

N

napkin   la servilleta
narrow   estrecho/a
national   nacional
nationality   las nacionalidad
native   natal
nature   la naturaleza
nature preserve   la reserva natural
near   cerca (de)
necessary   necesario/a
neck   el cuello
necklace   el collar
neighbor   el/la vecino/a
neighborhood   el barrio
neither   tampoco
neither . . . nor   ni ... ni
nephew   el sobrino
nerve   el nervio
nervous   nervioso/a
net   la red
network   la red
never   jamás; nunca
nevertheless   sin embargo
new   nuevo/a
New Year's Day   el Año Nuevo
New Year's Eve   el Fin de Año; la
    Nochevieja
news   la noticia
newspaper   el periódico
next to   al lado (de); próximo/a
Nicaraguan   nicaragüense
nice   agradable; majo/a; simpático/a
niece   la sobrina

Nigerian   nigeriano/a
night   la noche
night before last   ante(a)noche
nightgown   el camisón
nightmare   la pesadilla
no   ningún/ninguno/ninguna; no
no one   nadie
nobody   nadie
noise   el ruido
to nominate   nominar
none   ningún/ninguno/ninguna
normally   normalmente
North American   norteamericano/a
nose   la nariz
nostalgic   nostálgico
not   tampoco
not any   ningún/ninguno/ninguna
(not) ever   jamás; nunca
note card   la ficha
notebook   el cuaderno
nothing   nada
novel   la novela
novelist   el/la novelista
November   noviembre
now   ahora
nowadays   hoy en día
nurse   el/la enfermero/a

O

oath   el juramento
object   el objeto
to obtain   obtener
obvious   obvio/a
occupation   la ocupación
to occur   ocurrir
October   octubre
of   de
of course   claro; por supuesto;
    realmente; cómo no
to offer   ofrecer (zc)
office   la oficina
office (of doctor, dentist, etc.)   el
    consultorio
often   muchas veces
oil   el aceite
old   antiguo/a; mayor; viejo/a
olive   la aceituna
Olympics   las Olimpiadas
on, above   sobre
on demand   a petición
once   una vez
one hand   por un lado
onion   la cebolla
only (adv.)   sólo
only child   el hijo único/la hija única
to open   abrir

opening   la vacante
opinion   la opinión
opinion poll   la encuesta de opinión
opposing   contrario/a
optimistic   optimista
or   o
orange   anaranjado/a, naranja (adj.);
    la naranja
orchestra   la orquesta
to order   encargar; pedir (i)
organization   la organización
to organize   organizar
other   otro/a
other, another   otro/a
other hand   en cambio; por
    otro lado
outdoors   al aire libre
outside   afuera
outskirts   las afueras
outstanding   destacado/a
own   propio/a
ozone layer   la capa de ozono

P

package   el paquete
page   la página
pain   el dolor
painter   el/la pintor/a
painting   el cuadro; la pintura
pajamas   el/la piyama
palate   el paladar
Panamanian   panameño/a
pants   los pantalones
pantsuit   el traje pantalón
pantyhose   las pantimedias
papaya   la papaya
paprika   el achiote; el pimentón
parade   el desfile
Paraguayan   paraguayo/a
pardon me   con permiso, perdón
parents   los padres
parsley   el perejil
to participate   participar
partner   el/la compañero/a
party   la fiesta
passenger   el/la pasajero/a
passion fruit   el fruto de pasión
passive   pasivo/a
passport   el pasaporte
past   pasado/a
pastry   el pastel
patient   paciente; el/la paciente
patriotic   patriótico/a
to pay (for)   pagar
peach   el durazno; el melocotón
pear   la pera

peasant el/la campesino/a
pedestrian area la zona peatonal
pediatrician el/la pediatra
pen el bolígrafo
penalty el penalti
pencil el lápiz
people la gente
pepper la pimienta
percent por ciento
percentage el porcentaje
perfect perfecto/a
perfectionistic perfeccionista
perfectly perfectamente
performance el rendimiento
performer el/la intérprete
periodical el periódico
person la persona; la persona
perspective la perspectiva
Peruvian peruano/a
pessimistic pesimista
petroleum el petróleo
pharmacist el/la farmacéutico/a
pharmacy la farmacia
philology la filología
philosophy la filosofía
photo(graph) la foto(grafía)
physics la física
physiology la fisiología
to pick up recoger (j)
picture el cuadro
pie la tarta
pill la pastilla
pillow la almohada
pin el alfiler
pineapple la piña
pink rosado/a, rosa
to place colocar
place el lugar
plan el plan
to plan to pensar (ie) + infinitive
plane el avión
planet el planeta
plastic plástico
plastic arts los artes plásticas
plate, dish el plato
to play (a game, sport) jugar (ue)
to play (an instrument) tocar (un instrumento)
player el/la jugador/a
plaza la plaza
please por favor
pleased/nice to meet you encantado/a; mucho gusto
pleasure el placer
plumber el/la plomero/a; el/la fontanero/a
plus y

poem el poema
poet el/la poeta
poetry la poesía
point of view el punto de vista
policeman/woman el/la policía
Polish polaco/a
political science las ciencias políticas
poll la encuesta
polluted contaminado/a
poor pobre
popcorn las palomitas de maíz
popular popular
popularity la popularidad
to popularize popularizar (c)
population la población
pork el cerdo
port el deportes
to portray retratar
Portuguese portugués/ portuguesa
position el puesto
possible posible
poster el afiche
potato la papa
potter el/la ceramista
poultry, fowl las aves
poverty la pobreza
powerful potente
position la posición
to practice practicar
to precede preceder
to predict prever
to prefer preferir (ie)
preparation el preparativo
to prepare preparar
to prescribe recetar
prescription la receta
present actual; el regalo
present time actualmente; en la actualidad
preservation la conservación
president el presidente/la presidenta
presidential presidencial
preterit el pretérito
pretty bonito/a; lindo/a
price el precio
printer la impresora
prize el premio
probable probable
problem el problema
procession la procesión
to produce elaborar; producir
product el producto
professor el/la profesor/a
program el programa

progress el progreso
to prohibit prohibir
promising prometedor/a
proposal la propuesta
protein la proteína
proverb el refrán
provided that con tal (de) que
proximity la proximidad
psychiatrist el/la (p)siquiatra
psychologist el/la (p)sicólogo/a
psychology la (p)sicología
publicity la publicidad
publicity campaign la campaña de publicidad
Puerto Rican puertorriqueño/a
purple morado/a
purse la bolsa/el bolso
to put poner (g)
to put to bed acostar
to put makeup on oneself maquillar(se)
to put one's clothes on poner(se) (g) la ropa

Q

quality la calidad
quantity la cantidad
queen la reina
question la pregunta
quickly rápidamente
quiet callado/a
quotation la cita textual
to quote citar

R

race la carrera
racquet la raqueta
radiator el radiador
radio el/la radio
radio announcer el/la locutor/a
radiologist el/la radiólogo/a
rail el riel
to rain llover (ue)
rain la lluvia
rain forest el bosque tropical
raincoat el impermeable
to raise one's hand levantar la mano
rate la tasa
rather bastante
to reach out to comunicarse
to read leer
reading la lectura
ready listo/a
real estate bienes raíces
reality la realidad
really in en realidad/realmente

Really! ¡No me digas!
to reappear reaparecer
rearview mirror el espejo retrovisor
reason la razón
rebirth el renacimiento
receipt la receta
to receive recibir
recipe la receta
to recommend recomendar (ie)
recommendation la recomendación
to record grabar
recycled reciclado/a
red rojo/a
red pepper la pimienta roja
redhead pelirrojo/a
to reduce reducir
to reflect reflejar
to reforest repoblar
refrigerator el refrigerador; la nevera
regime el régimen
region la región
to regret arrepentirse (ie)
regularly regularmente
relative el pariente; el/la pariente
relatively relativamente
relief el alivio
to relieve aliviar
religious religioso/a
remedy, medicine el remedio
to remember recordar(se) (ue)
to rent alquilar
rent el alquiler
to repeat repetir (i)
to repopulate repoblar
reputation la reputación
to require exigir
to research investigar
research la investigación
resources los recursos
to respect respetar
to respond responder
responsible responsable
to rest descansar
restaurant el restaurante
result el resultado
résumé el currículum
to retire jubilarse
to return devolver; retornar; volver (ue)
review la reseña
to reward premiar
rib la costilla
rice el arroz
rich, wealthy rico/a
to ride (a bicycle) montar (en bicicleta)
right el derecho; la derecha

right? ¿verdad?
ring el anillo
river basin la cuenca
road el camino
to roast asar
robbery el robo
robe la bata
robot el robot
romantic romántico/a
roof el tejado
room la habitación
room; bedroom el cuarto
round trip de ida y vuelta
route el trayecto
routine la rutina
rug la alfombra
ruins las ruinas
to run correr

S

sad triste
safe la caja fuerte
salad la ensalada
salad dressing el aderezo
salary el sueldo
sale la rebaja; la venta
(sales) manager el/la gerente (de ventas)
salesman, saleswoman el/la vendedor/a
salesperson el dependiente/la dependienta
salt la sal
Salvadorian salvadoreño/a
sandal la sandalia
sandwich el sándwich
Saturday el sábado
to sauté saltear
to save ahorrar
savings los ahorros
sawdust el aserrín
to say decir (g, i)
to say goodbye despedir(se) (i)
to say hello mandar saludos
scared asustado/a
scarf la bufanda
scene la escena
schedule el horario
school la escuela
school, department la facultad
science la ciencia
scientist el/la científico/a
to score a goal meter un gol
screen la pantalla
sculptor el escultor/la escultora
sea el mar

search engine el buscador
seasoning el condimento
seat el asiento
security la seguridad
sedentary sedentario/a
to see ver
see you later hasta luego
see you soon hasta pronto
see you tomorrow hasta mañana
seed la semilla
to seem parecer (zc)
self-portrait el autorretrato
to sell vender
seller el/la vendedor/a
seminar el seminario
to send enviar; mandar
sentimental sentimental
September septiembre
serious grave; serio/a
to serve servir (i)
server el/la camarero/a
to set the table poner la mesa
several algún/alguno(s)/alguna(s)
shape la forma
sharp agudo/a
to shave (oneself) afeitar(se)
she ella
sheep la oveja
sheet la sábana
shell la concha
shellfish los mariscos
ship la nave, el barco
shirt la camisa
shoe el zapato
shopping las compras
shopping center el centro comercial
short (in length) corto/a
short (in stature) bajo/a; chaparro/a
short-sleeved shirt la camisa de manga corta
shorts los pantalones cortos
should deber
shoulder el hombro
to show mostrar (ue)
shower la ducha
shrimp el camarón; la gamba
sick enfermo/a
side el lado
to sign firmar
signal la señal
significant other la pareja
silence el silencio
silly, foolish tonto/a
simply simplemente
since desde; hace
sincere sincero/a
to sing cantar

single   soltero/a
sister   la hermana
to sit down   sentarse (ie)
size   el número; la talla; el tamaño
to skate   patinar
ski   el esquí
to ski   esquiar
skiing   el esquí
to skim   leer por encima
skin   la piel
skirt   la falda
sleep   el sueño
to sleep (to fall asleep)   dormir(se)
   (ue)
slipper   la zapatilla
slope   la bajada; la pendiente
slowly   despacio; lentamente
small   pequeño/a
smallpox   la viruela
smart   listo/a
to smoke   fumar
snack   la merienda
to sneeze   estornudar
snorkeling   el buceo
to snow   nevar (ie)
snow   la nieve
so that   para que
soap   el jabón
soap opera   la telenovela
sober   sobrio/a
soccer   el fútbol
social   social
society   la sociedad
sociology   la sociología
sock   el calcetín
soda   el refresco
sofa   el sofá
soft   blando/a; suave
soft drink   el refresco
soil   la tierra
some   algún/alguno(s)/alguna(s)
someone   alguien
something   algo
something else   otra cosa
something foolish   la babada
sometime   alguna vez
sometimes   algunas veces; a veces
son   el hijo
song   la canción
to soon as   as tan pronto (como)
sorcerer   el brujo
soul   el alma
to sound   sonar
soup   la sopa
sour   agrio/a
source   la fuente
souvenir   el recuerdo

spaghetti   los espaguetis
Spanish   español/a; el español
to speak   hablar
specialist   el/la especialista
specialty   la especialidad
speed   la velocidad
speed, haste   la prisa
to spend   gastar
to spend (time)   pasar
spice   la especie
spinach   las espinacas
spirit   el espíritu
to sponsor   patrocinar
spoon   la cuchara
spoonful   la cucharada
sports equipment   el equipo
   deportivo
sportswear   la ropa deportiva
to spray   rociar
to spread, to disseminate   difundir
spring   la primavera
square   la plaza
square meter   el metro cuadrado
stadium   el estadio
stairs   la escalera
to stand in line   hacer cola
to stand out   destacarse
star   la estrella
to start   empezar
statistics   las estadísticas
to stay in touch   mantenerse en
   contacto
steak   el bistec
steering wheel   el volante
step   el paso
stepbrother   el hermanastro
stepfather   el padrastro
stepmother   la madrastra
stepsister   la hermanastra
still   todavía
stockings   las medias
stomach   el estómago
to stop   detener
stopover   la escala
store   la tienda
store window   el escaparate
story   el cuento
stove   la cocina; la estufa
straight   derecho
strawberry   la fresa
street   la calle
to stroll   pasear
strong   fuerte
structure   la estructura
student   el alumno/a; el/la estudiante
student desk   el pupitre
studious   estudioso/a

to study   estudiar; investigar
to stumble   tropezarse
stupendous   estupendo/a
style   el estilo
stylish   de moda
subsidize   subvencionar
subway   el metro
success   el éxito
sugar   el/la azúcar
to suggest   sugerir (ie, i)
suit   el traje; el traje de chaqueta
suitcase   la maleta
to summarize   resumir
summer   el verano
sun   el sol
to sunbathe   tomar el sol
Sunday   el domingo
sunglasses   las gafas de sol
sunrise   la salida del sol
supermarket   el supermercado
supper   la comida
to support   apoyar; sustentar
surely, certainly   seguramente
surgeon   el/la cirujano/a
surgery   la operación
to surprise   sorprender
surprise   la sorpresa
surrealist   surrealista
to surround   rodear
survey   la encuesta
to survive   sobrevivir
sweater   el suéter
sweatshirt; jogging suit   la sudadera
to sweep   barrer
to swell   hinchar
swelling   la hinchazón
to swim   nadar
swimming pool   la piscina; la alberca
symbol   el símbolo
symptom   el síntoma

T

T-shirt   la camiseta
table   la mesa
tablecloth   el mantel
to take   llevar; tomar
to take a nap   to dormir (ue) la siesta
to take a seat   tomar asiento
to take a walk   dar un paseo; pasear
to take advantage   aprovechar
to take away   quitar(se)
to take care of   cuidar; cuidar(se) (de)
to take note   fijarse
to take notes   tomar apuntes/notas
to take off   quitar(se)
to take off (airplane)   despegar (u)

to take out sacar (qu)
to talk conversar; dialogar
talkative conversador/a
tall alto/a
tamale el tamale
tapas las tapas
task la tarea
tea el té
teacher el/la profesor/a
team; equipment el equipo
to tear romper
teaspoon la cucharita
technician el/la técnico/a
technology la tecnología
telephone el teléfono
television set el televisor
to tell contar (ue); decir (g, i)
tennis el tenis
tennis player el/la tenista
tennis shoe la zapatilla de deporte
terrace la terraza
terrorism el terrorismo
test el examen
thanks, thank you gracias
Thanksgiving el Día de Acción de
    Gracias
that ese/a (adj.); eso (pron.)
that is why por eso
that (over there) aquel/aquella
That's great! ¡Qué bien/bueno!
thaw, thawing el deshielo
theater el teatro
theater company la compañía de
    teatro
their su(s)
theme el tema
then entonces; luego
therapy la terapia
there allí
there is, there are hay
thermometer el termómetro
they ellos/ellas
thin delgado/a
thing la cosa
to think pensar (ie)
to think of/about pensar en
to think of/about (opinion) pensar de
third tercero/a
thirst la sed
this este/a; esto
thousand mil
throat la garganta
through por; a través de
to throw lanzar
Thursday el jueves
ticket el billete; el boleto, el pasaje
tie la corbata

tight estrecho/a
time la hora; el tiempo
timid tímido/a
tire la llanta
tired cansado/a
title el título
to a; para
toast el pan tostado/la tostada
to toast tostar
today hoy
Today is . . . Hoy es . . .
together juntos/as
toilet el inodoro
tomato el tomate
tomato sauce la salsa de tomate
tomorrow mañana
tone el tono
tongue la lengua
tonight esta noche
too también
tooth el diente
toothpaste la pasta de dientes
tourist class la clase turista
tournament el campeonato; el torneo
toward para
towel la toalla
toxic tóxico/a
toy el juguete
tradition la tradición
traditional tradicional
traditionally tradicionalmente
traffic el tráfico
train el tren
trainer el/la entrenador/a
training el entrenamiento
training resort el centro de
    entrenamiento
tranquil tranquilo/a
tranquilly tranquilamente
to translate traducir (zc)
trash la basura
to travel viajar
travel agency la agencia de viajes
travel agent el/la agente de viajes
tray la bandeja
to treat tratar
to treat, to be about tratar
tree el árbol
trips el viaje
true cierto/a; verdad
trunk el baúl; el maletero
trust la confianza
truth la verdad
to try probar; tratar
to try on probarse (ue)
Tuesday el martes
turkey el pavo

to turn doblar
to turn on encender (ie)
twin gemelo/a
to twist torcer(se) (ue)
typical típico/a

U

UFO el OVNI
ugly feo/a
umbrella el paraguas
umpire, referee el árbitro
uncle el tío
under abajo; debajo (de)
to underline subrayar
to understand comprender;
    entender (ie)
underwear la ropa interior
unemployment el desempleo
unforgettable inolvidable
to unify unificar (qu)
United States Estados Unidos
university la universidad
unless a menos que
unpleasant antipático/a
until hasta que
urgent urgente
Uruguayan uruguayo/a
U.S. citizen estadounidense
to use usar
useful útil

V

vacation las vacaciones
to vacuum pasar la aspiradora
vacuum cleaner la aspiradora
Valentine's Day el Día de los
    Enamorados; el Día del Amor y
    la Amistad
vanilla la vainilla
vegetable el vegetal, la verdura
vegetarian vegetariano/a
vein la vena
Venezuelan venezolano/a
verbs verbos
very muy
veterinarian el/la veterinario/a
video game el videojuego
view la vista
village el pueblo
vinegar el vinagre
virtual library la biblioteca virtual
virtually virtualmente
to visit visitar
vitamin la vitamina
voice la voz
volleyball el vóleibol; el volibol

W

waist   la cintura
to wait for   esperar
waiter/waitress   el/la camarero/a
waiting area   la sala de espera
to wake (someone up); to
   despertar(se) (ie)
to wake up   despertar(se)
to walk   caminar
wallet   la billetera
to want   querer (ie)
warehouse   el almacén
warming   el calentamiento
to wash (oneself)   lavar(se)
washer   la lavadora
wastebasket   el cesto
water   el agua
to water   regar (ie)
way   el camino
we   nosotros/nosotras
We are going to have a good time.   Lo
   vamos a pasar muy bien.
weak   débil
to wear   llevar
to wear a costume   disfrazarse
to wear a shoe size   calzar
weather   el tiempo; el tiempo
weather forecast   el pronóstico del
   tiempo
wedding   la boda
Wednesday   el miércoles
week   la semana
week ago   a una semana atrás
weekend   el fin de semana
weight   la pesa
well   bien; bueno/a
well-off   adinerado/a
what?   ¿qué?
What a pity!   ¡Qué lástima!
What a suprise/coincidence!   ¡Qué
   casualidad!
What day is it?   ¿Qué día es hoy?
What do you think?   ¿Qué te parece?

What for?   ¿para qué?
What is he/she/it like?   ¿Cómo es?
What is the date?   ¿Cuál es la fecha?;
   ¿Qué fecha es hoy?
What is the weather like?   ¿Qué
   tiempo hace?
What time is it?   ¿Qué hora es?
What's new?   ¿Qué tal?
What's up?   ¿Qué tal?
What's wrong (with you/them)?   ¿Qué
   te/le(s) pasa?
What's your name? (familiar)   ¿Cómo
   te llamas?
What's your name? (formal)   ¿Cómo se
   llama usted?
wheel   la rueda
when   cuando
when?   ¿cuándo?
where?   ¿dónde?
Where do we meet?   ¿Dónde
   quedamos?
Where is . . . ?   ¿Dónde está... ?
where (to)?   ¿adónde?
wherever   donde
which?   ¿cuál(es)?
while   mientras
to whistle   pitar
white   blanco/a
who?   ¿quién(es)?
Who is . . . ?   ¿Quién es... ?
whose?   ¿de quién?
why?   ¿para qué?; ¿por qué?
wide   ancho/a
wife   la esposa
wild   silvestre
will   el/la testamento
to win   ganar
wind   el viento
window   la ventana; la ventanilla
window seat   el asiento de
   ventanilla
windshield wiper   el limpiaparabrisas
wine   el vino
wine cellar   la bodega

winner   el ganador
winter   el invierno
to wish, to want   desear
with   con
without   sin; sin que
woman   la mujer
wood   la madera
wool   la lana
word   la palabra
work   la obra
to work   trabajar
work   el trabajo
worker   el/la obrero/a
workshop   el taller
World Cup   la Copa
   Mundial
world, worldwide   mundial
to worry   preocupar(se)
wound   la herida
wounded   herido/a
wrist   la muñeca
to write   escribir
writer   el escritor/la escritora

Y

year   el año
yellow   amarillo/a
yes   sí
yesterday   ayer
yet   todavía
yogurt   el yogur
you are (familiar)   eres; estás
you are (formal)   es; estás
you (familiar)   tú (familiar); vos
   (Argentina)
you (formal)   usted (formal)
you (plural)   ustedes (plural)
young   joven
young man/woman   el/la joven
your (familiar)   tu(s)
you're welcome   de nada
youth hostel   el albergue juvenil
yucca   la yuca

Credits

Text Credits

p. 48: "Un buen repaso a la Universidad de Salamanca" reprinted with permission from Alberto López Nájera; **p. 73:** ® All Rights Reserved by World Editors, Inc.; **p. 434:** "Dame la mano" by Gabriela Minstral. La Orden Franciscana de Chile autoriza el uso de la obra de Gabriela Mistral. Lo equivalente a los derechos de autoría es entregado a la Orden Franciscana de Chile, para los niños de Montegrande, de conformidad a la voluntad de Gabriela Minstral.; **p. 457:** El Entnógrafo by Jorge Luis Borges. ©1995 by Jorge Luis Borges, permission of The Wylie Agency Inc.; **p. 490:** Hombre pequenito by Alfonsina Storni. Editorial Losada S.A., Buenos Aires, 1997. Herederos de Alfonsina Storni. Used with permission; **p. 504:** Mafalda (#1126 and #104) por Joaquín S. Lavado, de QUINO. Ediciones de la Flor, 1997. Reprinted with permission of Caminito S.a.s.; **p. 520:** "Apocalipsis" © Denevi, Marco, Falsificaciones, Buenos Aires, Corregidor, 2007. Used with permission.

Photo Credits

Cover Image: Ferran Traite Soler/ IStockphoto.com: p. 2 © Jeff Greenberg/Alamy; p. 5 (top) Ian O'Leary/ Getty Images Inc.—Stone Allstock; p. 5 (center) Getty Images—Stockbyte, Royalty Free; p. 5 (bottom) Christina Kennedy/ PhotoEdit Inc.; p. 22 Dagli Orti (A)/Picture Desk, Inc./Kobal Collection; p. 23 (lower bottom center) Matt Trommer/Shutterstock; p. 23 (right) Pilar Echevarria/Shutterstock; p. 23 (top) Jarno gonzalez Zarraonandia/ Shutterstock; p. 23 (bottom) Rafael Ramirez Lee/Shutterstock; p. 23 (lower upper left) © Robert Frerck/Odyssey/Chicago; p. 24 (top) Grimberg, Marc/Getty Images Inc.—Image Bank; p. 24 (bottom) Goncharov Roman/ Shutterstock; p. 25 Embassy of Peru; Robert Frerck/Odyssey Productions, Inc.; p. 35 Richard Nowitz/National Geographic Image Collection; p. 44 Spencer Grant/PhotoEdit Inc.; p. 50 © Robert Fried/robertfriedphotography.com; p. 51 (top) Robert Fried/robertfriedphotography.com; p. 51 (bottom) Denis Doyle/AP Wideworld Photo; p. 54 © Cristena Cardenas; p. 55 (bottom) Robin Holden, Sr./Shutterstock; p. 55 (center) Graca Victoria/Shutterstock; p. 55 (center) April Turner/Shutterstock; p. 55 (top right) Aaron D. Settipane/ Shutterstock; p. 55 (right) Photo by Rico Torres © 2003 Miramax/ Columbia Pictures, All Rights Reserved, Kobal Collection—The Picture Desk; p. 56 (top left) © Jimmy Dorantes/Latin Focus.com; p. 56 (bottom right) Andresr/Shutterstock; p. 56 (top right) digitalskillet/Shutterstock; p. 56 (bottom left) Mira.com/Artist Name; p. 57 EyeWire Collection/Getty Images—Photodisc; p. 60 (left) Wallenrock/Shutterstock; p. 60 (center left) Dallas Events Inc./Shutterstock; p. 60 (center right) Laurence Gough/ Shutterstock; p. 60 (right) Yuri Arcurs/Shutterstock; p. 66 (top left) © Michael Germana/SSI Photo/Landov; p. 66 (top right) Jack Vartoogian/Front Row Photos; p. 66 (bottom right) © Steve Nesius/Reuters/ Landov; p. 66 (bottom left) © Ramon Espinosa/AP Wide World Photos; p. 67 Scott Harrison/Getty Images; p. 84 Courtesy of the Library of Congress; p. 84 Library of Congress; p. 85 (top) © 2008 Kendal Larson; p. 85 (bottom) Wikipedia, The Free Encyclopedia; Artist unknown. First wedding of Inca princess Nusta Beatriz to Spanish noble Martin de Loyola, 18th century; p. 88; © The Art Archive/Museo Pedro de Osma Lima/Mireille Vautier; p. 89 (center) Mike von Bergen/ Shutterstock; p. 89 (bottom) Marshall Bruce/Shutterstock; p. 89 (top left) Chris Howey/Shutterstock; p. 89 (bottom left) Paul Clarke/Shutterstock; p. 89 (top left) Nicholas Raymond/Shutterstock; p. 90 (top left) Todd B. Powell/Creative Eye/MIRA.com; p. 90 (top right) Nik Wheeler; p. 90 (center) Robert Frerck/Odyssey Productions, Inc.; p. 90 (bottom) © Bob Daemmrich/PhotoEdit; p. 94 Adalberto Rios Szalay/Sexto Sol/Getty Images, Inc.—Photodisc; p. 96 © John Van Hasselt/Sygma/ CORBIS; p. 103 (top) Getty Images, Inc.; p. 103 (top center) William Albert Allard/NGS Image Collection; p. 103 (bottom center) © Victor Englebert; p. 103 (bottom) Chad Ehlers/Stock Connection; p. 118 (top) © Scala/Art Resource; p. 118 (bottom) Dagli Orti/Picture Desk, Inc./Kobal Collection; p. 122 Fernando Botero, "En familia" (The Family). © Fernando Botero, courtesy of Marlborough Gallery, New York; p. 123 (center left) © Alejandro Velasquez; p. 123 (top) © Amra Pasic/Shutterstock; p. 123 (center right) © John Chang/Courtesy of www.istockphoto.com; p. 123 (bottom left) © Richard Gunion/Courtesy of www.istockphoto.com; p. 123 (bottom right) © Galyna Andrushko/Shutterstock; p. 124 (left) © Paloma Lapuerta; p. 124 (center) Tony Freeman/PhotoEdit Inc.; p. 124 (right) Michael Newman/PhotoEdit Inc.; p. 138 © Andre Schafer/Courtesy of www.istockphoto.com; p. 147 (top) Ellen Senisi; p. 147 (bottom) Bill Aron/PhotoEdit Inc.; p. 150 HERMANN BREHM/Nature Picture Library; p. 151 Colombia Information Service Tourist Office; p. 154 Mireille Vautier/ Woodfin Camp & Associates, Inc.; p. 155 (top) © Toon Possemiers/Courtesy of www.istockphoto. com; p. 155 (bottom left) Jeff Chevrier/Courtesy of www.istockphoto.com; p. 155 (bottom right) © Eli Coory/Fotolia; p. 155 (center right) Courtesy of www.istockphoto.com; p. 155 (center left) © Tatiana Popova/Shutterstock; p. 155 (center left) © Kmitu/Shutterstock; p. 155 (center left) © Valentyn Volkov/Shutterstock; p. 156 © Nik Wheeler/Alamy; p. 166 (top) Bruce Ayres/Getty Images Inc.—Stone Allstock; p. 166 (bottom) AP Wide World Photos; p. 166 (right) Robert Frerck/Getty Images Inc.—Stone Allstock; p. 170 (left) Laura Dwight/PhotoEdit Inc.; p. 170 (center) Tony Freeman/PhotoEdit Inc.; p. 170 (right) Robert Fried/robertfriedphotography. com; p. 184 Brennan Linsley/AP Wide World Photos; p. 185 (top) © Bettmann/CORBIS All Rights Reserved; p. 185 (bottom) Luis Romero/ AP Wide World Photos; p. 188 Simon Bolivar (1783–1830) (chromolitho) by Artist Unknown (pre 20th cenutry). Private Collection/Archives Charmet/Bridgeman Art Library; p. 189 (center) Jos? Enrique Molina/ AGE Fotostock America, Inc.; p. 189 (bottom right) Mark Cosslett/National Geographic Image Collection; p. 189 (bottom left) Rhodes, Leonard L T/ Animals Animals/ Earth Scenes; p. 189 (top) © Kimberly White/Reuters/ CORBIS All Rights Reserved; p. 190 (top) Ulrike Welsch/PhotoEdit Inc.; p. 190 (center) Beryl Goldberg; p. 190 (bottom) Jeff Greenberg/PhotoEdit Inc.; p. 202 (left) David Welling/Nature Picture Library; p. 202 (center) © Patrick Keen/Courtesy of www.istockphoto. com; p. 202 (right) © Yann Arthus-Bertrand/Bettmann/ CORBIS; p. 202 (bottom) Silva, Juan/Getty Images Inc.— Image Bank; p. 208 (left) Getty Images, Inc.; p. 208 (center) AP Wide World Photos; p. 208 (right) AP Wide World Photos; p. 210 Gordon, Larry Dale/Getty Images Inc.—Image Bank; p. 211 (left) © Lluis Gene/AFP/ Getty; p. 211 (center) Getty Images; p. 211 (right) Courtesy of Marshall Field's; p. 218 © Michael Stokes/ Shutterstock; p. 219 (top) Joese Caruci/AP Wide World Photos; p. 219 (bottom) © Javier Galeano/AP Wide World; p. 222 Xul Solar (Argentina 1887–1963), "Jefa (Patroness)". 1923. Watercolor on paper, set on cardboard. 10"x 10" (25.4 x 25.4 cm); Framed: 21 3/4" x 21 3/4" (55.2 x 55.2 cm). The Museum of Fine Arts, Houston; Museum purchase with funds provided by the Latin American Experience Gala and Auction; p. 223 (center left) © Mariano Heluani/Shutterstock; p. 223 (bottom center) © Wolfgang Kaehler www.wkaehlerphoto.com; p. 223 (bottom) © Ivonne Wierink-vanWetten/Courtesy of www.istockphoto.com; p. 223 (mid-center right) Daniel Rivademar/Odyssey Productions, Inc.; p. 223 (top) © Galina Barskaya/Shutterstock; p. 224 (top) © Marcos Brindicci/ Reuters/CORBIS; p. 224 (center) Bill Bachmann/PhotoEdit Inc.; p. 224 (bottom) © Chen Wei Seng/Shutterstock; p. 226 (left) © James M. Phelps, Jr./Shutterstock; p. 226 (center) © Kanwarjit Singh Boparai/ Shutterstock; p. 226 (right) © Adrees Latif/ Reuters/CORBIS; p. 249 (left) CARL SCHNEIDER/ Getty Images, Inc.—Taxi; p. 249 (right) © Monique Rodriguez/Courtesy of www.istockphoto.com; p. 249 (bottom) Courtesy of www.istockphoto.com; p. 252 © Stuart Cohen/The Image Works; p. 253 (top) Geoff Brightling © Dorling Kindersley; p. 253 (bottom) Getty Images Inc.—Hulton Archive Photos; p. 256 Frida Kahlo, "Self-Portrait at the Border Between Mexico and the United States". 1932. Museo Nacional de Arte Moderno, © 2001 Banco de Mexico Diego Rivera & Frida Kahlo Museums Trust. Av. Cinco de Mayo No. 2, Col. Centro, Del. Cuauhtemoc 06059, Mexico, D.F. Reproduction authorized by the Instituto Nacional de Bellas Artes y Literatura. © Christie's Images/CORBIS All

Language Functions Index

A

actions, describing, 138–139, 164–166, 484–485
advice, giving, 390, 425
affirmation, expressing, 440–442
agreement, reporting, 445
anecdotes, telling, 517
asking for what you need, 47
asking questions, 44–45
attention, getting someone's, 34
attitudes, expressing, 378–379
audience
    considering, 82
    focusing on, 319

B

brainstorming, 49

C

certainty, expressing, 477–480
characteristics, expressing, 70–72
chronological order, indicating, 217, 285
clarification, requesting, 45, 281
closings, 117
comparisons
    making, 273–279
    organizing information to make, 145
concern, expressing, 391
conclusions, drawing, 280
conditions, expressing
    changeable, 70–72
congratulating, 387
conjecture, expressing, 474–476, 477–480
content
    anticipating, 146
    focusing on, 319
    predicting and guessing, 248
    selecting appropriate, 183
context, using to figure out meaning, 214, 314
conversation, maintaining the flow of, 135

D

daily activities, talking about, 98–101, 142–143
decisions
    defending, 353
    gathering information strategically to express, 315
    giving, 353
    influencing, 353
details
    asking for, 245
    providing supporting, 251
    recording relevant, 352
disbelief, expressing, 34
dislikes, expressing, 76–77, 206–208
doubt, expressing, 443–446
duration, expressing, 111–113, 140–141, 245

E

emotional states, describing, 167–169
emotions, expressing, 378–379, 421, 490
empathy, showing, 281, 379
events
    describing, 209–211
    sequencing, 217, 285
expectations, expressing, 372–377

F

facts
    differentiating from opinons, 246
    using to support a view, 424
familiarity, expressing, 108–110
food, ordering, 94
formal tone, using appropriately, 148
future
    hypothesizing about the, 510–512
    talking about the, 348–351

G

gender, specifying, 39–41
goals, expressing, 380–383
greetings, 5–7, 21, 47
guessing, contextual, 214, 314

H

happiness, expressing, 387, 518
hopes, expressing, 372–377
humor, incorporating, 518, 521
hypothesizing, 447–450, 510–512
hypothetical situations, talking about, 406–409

I

ideas
    discussing, 247, 338, 391
    listening for main, 386
    organizing, 487
illustrations, using to anticipate content, 146
impersonal information, stating, 336–338

indirect objects, indicating, 203–205
inferences, making, 281
informal tone, using appropriately, 148
information
    clarifying, 241–242
    emphasizing, 241–242
    focusing on key, 247
    focusing on relevant, 388
    gathering, 315
    listening for, 78
    organizing, 317
    organizing for a presentation, 115
    organizing to make comparisons, 144
    presenting factual, 425
    requesting repetition, 281
    taking notes to recall, 212
instructions, giving, 310–313, 344–347
intention
    expresing, 111–113
    identifying, 454, 516
interest
    engaging, 421
    expressing, 245, 281
    maintaining, 247, 421
interviews, conducting, 281
invitations, 262–264

K

key words, looking for and using, 116
knowledge
    stating, 108–110
    supporting comprehension with, 420
    using background, 114

L

letter-writing, 117
likes, expressing, 76–77, 206–208
listening for the gist, 46
listening with visuals, 13
location, expressing, 12, 42–43, 42–43, 67–69
logical relationships, focusing on, 422

M

main ideas, listening for, 386
meaning, using context to figure out, 214
means, expressing, 111–113, 380–383

Subject Index